6.50

Oscar Wilde

Idylls of the Marketplace
Oscar Wilde and the Victorian Public

'HOW UTTER'

Idylls of the Marketplace

*Oscar Wilde
and the
Victorian Public*

Regenia Gagnier

Scolar Press

©1986 by the Board of Trustees of the
Leland Stanford Junior University
Published in England in 1987 by
Scolar Press
Gower Publishing Company Limited
Gower House, Croft Road
Aldershot GU11 3HR
First published in the USA in 1986 by
Leland Stanford Junior University
Printed in the United States of America

Sources of illustrations:
Frontispiece, pp. 2, 18, 46, 50, 102, 164, 178, Clark Library;
p. 138, Topham Picture Library.

Sources of endpaper illustrations:
Left page: *top left*, Clark Library; *top right*, courtesy of *Harper's Bazaar*,
the Hearst Corporation; *center*, estate of Sir Max Beerbohm;
bottom left, Bridgeman Art Library; *bottom right*, Mansell Collection
Right page: *top left and right, center*, Clark Library;
bottom left, Mary Evans Picture Library; *bottom right*, National Portrait Gallery (London)

British Library Cataloguing in Publication Data

Gagnier, Regenia A.
Idylls of the marketplace: Oscar Wilde
and the Victorian public.
1. Wilde, Oscar—Criticism and
interpretation
I. Title
828'.809   PR5824
ISBN 0-85967-730-3

*For my mother and father,
Jean and Clenton Gagnier,
ideal form of the public*

Acknowledgments

To my teachers at Berkeley, Frederick Crews, Thomas Laqueur, and Masao Miyoshi, who, in the early stages, criticized this book; my colleagues at Stanford, Herbert Lindenberger, Anne Mellor, Wilfred Stone, and Robert Polhemus, who continued to criticize it; my students in Aestheticism 304D, who live it; and my parents, who will buy it. Also to Joseph Di Prisco, who lived through it; and John Dupré, who—with his customary generosity—had nothing to do with it.

I am also grateful to the William Andrews Clark Memorial Library of the University of California, Los Angeles, for a term in its Wilde and His Circle archives; Norris Pope, Ellen Smith, and Helen Tartar at Stanford University Press, for their attentiveness to the text; *Genre* and *Criticism* for allowing me to reprint parts of chapters 3 (*Genre*, Fall 1982) and 5 (*Criticism*, Fall 1984); Merlin Holland, for permission to publish Wilde's photographs; and Edward Colman, for permission to quote from Alfred Douglas's unpublished correspondence.

R.G.

Contents

Introduction 1

1. Creating the Audience 17

2. Dandies and Gentlemen: or, *Dorian Gray* and the Press 49

3. Comedy and Consumers 101

4. Art for Love's Sake: *Salome* and *Reading Gaol* 137

5. *De Profundis*: An Audience of Peers 177

Appendixes
A. Art as Propaganda in Wartime: The Pemberton-Billing Trials on *Salome* 199
B. Alfred Douglas's Political Interpretation of Wilde's Conviction 205
C. Commodity Fetishism as Poetry in *A Florentine Tragedy* 208

Notes 213

Selected Bibliography 235

Index 245

Introduction

Delightful the path of sin
But a holy death's a habit.
Good man yourself there, Oscar,
Every way you had it.
      Brendan Behan,
   "Envoi" from "Oscar Wilde"

"I was a man who stood in symbolic relations to the art and culture of my age" (*De Profundis*); photo by Alfred, Ellis, and Wallery, 1892.

OSCAR WILDE wanted to have it all ways. "The artist can express everything," he wrote in the admonitory Preface to *The Picture of Dorian Gray*, meaning that the artist, with a sort of noblesse oblige, *ought* to be permitted to express everything.[1] In the attempt, Wilde expressed contradictions. "For the arts are made for life, and not life for the arts," he wrote in "A Note in Black and White on Mr. Whistler's Lecture" (1885), a response to Whistler's "Ten O'Clock" lecture; "art is not to be taught in academies. . . . The real schools should be the streets." Yet in "The Decay of Lying" (1889) and the Preface to *Dorian Gray* (1891), he found that "life imitates art" and "the proper school to learn art is not life but art." Again, in "London Models" (1889) he wrote that "the mere fact that [the acrobat] never speaks to the audience shows how well he appreciates the great truth that the aim of art is not to reveal personality but to please." But in an interview published in *The Sketch* (1895) after the opening of *An Ideal Husband*, Wilde told Gilbert Burgess, "The critics have always propounded the degrading dogma that the duty of the dramatist is to please the public. . . . A play is as personal and individual a form of self-expression as a poem or a picture." Wilde's rhetoric was like his behavior: as Richard Ellmann has said, given a choice of alternatives, he always chose both.[2]

In his political and aesthetic theory Wilde was romantic and cynical. In his drama he was sentimental and satirical. For critics he has been a martyr or a mannequin. In this book I argue, first, that the contradictions in his works can be understood only by reference to his audiences, and, second, that a consideration of his audiences can lead to a serious reconsideration of the aestheticism of the 1890's. This aestheticism was an engaged protest against Victorian utility, rationality, scientific factuality, and technological progress—in fact, against the whole middle-class drive to conform—but the emphasis is on engaged.

A figure as paradoxical as Wilde and an art as self-contradictory as his can only be understood by moving beyond the personal psychology and autonomy of the work to the audiences that affected the construction of both, to the social institutions in which art forms are developed and distributed. For example, critics of Wilde's comedies before *The Importance of Being Earnest* have noticed their divergent tendencies of melodrama and

Introduction

epigrammatic wit or melodrama and satire; I view these divergent components as Wilde's manipulations of his play-going public. Similarly, I argue that the British aesthetes' critique of purposiveness, productivity, and Nature was related to homosexuality and what amounted to a social revolution in domestic options, which means that the art world had significant community ties. Again, Wilde's experience of prison life had concrete effects on what is perhaps his greatest work of art, *De Profundis*—at once his own autobiography and a biography of Alfred Douglas—and the *absence* of an audience affected the form of that work as significantly as the presence of audiences affected his other works. Yet, like many artists of his generation, Wilde perennially feared the vulgarizing influence of those absolutely necessary audiences. He explored the relation of art to influence in *Dorian Gray*, as well as in his social and aesthetic theory.

In my use of "audience," however, I am not following the usual procedures of reception theory or the theory of reader response; nor by the relation of text to audience do I mean traditional associations of text and context or literature and historical background. For example, I do not provide a statistical analysis of novel-reading or play-going publics; nor do I isolate Wilde's texts from other historical texts at all. Rather I show that Wilde's texts are embedded in other historical discourse; that seeing the relevant discourse in relation to discernible audiences illuminates Wilde's work considerably; and that ultimately Wilde's works must be seen to have contributed to the creation of the texts and audiences of the time.

Readers accustomed to long analyses of literary texts may be surprised at the unusual amount of historical discourse included here. For example, in Chapter 1 I argue that Wilde developed two prose styles, one of Wildean wit, or critique, and one of jeweled seduction, to meet the challenge of the general public and of his own desire to attract a special audience. The first style, the language of wit, was technically the inversion of the language of the press. In Chapter 2 I situate both *Dorian Gray* and the scandal it provoked in a much broader crisis of images of dandies, gentlemen, and women, in art and life and in popular texts. In Chapter 3 I discuss the way Wilde's plays reflected the image and desires of his audience and therefore supported the continuation of that image and those desires. In Chapter 4 I show the relationship of a community of men whom Wilde considered his special audience to the larger Victorian public, and I discuss how with *Salome* Wilde attempted to transform the public according to the desires of this special community. I also indicate how *The Ballad of Reading Gaol* shows *Salome*'s failure to effect this transformation. Throughout the chap-

Introduction

ter I show how the artificial and anti-utilitarian emphases of the art-for-art's-sake movement were embedded in what one might call a sex-for-sex's-sake movement—a movement that opposed itself to "natural" sexuality and purposive reproduction. In Chapter 5 I claim that the material conditions of imprisonment in the 1890's and their resultant isolation of the prisoner from any audience determined the particular form of *De Profundis*, its peculiar mixture of romance and realism. Solitary confinement frequently resulted in the prisoner's insanity, and centralized control of the prisons inevitably resulted in the prisoner's anonymity and the trivialization of his labor. Wilde's literary style reflects the conditions within the prison environment even as he uses literary style to combat their threats.

These chapters therefore require, to greater and lesser degrees, considerable discussion of late-Victorian social institutions. Journalism, advertising, public schools, homosexual communities, criminology, etiquette, theater, and prisons are perhaps the most obtrusive of these institutions in my text. But they are also the most obtrusive in Wilde's works. Wilde as a dandy is often erroneously compared to Huysmans's hero in *A Rebours*, yet the comparison is negatively instructive. If Des Esseintes is solitary, neurotic, reactive against the bourgeoisie he despises, formally monologic, and concerned with perversion, Wilde is public, erotic, active, formally dialogic, and concerned with the inversion of middle-class language and life.[3] (The French decadents may also be more engaged than critics have made them out to be, but Wilde should not be treated as French, despite his threat to renounce his citizenship when *Salome* was banned in Britain.[4]) Understanding the relation of social to literary form is difficult and delicate, but my juxtapositions of Wilde's texts and history's should aid in doing so.

Moreover, a consideration of audiences is useful beyond just understanding Wilde's paradoxical style. Wilde is uniquely placed to contribute to an understanding of a much larger question: the place of art in a consumerist society. Except for the extremely partial and limited intellectual history that sees Wilde as a popularizer of Pater, intellectual historians of aestheticism have failed to recognize the extent to which late-Victorian aestheticism was embedded in popular culture, everyday social life, and common experience. Social historians in turn have failed to emphasize the emerging service and consumerist economy that determined late-Victorian aestheticism. Precisely because he was so famous, the figure of Oscar Wilde provides a fruitful subject and point of departure to remedy these failings. Wilde was one of the last celebrities to be identified in the public domain with an autonomous art, so that responses to him are highly suggestive for the historical place of traditional art in a consumerist society.

Heretofore probably the most useful theory of aestheticism in the idiosyncratic form it took in late-Victorian Britain has been that of the Frankfurt school. Although I do not believe that the theory is sufficient—nor was it developed with reference to the late Victorians—it is worth examining here. As elaborated by Theodor Adorno and recently rehearsed in Peter Bürger's *Theory of the Avant-Garde*, the elements of aestheticism include its detachment from praxis (a detachment that according to Adorno indicates a break with imperialist society) and a preoccupation with the formal or technical qualities of artistic media. Its function is to negate the means-end rationality of bourgeois everyday life by theorizing art as an autonomous, "useless" realm. In consequence it lacks both political content and social impact, and this in turn contributes to its repetition of worn-out forms and finally to unproductiveness on the part of its artists. Its production and reception are individual rather than collective; or, as Wilde would say, a genius is born but not paid.

Anglo-American literary critics have in general not viewed the late-Victorian writers as a specific protest against late-Victorian society, largely because they have seen them instead as attenuated and tired versions of earlier, for example, Romantic, protests or as commercial sellouts.[5] But Adorno's theory does contribute to an understanding of the decadent or aesthetic break with Victorian domestic and imperial ideology. The British aesthetes like Beardsley did perfect form and technique at the expense of political or social engagement; they did, like Johnson and Dowson, produce from classical models, produce little, and die young; and they did, like Wilde, write manifestos for autonomous art—"All art," said Wilde, "is quite useless."

Yet a theory of late-Victorian aestheticism as protest cannot limit its domain to the art world, as Bürger limits it. By locating in aestheticism the disintegration of art and life, art's lack of social consequence, its depoliticized production and reception, and finally its despair of changing life, Bürger can then gauge the avant-garde's reversal of these conditions. He would have avant-garde art responsible for making the institutional status of art recognizable and for attacking art as an institution, not as a style; for reintegrating art with life; for revealing the nexus between autonomy and absence of social consequence; for politicizing production and reception; and finally for wanting to organize a new way of life from a basis in art. But late-Victorian aestheticism, especially as advocated by Wilde, was not the divorce between art and life that Gautier's phrase *l'art pour l'art* may

Introduction

suggest. Beyond Bürger's Weberian sphere of "art-world," I would propose a theory of aestheticism from the point of view of consumption, or of the different publics that, in different ways, consumed it. Ultimately, I locate the interrelations of art world and life world in the practices of modern spectacular society.

For example, on one level the theme of *The Picture of Dorian Gray* is the problem of aestheticism. In turning Dorian into an ageless image, a work of art impervious to life, Wilde explored the possibility of art and life's disjunction. With Dorian's final destruction of his portrait and himself, Wilde suggests that the two cannot be divorced. The moralistic conclusion makes one wonder why the book was such a scandal, and here, as in most cases of scandalous works, it is probably more useful to look at the audience scandalized than to look at the work. As Chapter 2 shows, middle-class journalists resisted the aestheticism they saw in *Dorian Gray* because they resisted an art not accountable to public concerns. For Wilde's hero—or Wilde himself—to appear to be a transcendent work of art, unresponsive to his position as a gentleman, was unacceptable. Wilde also showed his awareness of this conflict in his short fiction, which contained the same themes as *Dorian Gray* but which, unlike the novel, integrated art with more familiar bourgeois life and concerns.

Related to Wilde's explicit treatments of the aesthetic dilemma is the problem of the dandy. The late-Victorian dandy in Wilde's works and in his practice is the human equivalent of aestheticism in art; he is the man removed from life, a living protest against vulgarity and means-end living. He provides commentary on a society he despises, in the form of wit at its expense; indeed this is his major form of participation in that society. The late-Victorian dandy, however, unlike Brummell and D'Orsay, had no patrons, so he needed a product. He produced himself. The commodification, or commercial exploitation, of the dandiacal self traced in Chapter 2 amounts to the reinscription of art into life.

Wilde was removed from life—as his British middle-class adversaries conceived of it—on several counts. By birth Irish, by education Oxonian, by inclination homosexual, he was an adjunct to Victorian imperial, commercial, and polite society. His legendary wit consisted in practice of a talent for inverting Victorian truisms, a style that from Hegel through Feuerbach, Marx, and Kirkegaard, to Guy Debord today has been called revolutionary. Yet the astonishing thing about his wit is not that he could always and so quickly find the right word to substitute for the key term of the platitude, but rather that he knew the platitudes so well to begin with.

Introduction

His mind was stocked with commonplaces, and these seem to have been there for the sole purpose of their subversion. The situation is one in which an outsider has to a stunning degree taken upon himself the reflective apparatus of the dominant group and then used this apparatus to mock the group on, and with, its own terms. The use of such tactics endears the speaker to the group at the moment he mocks it. This is the technique of ironic reference: the use of popular symbology by its critics in order to be both commercially competitive and critical.

To be commercially competitive and critical—or to marry and divorce art and life simultaneously—was the goal of Wilde's comedies. In their criticism of middle-class life, emphasizing the spectacle and the audience, the comedies bear historical analogy with Antonin Artaud's Alfred Jarry Theater of Cruelty. In Wilde's earlier plays, internal contradictions between Victorian sentimentality and dandiacal satire spell out the contradictory nature of Victorian bourgeois ideology. In *The Importance of Being Earnest*, Wilde moves to a higher, self-critical level, and his theater assumes the function of the historical avant-garde. Far from being autonomous, *Earnest* as performance negates those determinations that are essential in autonomous art. As Chapter 3 shows, the performance merges with the audience, thus obliterating the disjunction of art from life. Similarly, the author as individual producer merges with the audience as collective receiver when he compliments it from the stage on the quality of its performance. And the theater as collective and spectacular artifact, including both the stage and the opulently accoutred audience, reflects the conspicuous consumption that is the world of the play. Thus Wilde's theater, like Artaud's later, was a version of modern spectacular society. As Artaud was to theorize: "The encounter upon the stage"—for Artaud, the entire auditorium, the players and audience amid the mise-en-scène—"of two passionate manifestations, two living centers, two nervous magnetisms [i.e., of stage and audience] is something as entire, true, even decisive, as in life, the encounter of one epidermis with another in a timeless debauchery."[6]

The engagement of aestheticism as we are presenting it in the 1890's was grounded in the beginnings of modern spectacular and mass society and depended upon image and advertising. With *The Importance of Being Earnest*, first produced one year before Jarry's revolutionary insult to bourgeois audiences in *Ubu Roi* (*King Turd*, which began with Firmin Gémier strolling to the footlights to yell "Shit!" at the audience), the "society of the spectacle"—of image over substance—emerges. "Algernon is an extremely,

Introduction

I may almost say an ostentatiously, eligible young man," says Lady Bracknell. "He has nothing, but he looks everything."

Among commodity theorists, Guy Debord has analyzed precisely this twentieth-century, post-industrial society of the spectacle that one can begin to see in the relation of *Earnest* to its audience. Although this relation is the subject of Chapter 3, the nature of that audience is important from the outset, and it is worth citing Debord's analysis of the spectacle as the existing order's uninterrupted discourse about itself, the self-portrait of power. In the spectacle, one part of the world represents itself to the world and is superior to it. The fetishizing of the spectacle, as in the audience's fetishizing of its own image on stage in *Earnest*, prefigures the spectacle-commodity's total occupation of social life. Debord's analysis, in his *Society of the Spectacle* (1977), of the contempt in advertising and media of "specialists in the power of the spectacle" for their publics also applies to Wilde. "Specialists in the power of the spectacle," writes Debord, "an absolute power within its system of language without response"—a language not unlike the incestuous wit of *Earnest*—"are absolutely corrupted by their experience of contempt and of the success of contempt; and they find their contempt confirmed by their knowledge of the contemptible man, who the spectator really is."[7] Wilde's contempt was jolly and dazzling—in fact, he was himself dazzled by the dazzle—but the mixture of contempt and bedazzlement approaches more nearly to mass art than to the alleged detachment associated with aestheticism.

In analyzing the hypnotic effects of the spectacle, many commodity theorists accord a special insurrectionary value to speech, and here too Wilde may provide an instructive example of a practice in its early stages. Jean Baudrillard's critique of Marxism as "the mirror of production" shifts the search for potential revolutionary activity from production to consumption and specifically to advanced capitalism's consumption of the sign.[8] Baudrillard is interested in how capitalism invests things with value or controls the process of signification and hence produces its ideological hegemony. A productivist ideology, one based on the value of human labor, could not account for the articulated complexity of a symbolic exchange in consumption. But for Baudrillard consumption is not passively subsumed under the activity of production, as it appeared in classical political economy and classical Marxism; instead, it is active and relies on the active appropriation of signs. In a mass consumerist society, the signified and referent are abolished. This is what Wilde was speaking of when he lamented in "The Soul

Introduction

of Man Under Socialism" that in the current language of the press "words are absolutely distorted from their proper and simple meaning, and are used to express the obverse of their right signification." The signifying code refers not to any subjective or objective "reality" but to its own logic, like those post-modern, athermal fake logs used to give the illusion of homeliness to fake hearths. Wilde reacted in part at least to this state of language by perfecting a wit that was in its own way holistic, referring to nothing more than the Victorian platitudes on which it fed, but with a twist that will be discussed as critical. Baudrillard's critique of the productivist model allows for areas of analysis (consumption, language, the media) that can be better seen in relation to the repressiveness of the code than in relation to production.

In 1934 Walter Benjamin asked what it would mean to be a bourgeois artist invading the bourgeoisie on behalf of the proletariat, and he answered that it would mean to be a journalist breaking up the organic narratives presented to the bourgeoisie.[9] In Baudrillard's terms, this is to break down a false ethic of labor, or work ethic, with an aesthetic of nonwork, opposing a kind of nonsense to bourgeois sense. The nonworkers, like students, some women, underclasses, some intellectuals, and the Wilde who praised idleness and youth without cease, are mere marginals within the productive system. But precisely their marginality, their unmarked status, allows them—short of an international revolution—to revive the radicality of revolutionary romanticism with its poetry and machine-breaking over historical Marxism with its history of delays. The symbolic speech of the youth movement in Paris in 1968 or London in 1890 recaptures the essence of the revolution that was alienated along with human labor under political economy.

I do not share Baudrillard's or Michel de Certeau's optimism about the revolutionary value of speech or gesture (nonverbal sign, usually ironic), for our fin-de-siècle or for Wilde's. But, as described in Chapter 1, the "revolutionary style"—with its inversion of the established relations between concepts and the subversion of past critical conclusions that have become frozen into respectable truths, as Debord puts it in the last pages of *Society of the Spectacle*—was also Wilde's technique. Thinking in terms of the common perception of Wilde, in his day as in ours, as a plagiarist and of his wit as a mere easy trick of inversion of platitudes, one can cite Debord's hope for this speech of dialectical "diversion." Progress, says Debord, implies the necessity of a plagiarism that uses an author's expressions to replace a false idea with a right one. Diversion is thus the opposite of

Introduction

quotation, which tears a fragment from its context, from its movement, and ultimately from its epoch.[10] In Chapter 1, I hope to show that Wilde's aestheticism was more than a quotation from Pater.

A final aspect of the problematic of aestheticism in a spectacular society was revealed in the spectacle of Wilde's trials, which are treated in Chapter 4. The prosecutors attacked Wilde because his life, to them a low private life, was incommensurate with his putative and public aesthetic code. The press reporting the trials found in Wilde's life the same absence it had discerned in *The Picture of Dorian Gray*: the absence of middle-class life; he presumed to associate with aristocrats, artists, or grooms. As the prosecutors pushed the connections between the art world and domestic and sexual deviation, aestheticism came to represent a secret, private realm of art and sexuality impervious to middle-class conformity. In other words, aestheticism came to mean the irrational in both productive (art) and reproductive (sexuality) realms: a clear affront to bourgeois utility and rationality in these realms and an apparent indication of the art world's divorce from middle-class life. But at this point it also begins to appear that it was life—specifically middle-class life—that sought a divorce from art, not vice versa. And this suggests that the aestheticism of the 1890's was embedded in a concrete, local politics.

British Aestheticism as a movement ended in 1897, when Wilde left prison for Paris. Then the struggle between art and life was over, for middle-class life was left behind and Wilde was as free as his art. As one of life's criminals and outcasts, he found the proper audience for nonbourgeois, non-mass art—an audience of peers.

Up to this point I have been describing the genius of Wilde's life: he put, as he said, only his talent into his work. His distinction between genius and talent is useful. By genius he meant the spontaneous intelligence that had made him an easy success at Oxford. The commercialization of his "genius" amounted to channeling this spontaneous intelligence into a marketable "talent." This commercialized talent, in turn, leads us to consider his life's political economy, which again supports the case for the concrete embeddedness of Aestheticism in a late-Victorian market economy.

When Wilde went down from Oxford in 1878, he registered his profession as Professor of Aesthetics. This in part indicates his hopes for art, but his opinions on aesthetics were capricious enough to belie a coherent program. His self-styled title reflects as well late-Victorian specialization and growth of the professions, especially in the two domains Wilde knew best, the literary world and the university. Given the late-Victorian marketplace, even intellectuals, a sort of classless class above the concerns of the marketplace (as one says), had to specialize. Having been disappointed by sport and rejected as an inspector of schools, Wilde needed to specialize, so he chose art. (What he wanted was liberty.) The social conditions that prevent us from emphasizing the institution of art over the institution of specialization clarify the professionalization of the aesthete.

The first of these conditions was the rise of literary coteries and manifestos. The 1890's saw the collapse of Mudie's library and the three-volume novel, and the little magazines so prolific then were a conscious rejection of such massive and mass-oriented productions. From the Romantic period on, English literary figures had criticized industrial capitalist society, even as they developed increasingly aristocratic or individualistic poses for the artist. The Romantics and Aesthetes thus participated in a new tradition—the inevitable rupture between society and a specialized realm of art, and the felt duty on the part of some artists to assume antibourgeois attitudes. The intellectual, psychological, and emotional effects of the rise of natural science and the decline of orthodox Christianity, the failure of the tradition of cultural criticism to renovate industrial values, and the fracturing of the old, relatively compact reading public made the public appeal of an Eliot or a Tennyson impossible for late-Victorian artists. Some despaired of redeeming society and lost sympathy with bourgeois readers. For others, art for art's sake was a defense against what its proponents saw as a hostile environment. They rejected "external," especially utilitarian, standards for their work and created in their own minds a privileged public of fellow writers, largely so that they could pretend they had an audience. Thus the Rhymers' Club distinguished real literary artists, i.e., its members, from old-fashioned men of letters by their sophistication in formal matters. As I shall show in Chapter 1, Wilde, as spokesperson for this Aesthetic realm in his notorious essay "Pen, Pencil, and Poison," incriminated the entire bourgeois art world for its destructive isolationism.

A second condition, paralleling the late-Victorian literary protest, was the increasing isolation of the university as a research institute. In 1876 a group of Oxbridge scholars produced *Essays on the Endowment of Research*, expressing contempt for bourgeois utility and calling for "the pursuit of knowledge for its own sake." The scholars proclaimed that the university had higher functions than teaching. Mark Pattison wrote that England was beginning to see "that universities have other functions than that of educating youth. That liberal and scientific culture, intelligence, and the whole domain of mind, is a national interest, as much as agriculture, commerce, banking, or water-supply."[11] Just when the government wanted to give the property of the colleges ("idle fellowships") to the university in the form of professorships, the *Essays* called for the endowment of research by the annexation of college fellowships, the disendowment of teaching, and a break with the marketplace.

As Charles Edward Appleton argued in Essays 3 and 4, research should be endowed precisely because the marketplace failed to provide for it; but teaching should be thrown upon some kind of fee system insofar as the marketplace reflected a demand for it. If university fellows were expected to function as professors, teaching would "choke the spirit of original investigation altogether." With the rejection of professorships and disendowment of teaching, the essayists rejected the economic interest of the middle-class public, who they felt should be satisfied with having the universities train students to be middle-class at the parents' expense. As for the lower classes, who had traditionally counted on the rare scholarship, Appleton excluded them entirely: no student, he argued, should be subsidized, for the gifted working-class boy would do better to remain in his class and raise it up "as a class" (that is, to serve as one of Gramsci's "organic" intellectuals) rather than abandon it to profit from his individual mobility (or to move into the ranks of "traditional" intellectuals). Finally the essayists communicated that the proper criterion for measuring national progress was the development of academic culture, which required an intelligentsia.

Just such an intelligentsia arose with the university reform movement of the third quarter of the century, which sought to open the universities to students of all religious denominations, to broaden the curricula, and to convert the institutions into research establishments. The new idea of a university was national, secular, professional, and devoted to research. One of its products was the professional academic in a specialized discipline. Professionals accepted a common set of intellectual standards and procedures; concentrated on original research; emphasized "evidence"; expressed nonpartisanship in politics and theology; valued work according to its status as a "contribution" to the field; and accepted the circle of fellow researchers in the field as the significant audience.

Caught between cultural critics who were ignored by their society and academics who turned their backs on it in favor of their specialized "disciplines," the traditional man of letters, who gave moral as well as intellectual enlightenment and spoke on any subject without credentials, was not only an "amateur" but in danger of being unemployable. As Wilde's cultural criticism indicates (a small part of this criticism is the subject of

Introduction

Chapter 1), he was temperamentally a traditional man of letters. Chesterton called him (approvingly) "an Irish swashbuckler—a fighter," and Borges says that he was an ingenious man who was almost always right.[12] Yet when he came down to London in 1878 he understood his time well enough to know that he needed a profession and a specialty: hence, the Professor of Aesthetics. He immediately sought out the significant audience and set to rivaling the resident art expert James McNeill Whistler for "originality."

Specialization, with its seemingly independent realms of activity, and the possibilities for social mobility in Britain at the end of the nineteenth century made the notion of an aestheticized, or free, life not only possible but fashionable. These possibilities also indirectly contributed to the breakdown of Victorian "sincerity." Because Wilde aestheticized his life, he is famous for "posing." Yet the problem of his lack of sincerity exemplifies problems shared by the late Victorians in general. The social conditions in the London of the 1880's were ripe for posing: in this beginning of the age of modern advertising, the press was easily accessible for self-advertisement; the upper classes—which were now consolidating business, professional, and bureaucratic interests in addition to those of the older gentry and aristocracy—were enthusiastic for all kinds of fads and amusements; and the introduction of foreign-made fortunes and the decline of the landed aristocracy's economic base as a result of agricultural depression relaxed the traditional restrictions on entry into fashionable society. As Eric Hobsbawm has noted, the "making" of the working class as an identity in the period 1870-1914 was paralleled by the making of the middle class as we know it.[13]

Such conditions seemed to promise unprecedented social mobility to men of talent and education. Yet if posing was a solution in circles offering limited, but—as Wilde learned—deceptive, mobility, sincerity was another problem in the society of the spectacle. The groups that allowed for the possibility of social redefinition consistently overestimated social appearances. By the 1880's "sincerity" was, as Wilde said of the term "natural," one of the most debased coins in the currency of the language. The metaphor is appropriate, for the nineteenth century's confusion about sincerity was directly related to a mutable social economy. Aestheticism, the possibility of living one's life with the freedom of art, was possible only in a society with social mobility, economic security, and waning sincerity.

There was more margin in the 1890's, Ada Leverson reflected in the 1930's—margin for new entrants in Society, margin for activity, margin

Introduction

for credit, margin for interpretation. "Margin in every sense was in demand," wrote the woman whom young people called the Sphinx. She wanted to liberate the imagination when she suggested to Wilde that, unlike the minor poets whose verse trickled modestly down a page of massive white margin, he should publish a book *all* margin, full of beautiful unwritten thoughts. He should, said the Sphinx, have the blank volume printed on Japanese paper and bound in some Nilotic skin powdered with gilt nenuphars, smoothed with hard ivory, and decorated with gold by Ricketts. Wilde approved: "It shall be dedicated to you, and the unwritten text illustrated by Aubrey Beardsley. There must be five hundred signed copies for particular friends, six for the general public, and one for America."[14] The one copy in America would serve as the Ur-text for pirated editions, and in this best of all possible fantasy worlds the desired ratio of artistic to common readers would be 500 to 6.

Wilde wanted freedom from authority for the imagination and human society to develop. With their glittering packaging, their pages and performances mirroring the spectator, their illustrations by Beardsley—who never illustrated the text he was supposed to—Wilde's works give us both the images of advertising and the images of desire. In our analysis of art from the point of view of consumption, Wilde's works offer a site where the imagination—a romantic, indeed utopian, imagination—meets the marketplace that inevitably absorbs and transforms it.

I

Creating the Audience

But what completely fettered the artist was the pressure (and the accompanying drastic threats) always to fit into business life as an aesthetic expert. Formerly, like Kant and Hume, they signed their letters "Your most humble and obedient servant," and undermined the foundations of throne and altar. Today they address heads of government by their first names, yet in every artistic activity they are subject to illiterate masters. . . .

The blind and rapidly spreading repetition of words with special designations links advertising with the totalitarian watchword. . . . All the violence done to words is so vile that one can hardly bear to hear them any longer.

Max Horkheimer and Theodor Adorno,
"The Culture Industry: Enlightenment as Mass Deception," in *Dialectic of Enlightenment*

One of the results of the extraordinary tyranny of authority is that words are absolutely distorted from their proper and simple meaning, and are used to express the obverse of their right signification.

"The Soul of Man Under Socialism"

MR. OSCAR WILDE,

"Quite too utterly ecstatic"; from *Entr'acte*, 1881.

*I*N *The Trembling of the Veil,* Yeats says that Wilde had a genius for political life but that the corruption of the late-Victorian public was such that he could only indulge a contemptuous wit in set theatrical pieces. Yet Wilde's aesthetic and political theory, written before he turned to the stage, may be one of the last serious, if by no means solemn, attempts by an artist to construct a public not worthy of contempt. On the one hand, he exhibits the sadistic attitude toward a mass public that was characteristic of the great cultural critics since the Romantics. When he attacked an existing institution—the press, the academy, or the art world—he employed and subverted the very languages he criticized. When he considered the creation of an ideal audience, on the other, he changed his style. Perceiving a fallen art world and an unregenerate public, Wilde had two alternatives: to respond cynically or idealistically. He chose both alternatives and developed two distinct styles to represent them. He displays his cynicism in his technique of ironic reference, his idealism in imaginary dialogues of purple prose between two men. The first technique would lead to his theater and comedies; the second to a select audience of artful young men, romances, and prose poems. The first style was Wildean wit; the second, a prose jeweled and seductive. This doubleness constituted Wilde's response to the modern bourgeois artist's dilemma between private art and the need for a public.

Wilde composed his major theoretical works between 1885 and 1891, after he had toured the United States and during the period he was working as a journalist in London. The volume *Intentions* (1891), including four essays considerably revised from their first publication in periodicals, received predominantly favorable reviews in both London and the United States as a serious contribution to the contemporary debate over modern, or realist, art, although reviewers were quick to warn the public not to be put off by the "paradoxical," "bewildering" forms with which Wilde advanced his arguments for nonrepresentational art, or "lying."[1]

Two additional essays, "The Portrait of Mr. W. H." (1889) and "The Soul of Man Under Socialism" (1891), published only in article form, applied the principles introduced in *Intentions* to literary criticism and social theory.[2] Neither of these essays was formally reviewed, but both were to have resonance during Wilde's trials. His contemporary biographers Frank Harris and Robert Sherard wrote that "Mr. W. H." confirmed Wilde's homosexuality for many suspicious readers while it simultaneously affirmed the Cause for homosexual coteries. And Sherard wrote that although "The Soul of Man" was extremely popular in Central and Eastern Europe and among revolutionary groups in the United States, among the moneyed classes in England it produced a feeling of ill will against Wilde.[3] His plays would somewhat mollify the feeling, but the first reaction to the earlier essay would be remembered during the trials. Although Wilde's aesthetic and social theory has typically been treated as the popular manifesto of art for art's sake, by far the greatest part of these essays is devoted to the public and journalism—in fact, to the creation of an audience for art and life. I shall conclude the chapter, however, with a discussion of a poem rather than an essay, for "The Sphinx" illustrates in applied form what the essays theoretically propose with respect to the creation of an audience.

Playful and scintillating with wit, Wilde's essays also take up a sadistic attitude toward the public that attempted to influence artists and art. England ("the home of lost ideas"), he wrote in "The Critic as Artist," "has invented and established Public Opinion, which is an attempt to organize the ignorance of the community, and to elevate it to the dignity of physical force." And in "The Soul of Man Under Socialism":

> The public try to exercise over [art] an authority that is as immoral as it is ridiculous, and as corrupting as it is contemptible. . . . They are continually asking Art to be popular, to please their want of taste, to flatter their absurd vanity, to tell them what they have been told before, to show them what they ought to be tired of seeing, to amuse them when they feel heavy after eating too much, and to distract their thoughts when they are wearied of their own stupidity.
>
> With the decorative arts it is not different. The public clung with really pathetic tenacity to what I believe were the direct traditions of the Great Exhibition of international vulgarity, traditions that were so appalling that the houses in which people lived were only fit for blind people to live in.

By the public Wilde often means journalists, who produce a kind of anti-art that shares equally with art the focus of Wilde's theory. In "The Critic as Artist" he ironically concedes that

> there is much to be said in favour of modern journalism. By giving us the opinions of the uneducated, it keeps us in touch with the ignorance of the community. . . . [Journalists] give us the bald, sordid, disgusting facts of life. They chronicle, with degrading avidity, the sins of the second-rate, and with the conscientiousness

of the illiterate give us accurate and prosaic details of the doings of people of absolutely no interest whatsoever.

The public and journalists impede art and menace the imagination, first because they are entirely utilitarian ("Don't degrade me into the position of giving you useful information," says the older Gilbert to the younger Ernest in the dialogue of "The Critic as Artist"; "nothing that is worth knowing can be taught"); second because they have gone over to specialization ("Each of the professions means a prejudice," continues Gilbert; "we live in the age of the overworked, and the undereducated, the age in which people are so industrious that they become absolutely stupid"); and third because specialization has forced them to value evidence and proof above all. In the face of extreme purposiveness, productivity, and proof, Wilde opts, as in "The Decay of Lying," for the undirected, unproductive, and immature.

Many a young man starts in life with a natural gift for exaggeration which, if nurtured in congenial and sympathetic surroundings, or by the imitation of the best models, might grow into something really great and wonderful. But, as a rule, he comes to nothing. He falls into careless habits of accuracy . . . or takes to frequenting the society of the aged and the well-informed. . . . And in a short time he develops a morbid and unhealthy faculty of truth-telling, begins to verify all statements made in his presence, has no hesitation in contradicting people who are much younger than himself, and often ends by writing novels which are so like life that no one can possibly believe in their probability.

As I shall elaborate in a discussion of advertising in Chapter 2, Debord has observed how the false choices presented in spectacular abundance in the mass media gave rise to competitive oppositions like commercialized youth and age, which are meant to stimulate loyalty to quantitative trivialities. Wilde's oppositions here were shown to be false insofar as he discovered in the trials that the adult was not master of his life nor was youth the property of the young: both were subject to the dynamic of the system. Yet from these exhibitions two things become clear. Wilde wants public recognition as a Professor of Aesthetics who is able to lead the public toward art, and he wants a private life in which young men may realize their personalities, as he would say in "The Portrait of Mr. W. H.," "on some imaginative plane out of reach of the trammeling accidents and limitations of real life." The first desire can perhaps be seen most clearly in "The Soul of Man Under Socialism" and the second in "The Portrait of Mr. W. H." and "The Sphinx."

Yet before seeing Wilde's relatively controlled and stylized reaction, it is worth seeing the reactions of his cultural predecessors to their growing publics. For Wilde's jovial contempt at the expense of the public—or at the very least the bourgeois author's awareness of the distance between writer and general readers ("the quarter-educated" as Gissing calls them in *New Grub Street*)—was especially pronounced in the 1890's, but it was a well-established tradition. Images of print as self-devouring but paradoxically infinitely reproducible had multiplied during the century, not as the potentially positive collapse of the Benjaminian "aura" but as voracious vacuities, cheap thrills, implements of crime, and finally a total environmental hazard, an ecological disaster.

In 1831, Carlyle had complained about critics and reviewers who were stealing the market from authors: "At the last Leipzig Fair, there was advertised a Review of Reviews. By and by it will be found that all Literature has become one boundless self-devouring Review."[4] By the time he wrote "Shooting Niagara" (*Macmillan's Magazine*, August 1867), Carlyle was prepared to instruct the public to "leave Literature to run through its rapid fermentations . . . and to fluff itself off into Nothing, in its own way—like a poor bottle of soda-water with the cork sprung." *Culture and Anarchy* (1869) may be read as a lament for the British reading public's promiscuity: the newspapers Arnold mocks flaunt slogans as flat as Carlyle's soda-water. In 1872, in his letters to workers called *Fors Clavigera*, Ruskin associated the new reading public with thieves in a scorchingly contemptuous description of two rich American girls reading novels on a train—"cheap pilfered literature" Ruskin calls the new railroad fiction, which read like a form of rapid transit.[5] Wilde, in "The Soul of Man," coupled journalism and vandalism in describing journalists who "use the words very vaguely, as an ordinary mob will use ready-made paving-stones."

In "Fiction, Fair and Foul" (1880), Ruskin despaired over the vulgarity of fictional deathbed scenes—the drama most accessible to inhabitants of the city—tailored for the market, and he wished for audiences worthy of Scott rather than Dickens. The causes of the decline of health and dignity in literature were, of course, economic and social: "Nell, in *The Old Curiosity Shop*, was simply killed for the market, as a butcher kills a lamb," whereas Scott "never once . . . permitted the disgrace of wanton tears round the humiliation of strength, or the wreck of beauty."[6] One might recall Wilde's own bright response to the Dickensian public's sentimentality, that one would have to have a heart of stone not to laugh at the death of Little Nell, or Q. D. Leavis's correct observation that Bulwer Lytton's novels exploited each possible market: *Pelham*, novel of fashion, 1828; *Devereux*, historical romance, 1829; *Paul Clifford*, novel with a thesis, 1830; *Eugene Aram*, idealization of crime, 1832; *Godolphin*, philosophical-fashionable, 1833; *Last Days of Pompeii* and *Rienzi*, historical, 1834-35; *Ernest Maltravers*, realism and philosophy, 1837; *Zanoni*, supernatural, 1842.[7] Out of patience, Ruskin, Wilde's teacher at Oxford, simply condemns the urban public, railroads, readers, and writers and gathers "into one Caina of gelid putrescence the entire product of modern infidel imagination, amusing itself with destruction of the body, and busying itself with aberration of the mind."[8]

Print polluted the world. Literature had become litter, the very acme, as Deidre Lynch has said, of conspicuous consumption and built-in obsolescence. The narrator of *Our Mutual Friend* (1864) looks at London wondering: "That mysterious paper currency which circulates . . . when the wind blows . . . whence can it come, whither can it go? It hangs on every bush, flutters in every tree, is caught flying by the electric wires, haunts every enclosure, drinks at every pump, cowers at every grating, shudders upon every plot of grass, seeks rest in vain behind the regions of iron rails."[9] In Ruskin's close-up of the desecrated English landscape in "Fiction, Fair and Foul," the infamy is presided over by print, like flies over excrement:

Mixed dust of every unclean thing that can crumble in draught, and mildew of every unclean thing that can rot or rust in damp; ashes and rags, beer-bottle and old shoes, battered pans, smashed crockery, shreds of nameless clothes, door-sweepings, floor-sweepings, kitchen garbage, back-garden sewage, old iron, rotten timber jagged with out-torn nails, cigar-ends, pipe-bowls, cinders, bones, and ordure, indescribable; and variously kneaded into, sticking to, or fluttering foully here and there over all these, remnants, broadcast of every manner of newspaper, advertisement or big-lettered bill, festering and flaunting out their last publicity in the pits of stinking dust and mortal slime.[10]

Crowning it all is the image of the collapse of Mudie's circulating library in the 1890's because of the cost of storing thousands of ephemeral three-decker "latest novels" after their brief span of popularity.[11]

There were hundreds of cheap books and articles written on the problem of trashy literature. Literary dystopias from *Culture and Anarchy* to H. G. Wells's *Tono-Bungay: A Romance of Commerce* (1908) portrayed the proliferation of print for the quarter-educated with more energy and wit than had been expended on art in years. Gissing's *New Grub Street* (1891) is the most urgent treatment of a literary dystopia in all its appalling horror, and it presents the various components of the market in the 1890's. Gissing defined the quarter-educated and their subliterary wants:

No article in the paper is to measure more than two inches in length, and every inch must be broken into at least two paragraphs. . . . I would have the paper address itself to the quarter-educated; that is to say, the great new generation that is being turned out by the Board schools, the young men and women who can just read, but are incapable of sustained attention. People of this kind want something to occupy them in trains and on 'buses and trams . . . bits of stories, bits of description, bits of scandal, bits of jokes, bits of statistics, bits of foolery. . . . Everything must be very short, two inches at the utmost; their attention can't sustain itself beyond two inches.[12]

The hack writer inhabits a feverish, suppressed environment and, like his market, he suffers from a sort of consumption:

Mr. Quarmby laughed in a peculiar way, which was the result of long years of mirth-subdual in the Reading-room. . . . His suppressed laugh ended in a fit of coughing—the Reading-room cough.[13]

Another hack writer wonders whether she might not be replaced by a machine:

A few days ago her startled eye had caught an advertisement in the newspaper, headed 'Literary Machine'; had it then been invented at last, some automaton to supply the place of such poor creatures as herself, to turn out books and articles?[14]

She fears the insanity of the Reading-room:

Her eye discerned an official walking along the upper gallery, and . . . she likened him to a black, lost soul, doomed to wander in an eternity of vain research along endless shelves. . . . The readers who sat here at these radiating lines of desks, what were they but hapless flies caught in a huge web, its nucleus the great circle of the Catalogue? Darker, darker. From the towering wall of volumes seemed to emanate visible motes, intensifying the obscurity; in a moment the book-lined circumference of the room would be but a featureless prison-limit.[15]

The successful hack, on the other hand, has no time for such macabre fears. He recounts his day:

I got up at 7:30, and whilst I breakfasted I read through a volume I had to review. By 10:30 the review was written—three-quarters of a column of the *Evening Budget*. . . . At eleven I was ready to write my Saturday *causerie* for the *Will o' the Wisp*; it took me till close upon one o'clock. . . . By a quarter to two, [I had] sketched a paper for *The West End*. Pipe in mouth, I sat down to leisurely artistic work; by five, half the paper was done; the other half remains for to-morrow. From five to half-past I read four newspapers and two magazines, and from half-past to a quarter to six I jotted down several ideas that had come to me whilst reading. . . . Home once more at 6:45, and for two hours wrote steadily at a long affair I have in hand for *The Current*.[16]

This particular hack marries "the woman who has developed concurrently with journalistic enterprise":

> She read a good deal of that kind of literature which may be defined as specialism popularised; writing which addresses itself to educated, but not strictly studious, persons. . . . Thus, for instance, though she could not undertake the volumes of Herbert Spencer, she was intelligently acquainted with the tenor of their contents; and though she had never opened one of Darwin's books, her knowledge of his main theories and illustrations was respectable. She was becoming a typical woman of the new time, the woman who has developed concurrently with journalistic enterprise.[17]

As for the rest, those whom Gissing sees as artists, the stylist dies of starvation and exposure, deliriously apologizing for his relative lack of productivity to the wife who has abandoned him because of his poverty, and the realist commits suicide with the help of toxins researched in the British Museum. Moreover, in one of Gissing's better tragicomic ironies, the realist, who has devoted his life to the theory of the "essentially unheroic" embodied in a novel entitled *Mr. Bailey, Grocer*, at one point throws himself into a burning building to rescue the unpublished manuscript. Possibly the only more sinister treatment of late-Victorian letters is Arthur Machen's thriller *The Three Impostors* (1895), in which all information bears the duplicity of crime, all stories are deceptions, all professional writers are mystified, and any attempt at interpretation is fatal.

New Grub Street illustrates that we are not merely talking about one division—between artists and an inartistic public—but rather about many divisions among writers, publics, and writers and publics: the quarter-educated; the specialized popularized audience as defined above by Gissing; the new journalist; the old (amateur) man of letters; the specialists themselves, both readers and writers; and so on. Q. D. Leavis saw the eighteenth-century novelists as writing for the best—and only—reading public, at the very least the novelist's peers. In the nineteenth century, they wrote for the shopkeeper and worker as well. In some cases the writer and a public *were* peers: Leavis cites Dickens as one such case.[18] The Thackeray/Trollope/Eliot public may have had occasion to despise the Dickens/Reade/Collins public, but in any case what could conceivably be called incipient middlebrow and lowbrow tastes were represented side by side in the shilling magazines and twopenny weeklies.

Leavis was hesitant to claim more than the beginnings of a split between popular and cultivated taste in the mid-Victorian period, but most historians agree that one occurred in the 1880's, about the time of *Treasure Island* (1882). By this time the standardizing effects of the public schools (discussed in Chapter 2), the rise of the new journalism facilitated by the expansion of advertising, and academic specialization had divided the market and was effectively silencing the former man of letters. The biographer of the newspaper entrepreneur Northcliffe recited the differences between the old elite and the democratic new journalists:

The props of the Old Journalism feel bewildered. Their task, they believe, is to enlighten such of the public as can profit by enlightenment on political questions, on foreign policy. Their duty, they maintain, is to guide opinion concerning matters which may affect national well-being, cause changes of Government, raise the issue of peace or war. They have nothing to do with increase of circulation. They call this "pandering to mob interest in trivialities," commercial, undignified. Their standard of importance is set by the chiefs of political parties, Foreign Office, and the Treasury; by the famous Clubs (Reform, Carlton, Athenaeum); by the great country houses, the country rectories; by the Universities, by Bench and Bar. Now the standard is to be set by the mass of the people; the New Journalism will put in the foreground whatever is of interest to them, whatever will make them "hand the paper about."[19]

The growth and splintering of the reading publics, the marketing changes of 1840-80 that resulted in the professionalization of authorship—for example, specialist readers at publishing houses, literary agents, author's royalties, the Society of Authors—and the high and low culture industries contributed to the hostility rampant in the press. Far from appreciating the new platforms for exposure and the more respectable status of authors, the traditional men of letters and great social critics more often than not felt drowned out by triviality and claptrap.[20] The new journalists, they felt, represented not democracy but demagoguery. By the 1880's, according to John Gross's *Rise and Fall of the Man of Letters*, Oxbridge produced as many journalists as philosophers, and the ambitious graduates plagued traditional men of letters like Gissing's Alfred Yule in *New Grub Street*. After a life of unappreciated scholarly toil—that is, he was never even offered an editorship—the embittered Yule goes mad and blind and must be supported until his death by a hack-writing daughter. Within the universities, research experts exposed inaccurate and insufficient information in amateur writing—of the sort that Lady Carbury produces in Trollope's *The Way We Live Now*. Sidney Colvin finally formulated the brutal choice: "There comes a time when you must choose between the dispersion and fragmentariness, which is the habit of journalism and life in a hurry,

Creating the Audience

and the concentration and completeness which is the habit of serious literature."[21]

Reading all that trash, however, had an effect on its critics. Arnold studied it to mock it, and the result was a work of satiric genius richer and livelier than anything he had written before.[22] The texts that make up his *Culture and Anarchy: An Essay in Political and Social Criticism* provide excellent examples of the encroachment of anarchy on Culture, for they include more anarchy than Culture. With the skill of a caricaturist, Arnold labels an unpleasant audience and attempts to construct a pleasant one. He pilfers clichés out of newspapers and parodies them with his own clichés, absorbing them with the intention of subverting them. Like his labels Barbarians, Philistines, and Populace, even his central terms Hebraism and Hellenism smack to a classicist of tags or slogans soliciting a congeries of slightly evangelical attitudes toward education and reform.

With low cunning he quotes the classes on themselves: "the great broad-shouldered genial Englishman"; "the great middle class of this country, with its earnest common-sense penetrating through sophisms and ignoring commonplaces"; "the working man with his bright powers of sympathy and ready powers of action." He parodies religions "with their so many thousand souls and so many thousand rifles" and their "Dissidence of Dissent and Protestantism of the Protestant Religion." He parodies John Bright's "commendable interest in politics." He parodies himself as he is represented in the press, "a plain, unsystematic writer, without a philosophy." Against these he shoots his own slogans—phrases that sound like advertisements: "From Maine to Florida, and back again, all America Hebraises"; "Take care that your best light be not darkness" (pilfered from Bishop Thomas Wilson). One must cultivate, Arnold reiterates, one's Best Self, Right Reason, Sweetness, and Light. Here again we find the primitive form of the spectacular society's competitive oppositions, as if Arnold's readers could choose to be Barbarian, Philistine, or Populace.

Arnold probably deliberately permitted the forms of newsprint to dominate his style: he knew his market. By depoliticizing society and proposing the impossible conjunction of hypostatized qualities like Hebraism and Hellenism, Arnold thought to create something out of nothing, a solid State out of anarchy, an audience out of the public. He tried to sell Culture, and so, like most advertisers, he sloganized, reasoning by definition or tautology. Yet because his definitions generally took care to be idiosyncratic, nominal identities rather than empirical or functional consensus, he often succeeded in excluding from the definitions any ordinary (or practical) point of view. Therefore he produced rhetoric, but few sales. Thus he was able to say that culture is spiritual, therefore machinery (materialism) is not culture; or that criticism alone, "the free disinterested play of mind," rather than the practical point of view, can see the object as it really is ("The Function of Criticism at the Present Time"). The resultant slogan could be *Criticism alone sees the object as it really is*.

In a country where there is no "sovereign organ of opinion" or "recognised authority in matters of tone and taste"—that is, nothing like the French Academy—there may be poetry and genius, writes Arnold, but prose and intelligence will always bear "a note of provinciality" ("The Literary Influence of Academies"). This exemplifies reasoning by tautology, for the key roots are "centre" (the academy) and "province," which are by definition mutually exclusive. The resultant slogan could be *For tone and taste, try an Academy*.

Arnold could also write that "human nature" is the impulse to relate all knowledge to our sense of conduct and beauty, and so he could deduce that since science is only instrumental knowledge, which has nothing to do with conduct and beauty, the study of science alone can never satisfy human nature. Art, on the other hand, is one manifestation of the human relationship to beauty, and the great actions in great art refer to conduct, so literature by definition is sufficient ("Literature and Science"). The resultant slogan: *Only art can satisfy*. In *Seven Types of Ambiguity* (1947), William Empson felt that the "increasing vagueness, compactness, and lack of logical distinctions" in English journalism may "yet give back something of the Elizabethan energy to what is at present a rather exhausted language."[23] Although Empson was half-ironic here, in Arnold's case the exuberant, exploitative wordplay resulted in a sort of un-self-conscious poetry. One might even say that it resulted in his best poetry.

Of course, Arnold's word games were in the service of proclaiming that—again a slogan—"the men of Culture are the true apostles of equality," much as Wilde would claim that "the new Individualism is the New Hellenism" in the conclusion of "The Soul of Man Under Socialism." But without wit, slogans are no less than mental bondage. If *Culture and Anarchy* were not so exuberant in Arnold's destruction of his adversaries' speech, the reader who accepted Arnold's pious nomenclature would suffer a sort of textual bondage. Those who do not like his slogans find themselves alienated from the text or reduced to an epithet. Those who do not share his concept of Culture and its "disinterested study" are in bondage to the Ordinary—not Best—Self.

Wilde admired Arnold, but he discerned both this verbal bondage, duplicating the press's power over the public, and Arnold's tendency toward authoritarianism. As Gilbert shrewdly observed in "The Critic as Artist," the logical culmination of Arnold's disinterested study was in fact "to see the object as in itself it really was not." Art, for Wilde in "The Soul of Man Under Socialism," is no more autonomous than it is for Ruskin and Arnold: it is political.

Despite the seasoned debate among twentieth-century critics over whether Wilde was individualist, socialist, or anarchist,[24] "The Soul of Man" is in fact about the press and media control. Early in the essay Wilde establishes that the two problems of the modern world are pain and poverty; he predicts that inevitably the first will be solved by medical science and the second by socialism. Once the State, "a voluntary association that will organize labour, and be the manufacturer and distributor of necessary commodities," takes over the production of "useful things," it will be left to the individual "to make what is beautiful."

Here Wilde raises to an ideal level the socialist position, common not only to Kropotkin and Marx but also to local labor leaders like John Burns and Tom Mann, that technology would level the workers. But beyond leveling them, it would liberate them to be artists, or people who produce according to their own desires and natures, rather than people like journalists, who produce for the status quo. The best that a journalist can do, under the current regime, is to do what Wilde did in "The Soul of Man"—to use the techniques of satire, the revenge of beauty upon ugliness; and at this point Wilde launches into the kind of Juvenalian invective toward the public that was cited earlier. On the other hand, it is for the artist to try to revive a language mortified by the system. Just as the authority of the State will pass away, just as ecclesiastical and governmental authority had passed away from the pursuit of speculative thought in the universities, so too must the public authority over art through the form of journalism wither away.

In the remainder of the essay, Wilde instructs the public how to be receptive rather than authoritative toward art. Instead of calling books, like his own *Dorian Gray*, "immoral, unintelligible, exotic, and unhealthy"—typical journalistic favorites—the public should concede that "the work of art is to dominate the spectator." Having instructed the public, Wilde concludes the essay with the reinscription of art into life: "One of the results of the extraordinary tyranny of authority is that words are absolutely distorted from their proper and simple meanings, and are used to express the obverse of their right signification. What is true about Art is true about Life. . . . Under Individualism people will be quite natural and absolutely unselfish, and will know the meanings of the words, and realise them in their free, beautiful lives." In teaching the spectator how to be receptive to art, Wilde teaches the public the political message of how to be receptive to the lives of others not like oneself: "Selfishness [like censorship] is not living as one wishes to live, it is asking others to live as one wishes to live."

There is no question but that Wilde's socialism includes elements of the strange miscellany characterizing the socialist and labor platforms of the last 25 years of the nineteenth century: the Marxists of the Socialist Democratic Federation; the Fellowship of the New Life, modeled on the American transcendentalists; William Morris's Socialist League; the Fabians; the Independent Labour Party; and the ethical idealists like Edward Carpenter.[25] The religious and ethical socialism of Ruskin's Guild of St. George had been increasingly exposed for what it was: a paternalistic return to harmonious master-servant relations, intended to solve the class conflict brought about by competition and the cash nexus.[26] Unlike Ruskin, Wilde and others were not content to make of the laborer a glorified beast of burden, although they were not always in agreement about the alternatives.

"The Soul of Man" combines elements from many of these representative versions of socialism, as well as remnants of Renan's primitive, revolutionary Christianity in *The Life of Jesus*, a book Wilde admired throughout his life. Wilde had learned their language and catch phrases as well as Blatchford would for *Merrie England* (1894). Nor is there any question but that Wilde was sympathetic to socialism.[27] Although he was not actively involved with the various socialist and labor programs, his sympathies with those who were extended considerably beyond his youthful admiration of, and later friendship with, Morris.

Yet beyond Wilde's socialism, his essay presents a more significant attack on the fin-de-siècle culture industry, and this is where he perfects Arnold's tactics against the press he despises. Shaw blasted Wilde's "snobbery" in declaiming against the vulgarity of the British journalist in a manner, he said, that displayed "the odious feeling that is itself the vilest vulgarity."[28] Yet Shaw was among the minority of progressive and radical thinkers in not attacking the press. In *News from Nowhere*, published just before "The Soul of Man" and undoubtedly influential on Wilde's work, Morris presented a fantasy of a perfect socialist community set in England in 2050 A.D. The time-traveller William "Guest" hears from an old man that the nineteenth-century press was almost entirely reactionary. Only through a general strike that prevented publication and the defection of one sole courageous editor to the side of the revolution did the revolutionaries gain control of the papers and institute the great "Change," or socialism. Given the British press, good news came from nowhere.

Part of this concern with the language of the media may be attributable to the free speech movement of the time, which linked radicals and socialists and had organized demonstrations like what came to be called "Bloody Sunday" (13 November 1887) in Trafalgar Square. Part was due to cultural critics like Arnold, whose success in publicizing the press's corruption of language was considerable. As early as 1844 Engels had noticed that the English language was "permeated" by the ideology of the bourgeoisie.

Even the English language is permeated by the one idea that dominates the waking hours of the bourgeoisie. People are "valued" in terms of hard cash. They say of a man: "He is worth £10,000," and by that they mean that he possesses that sum. Anyone who has money is "respectable." He belongs to "the better sort of people." He is said to be "influential," which means that what he says carried weight in the circles in which he moves. The spirit of petty bargaining permeates the whole language.[29]

Although in his 1892 preface to the English edition of *The Condition of the Working Class in England*, Engels disparaged Wilde's socialism, which "has not only become respectable, but has actually donned evening dress and lounges lazily on drawing-room *caseuses*," even in 1844 he had begun to perceive the distortion of language or rigidification of bourgeois ideology in the press that Wilde considered a threat to art and liberty. In its use of middle-class newspapers, Engels's method, like Wilde's, had been to subvert the speech of his adversaries. "Charity," Engels raves, continuing the passage above on language, "—when he who gives is more degraded than he who receives. Charity—when the recipient is trodden even deeper into the mud than he was before. Charity—when those who dispense alms insist that those who receive them must first be cast out of society as pariahs and must be deprived of their last shred of self respect by being *forced to beg*!" "I enjoy," he writes, "making my opponents provide me with evidence."[30] "Charity," Wilde writes in "The Soul of Man," "creates a multitude of sins."

For this kind of language, which deconstructed bourgeois categories of thought, one might use the term "dialogical." In *Problems of Dostoevsky's Poetics*, Bakhtin cites Wilde—from Wilde's reviews of Dostoevsky—as one of the first readers to accurately understand Dostoevsky's most significant contribution to literary modernism, that is, what Bakhtin terms the "inner unfinalizability" of Dostoevsky's characters.[31] Bakhtin calls this quality "dialogicality" or "polyphonism," as opposed to the monologicality of traditional novels. Through his characters, Dostoevsky is multi-voiced, dialogic; all views are enunciated in dialogue between characters or in a character's dialogue with itself. In the case of a character's dialogue with itself, Bakhtin cites the phenomenon of "double-voiced words," in which an interior monologue consists of rephrasing and altering the words of an external adversary. The heroes in Dostoevsky *are* their ideas, but these ideas are constantly in flux, "unfinalizable." Bakhtin contends that previous readers have finalized (or "monologized") this openness by trying to identify the man Dostoevsky (the man with social and religious beliefs) with certain of his characters, and then by "dialoging" with a particular character as if it represented the views of Dostoevsky. This dialogicality of double-voiced words amounts formally to what Debord calls the revolutionary and dialectical style of diversion, the style connecting Hegel, Feuerbach, and Marx.

In creating his characters as generating subjects rather than finalized objects or finished products, Dostoevsky's works posed significant alternatives to society as he saw it as well as to previous literature. Like Bakhtin's "double-voiced" words, Wilde's epigrams and paradoxes exploit the self-critical possibilities of Victorian language and thought patterns. As Debord writes:

Diversion leads to the subversion of past critical conclusions which were frozen into respectable truths, namely transformed into lies. . . . It is the obligation of *distance* toward what was falsified into official truth which determines the use of diversion. . . . Ideas improve. The meaning of words participates in the improvement. Plagiarism is necessary. Progress implies it. It embraces an author's phrase, makes use of his expressions, erases a false idea, and replaces it with the right idea. Diversion is the opposite of quotation . . . [which is] a fragment torn from its context, from its movement, and ultimately from the global framework of its epoch. . . . Diversion is the fluid language of anti-ideology.[32]

In addition, the larger forms of Wilde's essays are dialogical. "The Truth of Masks" proposes and defends a theory of dramatic coherence and interpretation only to conclude with Wilde's disavowal of the theory: "Not that I agree with everything that I have said in this essay. There is much with which I entirely disagree. The essay simply represents an artistic standpoint, and in aesthetic criticism attitude is everything. . . . It is only in art-criticism, and through it, that we can realize Hegel's system of contraries." "The Portrait of Mr. W. H." presents a dialogical production of a theory through three separate advocates, and the narrator's ambivalence at the end emphasizes its unfinalizability. And "Pen, Pencil, and Poison" is an ironic, or double-voiced, treatment of the art/life dichotomy.

In "The Soul of Man Under Socialism" Wilde focuses directly on the press's distortions of language—its "respectable truths"—and employs wit to subvert their bourgeois meanings, using, as had Arnold, the language he is criticizing. The first part of the tract argues against current notions of philanthropy, individualism, and the Christian virtues. "Altruism" or otherness, it turns out, is a mere distortion of language in a society based on competition rather than cooperation:

With admirable though misdirected intentions, [altruists] very seriously and very sentimentally set themselves to the task of remedying the evils that they see. But their remedies do not cure the disease: they merely prolong it. Indeed, their remedies are part of the disease.

They try to solve the problem of poverty, for instance, by keeping the poor alive or, in the case of a very advanced school, by amusing the poor.

But this is not a solution: it is an aggravation of the difficulty. *The proper aim is to try and reconstruct society on such a basis that poverty will be impossible.* . . . Charity creates a multitude of sins. . . . It is immoral to use private property in order to alleviate the horrible evils that result from the institution of private property.

With such subversive phrases as "Charity creates a multitude of sins," "In the interest of the rich we must get rid of private property," "Disobedience is man's original virtue," and "Democracy is the bludgeoning of the people by the people for the people," Wilde cheerfully advocates agitators, demagogues, and violence for the temporary relief of the poor. In the long run, all authority must be abolished altogether.

But Wilde argues that the tyranny exercised by journalists over public opinion is the worst sort of tyranny, for "the pen is mightier than the paving-stone, and can be made as offensive as the brickbat." To return to words "their proper and simple meanings," their "right signification," he wields his tricks of paradox. One such use is his treatment of the word "unpractical," which the popular press frequently applied to utopian schemes such as his:

It will of course be said that such a scheme as is set forth here is quite unpractical, and goes against human nature. This is perfectly true. It is unpractical, and it goes against human nature. This is why it is worth carrying out, and that is why one proposes it. For what is a practical scheme? *A practical scheme is either a scheme that is already in existence, or a scheme that could be carried out under existing conditions.* But it is exactly the existing conditions that one objects to; and any scheme that could accept these conditions is wrong and foolish. The conditions will be done away with, and human nature will change. . . . The systems that fail are those that rely on the permanency of human nature, and not on its growth and development.

In "Pen, Pencil, and Poison: A Study in Green," Wilde included in his attack the current art world as well as the press, again using the institutional style to criticize the institution. He ironically parodies a topical genre, aesthetic appreciations of bizarre, perverse, often criminal, historical figures, in order to indicate the art world's incriminating engagement with culture. In doing so, he confirms the impossibility of separating creation from criticism, doing from talking, and, ultimately, life from art.

By the 1870's, novelists and dramatists had exhausted the material in the *Newgate Calendar*, the last nineteenth-century edition of which was published in 1845. First published in 1773, the calendar offered memoirs of notorious malefactors and transcriptions of their last exclamations, generally from the scaffold. Bulwer Lytton and Harrison Ainsworth were only the most prominent of novelists who ransacked its pages for material on burglary, highway robbery, swindling, and murder, and they were imitated by hack novelists as well as dramatists, who plagued the censors with law-defying brigands like Jack Sheppard. The Newgate novel and drama, sensational permutations of the historical romance that were suspected by the authorities of making crime attractive to the young and ambitious, were eventually superseded by contemporary accounts of murder readily available in all gruesome detail in the press.[33] In "Pen, Pencil, and Poison," however, Wilde was not so concerned with popular forms of literature and drama as he was with their offspring, the critical appreciations of criminals, which claimed more objective status and more psychological subtlety. That is, the essay is directed against academic, as well as popular, representatives of the art world.

Critics have always interpreted "Pen, Pencil, and Poison," Wilde's aesthetic appreciation of the artist and murderer Thomas Griffiths Wainewright, as forwarding Wilde's alleged view that ethical judgments have no place in assessments of art works, that art works are autonomous objects of beauty independent of spectatorial exigencies. Recently Lance Morrow in *Time* magazine used the conclusion of Wilde's essay—"The fact of a man being a poisoner is nothing against his prose"—to represent Mailer's defense of Jack Abbott.[34] Yet this interpretation, imputing to Wilde a simplicity and transparency entirely uncharacteristic, is wrong; the key passages of the essay containing authorial comment are best understood as ironic.

First, Wilde suggests that the aesthetic, impressionist, or Paterian school of criticism mystified the past, that is, that critics primarily concerned with art and artists obfuscated certain unconscionable facts of history in order to justify their own sense of the primacy of art. Second, he says explicitly that although such an obfuscation of history may have been attractive, it was dangerous for the present. Third, he demystifies "gentlemen" of the present, exposing their own pose of "culture" as historically linked with "criminal" behavior. And finally, he undercuts art as a bearer of absolute value and takes artists to task for their lack of critical, that is, dialogical, perspective. It is increasingly clear that the essay is ironic if we also consider the view advanced in every other of Wilde's essays, that art should be normative, and if we also remember that Wilde, unlike some of his French and English contemporary "decadents," never once wrote a story or scenario without a "moral." (*The Importance of Being Earnest* is a possible exception. The obscurity of the moral here has, for some, redeemed Wilde as a modern writer.)

The essay begins benignly enough with the observation that artists and men of letters generally lack wholeness and completeness of nature. "This must necessarily be so," writes Wilde, "for that very concentration of vision and intensity of purpose which is the characteristic of the artistic temperament is in itself a mode of limitation." As the essay progresses, the emphasis will fall increasingly on the limitations. Here Wilde introduces apparent exceptions: Rubens serving as ambassador, Goethe as state councillor, Milton as Latin secretary to Cromwell, Sophocles in civic office, American artists as diplomatic representatives—and Wainewright, "being not merely a poet and a painter, an art-critic, an antiquarian, and a writer of prose, an amateur of beautiful things, and a dilettante of things delightful, but also a forger of no mean or ordinary capabilities, and as a subtle and secret poisoner almost without rival in this or any age." The conjunction of the lawless Wainewright and accepted geniuses who were also civil servants anticipates the link between art, or "culture," and crime that will later surface as the dominant view of the essay.

Throughout the biographical summary of Wainewright's occupations and avocations, there are equally remarkable elisions between his art and criminality: "Indeed, painting was the first art that fascinated him. It was not till much later that he sought to find expression by pen or poison"; and "However, we must not forget that the cultivated young man who penned these lines, and who was so susceptible to Wordsworthian influences, was also, as I said at the beginning of this memoir, one of the most subtle and secret poisoners of this or any age." Wilde deftly juxtaposes Wainewright's poisoning of his sister-in-law with the drawing he made of his victim: "After the doctor's morning visit, Mr. and Mrs. Wainewright brought her some poisoned jelly, and then went out for a walk. When they returned Helen Abercrombie was dead. She was about twenty years of age, a tall graceful girl with fair hair. A very charming red-chalk drawing of her by her brother-in-law is still in existence, and shows how much his style as an artist was influenced by Sir Thomas Lawrence. . . ." When Wainewright gratuitously poisons a friend, Wilde mentions his immediate embarkation on a sketching tour: "His friend died the next day in his presence, and he left Boulogne at once for a sketching tour through the most picturesque parts of Brittany." And art and crime are again linked, with more general culpability, when "Dickens, Macready, and Hablot Browne came across [Wainewright] by chance" in jail: "They had been going over prisons of London, searching for artistic effects, and in Newgate they suddenly caught sight of Wainewright. He met them with a defiant stare, Forster tells us, but Macready was 'Horrified to recognize a man familiarly known to him in former years, and at whose table he had dined.'"

Wilde's prolonged, controlled discussion of Wainewright's art, with its casual but insistent repetition of its customary result in murder, produces in readers, depending upon their mood, either a gleeful recognition of Wilde's masterly use of irony, the master trope, or a mad, nightmarish sensation, rather like that produced by Swift's "Modest Proposal." In neither case can one take the essay as a defense of the autonomy of art, despite the fact that bourgeois art critics have done so for a century. Like "A Modest Proposal," Wilde's essay builds a case, through irony, against specialization (including a specialized "art world"), the division of labor, scientific standards, and, in this case, journalism.

If we set aside his achievements in the sphere of poison, what he has actually left to us hardly justifies his reputation. But then it is only the Philistine who seeks to estimate a personality by the vulgar test of production.

The fact of a man being a poisoner is nothing against his prose. The domestic virtues are not the true bases of art, though they may serve as an excellent advertisement for second-rate artists.

[Historical felons] have passed into the sphere of art and science, and neither art nor science knows anything of moral approval or disapproval.

The exotic aura with which Wilde surrounds Wainewright, his strange room and library, his fascination with cats and hermaphrodites, Wilde's repetition of "strange," "mysterious," "fascinating," also suggest a parody of the Paterian school of criticism. At the conclusion of the essay Wilde ironically remarks that had Wainewright lived during a more distant time, we might have been better able to assess his aesthetic work: "It is impossible not to feel a strong prejudice against a man who might have poisoned Lord Tennyson, or Mr. Gladstone, or the Master of Balliol. But had the man worn a costume and spoken a language different from our own, had he lived in imperial Rome, or at the time of the Italian Renaissance, or in Spain in the seventeenth century, or in any land or any century but this century and this land, we would be quite able to arrive at a perfectly unprejudiced estimate of his position and value."

Also ironically, Wilde goes on to disclaim any moral judgments applied to history or to history as represented through art, saying that we need not judge Tiberius or Cæsar Borgia because we no longer fear them. But the corollary of this is that we must judge what we fear. And since we fear Wainewright as one of our own contemporaries, he should not be the subject of "charming studies":

At present I feel that he is just a little too modern to be treated in that fine spirit of disinterested curiosity to which we owe so many charming studies of the great criminals of the Italian Renaissance from the pens of Mr. John Addington Symonds, Miss A. Mary Robinson, Miss Vernon Lee, and other distinguished writers. However, Art has not forgotten him. He is the hero of Dickens's *Hunted Down*, the Varney of Bulwer's *Lucretia*; and it is gratifying to note that fiction has paid some homage to one who was so powerful with "pen, pencil, and poison." To be suggestive for fiction is to be of more importance than a fact.

That last sentence, a statement that critics have read solemnly, is ironic, as are Wilde's praises of "charming studies" of Renaissance criminals. The pen and pencil, he suggests, are poison.

Wilde himself is critical of his object, and he does not hesitate to demystify Wainewright's false status as an artist—while he simultaneously identifies him with the journalists who have brought his kind of "art" up to the present. He deftly exposes Wainewright's (and by extension others') artistic "sensitivity": "His delicately strung organization, however indifferent it might have been to inflicting pain on others, was itself most keenly sensitive to pain." He is suspicious of Wainewright's status as an artist: "His life-work falls naturally under the three heads suggested by Mr. Swinburne [pen, pencil, and poison], and it may be partly admitted that, if we set aside his achievements in the sphere of poison, what he has actually left to us hardly justified his reputation." He quotes at length from Wainewright's impressionistic art criticism and says of it that "there is much that is terrible, and very much that is quite horrible, but it is not without a certain crude form of power, or at any rate, a certain crude violence of words, a quality which this age should highly appreciate, as it is its chief defect."

In fact, the most that Wilde can say of Wainewright's "art" is that it is the Ur-form of modern sensational journalism; and far from presenting the object as it really was, Wainewright's gorgeous style, like that of Wilde's own contemporary impressionistic critics, concealed and mystified the object: "One side of his literary career deserves especial notice. Modern journalism may be said to owe almost as much to him as to any man of the early part of this century. He was the pioneer of Asiatic prose, and delighted in pictorial epithets and pompous exaggerations. To have a style so gorgeous that it conceals the subject is one of the highest achievements of an important and much admired school of Fleet Street leader-writers." Wilde adds that if we are to make a literary spectacle of Wainewright, it should be for his crime of journalism: "There is, however, something dramatic in the fact that this heavy punishment [for forgery] was inflicted on him for what, if we remember his fatal influence on the prose of modern journalism, was certainly not the worst of all his sins."

Wilde claims that the fascination of respectable critics and artists with criminals is indivisible from and implicated in their own personalities—a recurrent Wildean claim for the Unconscious against the progressive moral cant of the day—and that their own perverse personalities quite frequently falsify their subjects: "M. Zola, in one of his novels, tells us of a young man who, having committed a murder, takes to art, and paints greenish impressionist portraits of perfectly respectable people, all of which bear a curious resemblance to his victim." Similarly, Wainewright's "cultured," gentlemanly qualities, like those of many of Dickens's gentlemen, are merely a shiny veneer to cover his crimes. Wainewright reportedly told a visitor to his jail cell, which "was for some time a kind of fashionable lounge": "But, sir, I will tell you one thing in which I have succeeded to the last. I have been determined through life to hold the position of a gentleman. I have always done so. I do so still. It is the custom of this place that each of the inmates of a cell shall take his morning's turn of sweeping it out. I occupy a cell with a bricklayer and a sweep, but they never offer me the broom!"

Wilde stresses that in fact the only thing that makes Wainewright interesting to gentlemen is that he was a "cultured" man who sinned through leisure. In this way Wilde leaves the critics with the uncomfortable association of crime and their own class rather than with the lower class and its uninteresting criminality that resulted from poverty: "From Newgate he was brought to the hulks at Portsmouth, and sent from there in the *Susan* to Van Diemen's Land along with three hundred other convicts. The voyage seems to have been most distasteful to him, and in a letter written to a friend he spoke bitterly about the ignominy of 'the companion of poets and artists' being compelled to associate with 'country bumpkins.' The phrase that he applied to his companions need not surprise us. Crime in England is rarely the result of sin. It is nearly always the result of starvation."

Finally, in a notorious concluding statement, Wilde says that crime constitutes a large part of the aesthetic past and that present fascination with this past indicated the conservative function of the art world: "That [Wainewright] had a sincere love of art and nature seems to me quite certain. There is no essential incongruity between crime and culture." (Earlier in the decade Wilde had lectured in Boston on "that dreadful record of crime known as history," admonishing parents of undergraduates that "You give the criminal calendar of Europe to your children under the name of history."[35]) That is, men of "culture" had justified their own culture by mystifying the past, by taking Wainewright's gaudy career as the object of art rather than by seeing the larger movements of history (like the colonial deportation of 300 starving convicts) and offering a solution or alternative to these. That "there is no essential incongruity between crime and culture" is understatement: it accused culture, just as many critical "appreciations" valorized crime. The cultured man's "very concentration of vision and intensity of purpose" amounts to a limited conception of social life and a dangerously isolated egocentrism. The essay becomes a critique of what is commonly understood to be *l'art pour l'art*.

In a striking contrast, "The Portrait of Mr. W. H." presents a meaningful and engaged, indeed a seductive, art, an art not criminal, in a very dramatic form. At the same time the essay is a satire on standards of evidence and proof in a scientific, utilitarian age and a kind of parable of the loss of faith—for Wilde, imagination—in the nineteenth century. In the sensational conclusion to the essay, the skeptical narrator cries out, "To die for one's theological opinions is the worst use a man can make of his life; but to die for a literary theory! It seemed impossible." Yet "The Portrait of Mr. W. H." is a story of two characters who die for their belief in a literary theory that is never proven and of the narrator who finally thinks that there is "really a great deal to be said" for that theory.

Erskine, an older man, tells the young narrator the history of his friend Cyril Graham, a boy actor who invented a theory that the Mr. W. H. to whom Shakespeare's Sonnets were dedicated was a boy actor named Willie Hughes. Graham's theory was based on purely "internal evidence," that is, evidence within the Sonnets themselves—although for the reader the term "internal evidence" will have increasing relevance to the internality of the theorists. Despite Graham's extensive exegesis and intense desire that it persuade Erskine, his friend, a hard-headed rationalist, remained skeptical, insisting that the theory assumed the existence of the Willie Hughes that it had intended to prove; he demanded "independent evidence." Cyril Graham consequently had a portrait forged of W. H., by which he finally persuaded Erskine. By chance, however, Erskine detected the fraud, had words with Graham, and Graham, in a state of extreme abjection, killed himself as a final testimony to his belief in the theory.

The narrator is convinced by Graham's theory and goes off to lock himself up with the Sonnets to develop it further, despite Erskine's admonition that "a thing is not necessarily true because a man dies for it." He considerably expands the theory, and at this point Wilde's text is saturated with quotations from the Sonnets. Through Willie Hughes, the narrator comes to understand Shakespeare's theory of drama; he writes a history of English boy actors of the sixteenth and seventeenth centuries; he discovers the relationship of Shakespeare and Willie Hughes to the Dark Lady; and he finally comprehends the actual "drama" of the Sonnets.

He writes the expanded theory to Erskine, but in the process he loses his belief. That is, once he extracts himself from the absorbing drama to produce an argument, the unilateral form of rhetoric reduces the theory to one polemic among many. As such, it is exposed to the sorts of rational constraints that are expected of theories—for example, that they not assume the thing they are to prove. Erskine, however, is now persuaded and, agitated by the narrator's admission that he had assumed all of what he intended to prove, removes himself to Germany, where the narrator had speculated that Willie Hughes died. Failing to find proof in Germany, Erskine writes to the narrator that he intends to offer his own life as the second martyrdom to the theory. The narrator rushes off to prevent the suicide, but arrives after Erskine has died. He learns that Erskine had not killed himself at all, but had expected for some time to die of consumption. The narrator inherits the forged portrait, but skeptically echoes Erskine to Cyril Graham to the effect that the "pathetic fallacy" of martyrdom proves nothing, that it "is merely a tragic form of scepticism, an attempt to realise by fire what one had failed to do by faith." But sometimes, alone in his library with the forged portrait, the narrator thinks that "there really is a great deal to be said for the Willie Hughes theory of Shakespeare's Sonnets."

The argument here is not only in favor of other truths than the scientific, which Wilde had argued in "The Truth of Masks," but it also opposes Wilde's version of hermeneutics to the public and journalistic value of objectivity. "For in art," "The Truth of Masks" concludes, "there is no such thing as a universal truth. A Truth in art is that whose contradictory is also true.... It is only in art-criticism, and through it, that we can realize Hegel's system of contraries. The truths of metaphysics are the truths of masks."[36] It is precisely his belief in interpretation, or the practice of criticism, that prevents the divorce, despite his contempt for the public, between art and life. The hermeneutic was contained in "The Decay of Lying": "There may have been fogs for centuries in London. I dare say there were. But no one saw them, and so we do not know anything about them. They did not exist till Art had invented them. Now, it must be admitted, fogs are carried to excess. They have become the mere mannerism of a clique, and the exaggerated realism of their method gives dull people bronchitis. Where the cultured catch an effect, the uncultured catch cold."

"The Portrait of Mr. W. H." presents a theory that Wilde understood to be no more than a fanciful construction answerable to the private exigencies of his own personality. Not only did it confront bourgeois standards of truth, it also affronted professional standards of originality and honesty, for it is a plagiarism, having been first advanced in 1766 by a Shakespearean scholar named Thomas Tyrwhitt and then duly incorporated in Malone's 1780 edition of *The Poems of Shakespeare*. Moreover, in the *Woman's World* of September 1888, Wilde had edited an article by Amy Strachey entitled "The Child-Players of the Elizabethan Age," from which he had also borrowed significantly. As Debord says, a dialectical and historicizing plagiarism is necessary for progress, and Wilde is clearly using Tyrwhitt's theory in the service of his own freedom.

In the introduction to his anthology of Victorian texts dealing with homosexual subjects, Brian Reade places this as the first short story in English to dwell upon pederasty, although Sir Richard Burton had already called Shakespeare "that most debauched genius" in his "Terminal Essay," the history of pederasty, to his translation of *The Book of the Thousand Nights and a Night* (1885).[37] Significantly, Wilde's essay begins with Erskine and the narrator, a much younger man, discussing literary forgeries. The narrator claims that "all Art being to a certain degree a mode of acting, an attempt to realize one's own personality on some imaginative plane out of reach of the trammeling accidents and limitations of real life, to censure an artist for a forgery [is] to confuse an ethical with an aesthetic argument." In the story, the characters enact this notion that the experience of art, for spectator as well as artist, is a kind of forgery. After working out the "drama" of Shakespeare's Sonnets, the narrator will say, "I had lived it all." In "The Critic as Artist," Gilbert calls literary criticism "the highest form of autobiography": "give the artist a mask, and he will tell you the truth." And Wilde does tell the truth in the story, realized "on some imaginative plane."

Erskine, Cyril, and the narrator seek themselves and their own homoeroticism in Shakespeare's art. Erskine fails because he can only go as far as reason; he seeks external authority (facts) for artistic interpretation. Cyril recognizes and acknowledges his homoeroticism, he can trust "internal evidence," but he is too dependent upon Erskine's approbation; he seeks external authority in the other (the art world). The narrator believes and doubts at once, allowing himself a sort of conscious repression, unfinalizability, or, if you will, a willing suspension of disbelief. He does not act on what he learns of Shakespeare and his boy, but he contemplates the portrait alone in his library and sometimes thinks that "there really is a great deal to be said for the Willie Hughes theory of Shakespeare's Sonnets." He also shows the forged portrait to his friends as a test of either their gullibility or seducibility: "They have decided that it is not a Clouet, but an Ouvry."[38]

At this point one need hardly say that as he composed "The Portrait of Mr. W. H." in conversations with Robert Ross, Wilde was practically concerned with what the narrator calls "the ambiguity of the sexes." He was meeting with a number of young actors; and, if Croft-Cooke is right in his characterization of Wilde's emotional make-up, he was much like his own picture of Willie Hughes: "He could act love, but could not feel it, could mimic passion without realising it."

The narrator writes that the creative energy of art is "objective," whereas such seemingly "real," substantial attributes as sex are "mere accidents"; this is consistent with Wilde's characteristic devaluation of science. The narrator also surmises that Willie Hughes died in Germany, having brought "the Romantic Movement," equal to playacting or imaginative posing, into that land; and Vivian had heralded "the return of Romance" in "The Decay of Lying." The idea that Shakespeare had worked out his theory of the drama in his Sonnets is duplicated in Wilde's working out his theory of the drama in "The Portrait of Mr. W. H." The Sonnets become a drama of Shakespeare's life, and "Mr. W. H." is also a drama, in five acts, dramatizing Wilde's theories of art and love.

Two bizarre notes to the story indicate the extent to which Wilde's fiction affected the lives of real boys for a half-century and thus the extent to which Wilde succeeded in creating an audience, fit though few. John Moray Stuart-Young's long poem *Osrac, the Self-Sufficient* (1905) is prefaced by two forged photographs: one of Johnnie, signed "Yours sincerely J. M. Stuart-Young," holding a volume of Wilde's *Poems*, and one of Wilde, bearing the forged autograph "Oscar Wilde to Johnnie September 1894." The epigraph to the poem is *"Rien n'est vrai que le beau."*[39] The homosexual Johnnie apparently fabricated a relationship with his much-admired master, Wilde, as Wilde had fabricated a precedent relationship between Shakespeare and Willie Hughes. Moreover, Johnnie went on in *Osrac, the Self-Sufficient* to attribute Wilde's downfall to what the boy considered his own downfall to have been: masturbation, or "the witchery of the hand"—hence "self-sufficient." Johnnie's own eventual prison sentence even further enforced his identification with his idol.

Perhaps not surprisingly, it was Wilde's own dear boy who proved—at least to the satisfaction of many of his contemporaries, including Shaw—the theory of Shakespeare's boy that Wilde had taught him and that Erskine had taught the young narrator. In 1933 Alfred Douglas published the *True History of Shakespeare's Sonnets*, the research for which, he claimed, destroyed his eyesight. In Part I, as well as in his unpublished letters to Adrian Earle, Douglas explains that whereas Wilde did not acknowledge his predecessors Tyrwhitt and Malone, and whereas Samuel Butler, who "spent years of his life trying to find a Will Hewes," did not acknowledge Wilde, Douglas acknowledges them all and adds his own touches to the theory.

Although Douglas's book still relied on "internal" evidence, after it was published he acquired the evidence that everyone but Wilde had sought. In a letter to Earle of 18 August 1942, he wrote that reference to a William Hewes had been discovered in the archives in Canterbury: he had been a freeman by apprenticeship to John Marlowe (Christopher's father), shoemaker, in 1593. Hence Willie Hughes's connection to Marlowe's and Shakespeare's companies. A scholar had read Douglas's book, recalled something he had seen in Canterbury, and Douglas had forthwith made the fruitful inquiries. Douglas's later correspondence with Earle indicates that the young Earle and other devotees of the now aged Douglas continued to refine the theory. While its literalism at their hands entirely missed the point of Wilde's essay, its power of influence was right in its spirit.[40] An artistic community, of a sort, had been created.

In tracing alternatives, like "Mr. W. H.," to the institutional languages that Wilde inverted as a form of critique, "The Sphinx" is the summa of Wilde's art-as-seduction. Rather than the measured substitutions and inversions of wit, here the language is excessive and unrestrained, indiscriminate, not deriding an existing audience, but teasing an ideal one. In the poem the boy of hardly "twenty summers" ultimately banishes (represses) his uninnocent desires, but not without an excess of eroticism.

> In a dim corner of my room for longer than my fancy thinks
> A beautiful and silent Sphinx has watched me through the shifting gloom.

Whether these opening lines refer to an objet d'art or are entirely a product of the student's imagination, in the course of the poem that imagination destroys any illusions of innocence in the human psyche. Trying to imagine the (Paterian) Sphinx's "thousand weary centuries" of experience, the student exhausts a vocabulary of rhymes from a schoolboy's classics, depletes the excesses of school sexuality: Hieroglyphs/Hippogriffs, obelisks/Basilisks, Cyprian Kiss/Heliopolis, catafalque/Amenalk, odorous/Antinous, corridors/Mandragores, sarcophagus/Tragelaphos, cubits' span/Kurdistan, new-made wine/insapphirine, Corybants/elephants, Nubians/peacock fans, Bedouin/paladin, striped burnous/Titan thews, figured coins/barren loins, amorous jests/agate breasts, and so forth.

"Inviolate and immobile," the Sphinx, clandestinely come to inhabit the student's "cell," suffers him to interrogate her about her lovers:

> Did Gryphons with great metal flanks leap on you in your trampled couch?
>
> Did monstrous hippopotami come sidling toward you in the mist?

As his imagination grows bolder, the student's queries become assertions.

> White Ammon was your bedfellow! Your chamber was the steaming Nile!

After hundreds of lines of this, he energetically encourages her to

> Follow some roving lion's spoor across the copper-coloured plain,
> Reach out and hale him by the mane and bid him be your paramour!
>
> And take a tiger for your mate, whose amber sides are flecked with black,
> And ride upon his gilded back in triumph through the Theban gate.

Under the delusion that his Sphinx is not his own imagination, he sends her packing; and with a gesture toward the deconstruction of Roman Catholicism in the nineteenth century, he repositions his meditation on another objet d'art, his crucifix,

> Whose pallid burden, sick with pain, watches the world with wearied eyes,
> And weeps for every soul that dies, and weeps for every soul in vain.

In exhibiting "The Sphinx" in standard accounts of the subject as the quintessentially decadent poem—in the sense of exhausted, erethistic, and esoteric—critics have overlooked the fact that it is a very funny and very sexy piece: it should be read among friends, like many of John Ashbery's new poems with equally clunky rhythms. Part of its charm lies in the generosity of the poet who pours into the ear of his beloved a ten-year treasure trove of research in improbable rhymes, a textbook-complete catalogue, as Ira Livingston has put it, of polymorphous perversity. The poem is a poem of excess in the sense that the object of desire is technically absent; the desire compulsively flows from the subject's brain. But the consummate mastery, the *style*, of having the shy beloved *seduce himself* must be admired.

"To Marcel Schwob in friendship and admiration" Wilde dedicated the poem. Although he began the poem at Oxford sometime in 1874-76, he did not finish it until he was in Paris in 1883 and did not publish it until 1894. Since he was 40 years old in 1894, hyperliteral critics ridiculed him for presenting himself as hardly having seen "some twenty summers." Yet Wilde was neither vain nor posing as an innocent. The student represents Schwob, a French symbolist writer, who was 16 when Wilde met him in Paris and 27 when the poem was published. In writing the poem, Wilde the seducer/Sphinx confronted the reticent student/Schwob with Schwob's own thinly repressed desires. That Schwob was at least theoretically seducible by this schoolboy chant is suggested by the fact that the most puerile of all insurrectional works of art, *Ubu Roi*, was also dedicated to him in 1896. Ada Leverson evidently penetrated the mystery as a Wildean strategy for seduction when she parodied the poem in *Punch* (21 July 1894) under the title "The Minx." More importantly for our thesis, Wilde himself drew the line between his public and private arts when he informed John Lane in 1892 that the poem could not be brought out in a popular or cheap edition.[41]

A private art-as-seduction or a public diversion-as-critique were Wilde's

Lecture tour of the United States; "Oscar Wilde" by Sarony of New York, 1882.

options as engaged bourgeois artist. He employed both styles: one to criticize an irresponsible mass audience and the other to create an audience of intimates. "The Critic as Artist," which, like "The Decay of Lying," is set in a private library intentionally far from the madding crowd, presents the play of two men, again an older and a younger. The older man wants to play for the younger "a fantasy by Dvorak. He writes passionate, curiously-coloured things," but Ernest (the younger) wants him to "Turn round and talk to me. . . . There is something in your voice that is wonderful." Undoubtedly, the heightened purpleness of the prose throughout the lengthy dialogue is intended as a seduction, especially since the man with the magical voice will not be "degraded into the position of giving you useful information. . . . Nothing that is worth knowing can be taught."

On the other hand, the thesis of "The Critic as Artist" is a political one: if everyone were a literary critic, no one would make war. Cultural criticism would render invidious nationalism obsolete:

> It is Criticism that makes us cosmopolitan. The Manchester school tried to make men realize the brotherhood of humanity, by pointing out the commercial advantages of peace. It sought to degrade the wonderful world into a common marketplace for the buyer and the seller. It addressed itself to the lowest instincts, and it failed. . . . Criticism will annihilate race-prejudices, by insisting upon the unity of the human mind in the variety of its forms. If we are tempted to make war upon another nation, we shall remember that we are seeking to destroy an element of our own culture, and possibly its most important element. . . . [People] will not say "We will not war against France because her prose is perfect," but because the prose of France is perfect, they will not hate the land. Intellectual criticism will bind Europe together in bonds far closer than those that can be forged by shopman or sentimentalist. It will give us the peace that comes from understanding.

Understanding the importance of the culture industry as a transnational political force, Wilde both satirized and exploited it. Since journalism ruled, he became a critic, but he insisted that his criticism was creative: "The highest criticism really is the record of one's own soul. . . . I am always amused by the silly vanity of those writers and artists of our day who seem to imagine that the primary function of the critic is to chatter about their second-rate work." Since criticism had become a profession, he opted for talking over acting, and finally, in a parody of Gramsci's "traditional" intellectual, doing nothing at all. "I said to you some time ago that it was far more difficult to talk about a thing than to do it. Let me say to you now that to do nothing at all is the most difficult thing in the world, the most difficult and the most intellectual." The lines are Gilbert's in "The Critic as Artist," in which the subtitles indicate the importance of "doing nothing" and "discussing everything." This is the philosophy of a dandy who is satirizing the pose of a gentleman: for what a gentleman *was*, as A. Smythe Palmer wrote in *The Ideal of a Gentleman*, was infinitely more significant than what he *did*.[42] ("Do you smoke?" Lady Bracknell asks Jack. "Well, yes, I must admit I smoke." "I am glad to hear it. A man should always have an occupation of some kind.") Short of any serious social change as envisioned in "The Soul of Man Under Socialism"—that is, short of any real alliance between Gramsci's traditional intellectuals and "organic" intellectuals in a productive or creative economy—seduction was the alternative to the slogans and inversions of slogans.[43]

2

Dandies and Gentlemen:
or, 'Dorian Gray' and the Press

> The nineteenth-century dislike of romanticism is the rage of Caliban not seeing his own face in a glass.
>
> Preface to *The Picture of Dorian Gray*

> The world was more than ordinarily alive because of Melmotte and his failures.
>
> Trollope, *The Way We Live Now*

DAYS WITH CELEBRITIES. (32).
MR. OSCAR WILDE.

Reception at home after U.S. tour.

*I*N THE 1984 FILM *The Picture of Dorian Gray in the Yellow Newspaper*, German director Ulrike Ottinger brilliantly probes the idea of total media control: Frau Dr. Mabuse, head of an international press cartel, creates the stunner and personality Dorian Gray. A bizarre, simultaneous double ending has Dorian both the victim of the media tycoon and the image that she cannot control. Wilde's *Picture of Dorian Gray* is not German expressionist cinema about total media manipulation, but it is about the relationship between the image and the real, between art and life. Under the influence of its Mabuse, Harry Wotton, Dorian's image dominates his life and others', and life responds with a vengeance—or according to an alternate reading, with a final concession to a moralistic marketplace. But more important than the novel itself is the controversy it generated, for it recapitulated the novel's themes. Dorian attempted to divorce himself from life and history through an image impervious to experience, an attempt to live "aesthetically." The press attacked Wilde because his book and, it was feared, he were divorced from middle-class life: in *The Picture of Dorian Gray* the press could see nothing of itself. For his part, Wilde responded by perfecting an adversarial image to that of their gentleman: that of the dandy. Both received considerable publicity.

Although the controversy surrounding *Dorian Gray* couched itself in terms of art and morality, it was a product of social tensions that had been brewing for decades. These concerned the much-advertised images of dandies and gentlemen, and to a lesser extent, they also concerned the much-advertised images of women. The meaning of decadence in British literature of the 1890's is revealed in these tensions, rather than in any particular literary style. The images of the dandy, the gentleman, and the woman—comprising the relatively primitive form of the cult of personality in the 1890's—cannot be divorced from an advertising, consumerist culture. For what might have begun as the gentleman's self-reliance, the woman's self-help, or the dandy's "burning need to create for oneself a personal originality" (Baudelaire) often ended in self-promotion. If we uncover the history of these conflicts, which amount to a crisis of the male, we shall see that the dandy's rubric of "Art" counteracted an entire spectrum of perceived losses in the age of mechanical reproduction, advertising, and middle-class conformity.

Therefore we must shift our analysis from the artwork alone to encompass a number of interrelated phenomena of the time: the art of advertising in the 1890's that reflected the crisis of images, for the dandies in *Dorian Gray* could not have arisen except as rejections of, and counterparts to, the normative image of the gentleman; *Dorian Gray*'s very public production, from Wilde's addition of the inflammatory Preface to his responses to critics; the broader social conflicts between the dandy, rooted in high Society, and the gentleman, rooted in the public schools then producing a standardized middle class; and ultimately the popularized images of dandy and gentleman in cheap productions for the general public. *Dorian Gray* comes to us as an exemplum of decadence with a history of scandal. An analysis of the scandal will reveal the real story behind the novel and the nature of British decadence.

For the researcher in Wildeiana, perhaps the most surprising data are the astonishing numbers of popular cartoons, songs, scores, dances—like "The Oscar Wilde Forget-Me-Not Waltzes" in the United States—and parodies that the public figure Wilde generated on both sides of the Atlantic. Then there are the novels, stories, essays, apologies, biographies, and tributes very different in tone that began to flood the market in 1895. When Wilde went down from Oxford to London, he entered a world in which product advertising was matched by the ability of persons to advertise themselves. Reviews of his plays are especially interesting in this context. Not only were his first successes reviewed exhaustively in the London press, but the provincial papers also duly responded to his first nights in London. Moreover, reviewers then did not criticize the drama so much as they advised the dramatist. Wilde and theater managers were instructed to delete acts, eliminate characters, revise scripts, and modify their own behavior during curtain calls and were generally subjected to the opinions and directorial talents of writers and reviewers who today often seem barely literate. But this treatment and self-treatment of work and artist as improvable and sellable commodities partook of the same odd mixture of idealism and commerciality that product advertising exhibited.

For Wilde to employ the tactics of advertising and publicity at the very time he was expressing a socialist theory is not so contradictory as it has appeared to critics. The late-Victorian socialist propaganda and the management of advertising in the last decades of the century used similar techniques of dissemination—for example, the engaging of the lower classes—and a similar rhetoric of "free choice," "promise," and "the goal of a better life." Sidney Webb worried that as monopoly trusts came to dominate business, advertising would become, not the herald of better products and services, but rather the competitive means of various industries to gain the largest share of the consumer's income. In his introduction to G. W. Goodall's *Advertising: A Study of a Modern Business Power* in May 1914, a year in which Britain was spending as much on advertising—£10,000,000—as on its Army and Navy combined, Webb discussed the potential of advertising as well as its perversion in a capitalist state.[1] Thomas J. Barratt's £3,000,000 on soap advertisement represented for Webb "the value of the wrecks to which the competition of this giant soap manufacturer has reduced so many old-fashioned soap boilers." Better, thought Webb, to imagine advertising in a "co-operative commonwealth," where it would serve as an educational force and a tool for freedom of choice:

Even when all our various manufacturers and stores have become public services, and when no capitalist levies a toll upon our supplies, we can easily imagine the various public health departments advertising their baths and other hygienic opportunities; the educational authorities importuning every young man and maiden to try their attractive lecture courses and organised games; the municipalities of the various pleasure resorts commending their holiday attractions; the national railway and steamship administration tempting us to enlarge our minds by travel; the State Insurance Department urging us all to insure for allowances in old age or sickness, supplementary to the common provision; in short no end of advertising intended to influence our decision as to how to spend our incomes in the ways the 'general will' of the community felt to be good.[2]

The years 1914 to 1918 brought about enormous increases in state advertising to produce a new national identity, but one very different from that imagined by Webb. Yet if Webb saw that the current practice of advertising benefited the capitalist rather more than the worker, others saw it in more democratic terms.

As early as the *Tatler*, Addison had called advertisements "instruments of ambition . . . of great Use to the Vulgar": "A man that is by no means big enough for the *Gazette* may easily creep into the advertisements; by which means we often see an Apothecary in the same paper of news with a Plenipotentiary, or a running Footman with an Ambassador" (14 September 1710). Samuel Johnson admonished that every advertiser "should remember that his name is to stand in the same paper with those of the King of Prussia and the Emperor of Germany, and endeavor to make himself worthy of such association" (*Idler*, 20 January 1759). Through the work of Bulwer Lytton, Brougham, Gladstone, and Disraeli, the advertising tax was abolished in 1853, the stamp duty on newspapers in 1855, and the last "tax upon knowledge," a duty on paper, in 1861. Macaulay was quoted with approbation by Gladstone that "advertising is to business what steam is to machinery—the great propelling power."[3] And by 1901 the Prince of Wales spoke the sentence that was elaborated by the press and publicized by manufacturers as the "Wake up, England!" speech at the Guildhall. He encouraged manufacturers to advertise internationally: "To the distinguished representatives of the commercial interests of the Empire, whom I have had the pleasure of meeting here, I venture to allude to the impression which seems generally to prevail among their brethren across the seas, that the Old Country must wake up if she intends to maintain her old position of pre-eminence in her colonial trade against foreign competitors."[4]

"Advertising," declaimed Churchill, "nourishes the consuming power of men. It creates wants for a better standard of living. It sets up before a man the goal of a better home, better clothing, better food for himself and his family. It spurs individual exertion and greater production. It brings together in fertile union those things which otherwise would never have met."[5] Like the dreams of the socialists, advertising imaged infinite possibility—personal, national, global. The consumer need not be recognized by the Queen to be successful, for the arena of success was shifting; the symbols of status, industry, and comfort were as plentiful as the ads, and the ads determined the "wants." Thus in "The Soul of Man Under Socialism," Wilde would regret people wasting their lives "in accumulating things, and symbols for things" and deplore the culture that encouraged it: "So completely has man's personality been absorbed by his possessions that the English law has always treated offenses against a man's property with far more severity than offenses against his person, and property is still the test of complete citizenship." (Students of British culture should recall that respect for private property was one of the Thirty-Nine Articles of Religion. Article 38 begins, "The Riches and Goods of Christians are not common. . . .")

The 1890's in England, a time of overproduction (or underconsumption) at home, initiated modern practices of advertising, those that identified products with desired modes of living. The significance of these practices cannot be overestimated insofar as they initiated an ideology of choice dependent on the proliferation of images: the consumerist ideology of a free life-*style*.

On the other hand, Samuel Johnson (like John Berger today) had discerned that the democratic practice more often than not debased and leveled all to the status of objects. He protested the humiliation of "a famous Mohawk Indian warrior" who was advertised as on exhibition with his war-paint and scalping knife but was juxtaposed in the ads with Dublin butter. By the 1890's, the *Times*'s reports of advertising excesses had spurred enough indignation to found the S.C.A.P.A. (Society for the Checking of Abuses in Public Advertising), predominantly directed against posters and billboards; and the battle still raged at the end of the century when the moon lay fair on two monstrous signs for oats competing halfway up the cliffs of Dover. Although in *The Sorrows of Satan* (1895) Marie Corelli wrote that Millais's "Bubbles" poster, exploited by Pears soap, "[would] prevent [Millais] ever standing on the dignified height of distinction with such masters in Art as Romney, Sir Peter Lely, Gainsborough, and Reynolds,"[6] and W. P. Frith complained when his little girl with "The New Frock" was turned into a soap poster entitled "So Clean," the Royal Academy continued to be ransacked by meat extract firms for portraits of healthy cows; art and advertising were inextricably tied.

The great proliferation of the ephemeral "little" (art) magazines may have begun in the spirit and tradition of arts and crafts in the manner of Morris, but they survived only when they were commercially viable. The most successful of the little magazines, the *Yellow Book*, was successful precisely because it was directed toward an inclusive market beyond traditional coteries, individual arts, and esoterica. After its death in 1895 because of its association in the public's mind with Wilde, its successor, the *Savoy*, failed largely because its management rejected advertising. Even that marvel of craftsmanship, the Bodley Head book, dedicated to the Revival of Printing in the (simplified) mode of Blake, Rossetti, and Morris, owed its success to the very shrewd and firm business practices of John Lane, whose strategies were much scrutinized and criticized by the reading public and bookselling competitors.[7]

Regardless of the concerns of gentlemen journalists and women novelists about the effects of advertising, the liberals had abolished the taxes on both advertising and paper. The result was not only to increase the number of newspapers in Britain from 640 to 3,000 between 1855 and 1900, to decrease the costs of advertising, and to make the papers more affordable for the masses, but also to eliminate numerous shady practices on the parts of tax collectors—for example, that of taxing favorable book reviews as advertisements. (This practice may have interesting implications for literary reception theories of the first half of the nineteenth century. As Turner writes in his history of advertising, "An author whose book was savaged by an impecunious periodical could be pardoned for harbouring base suspicions."[8]) When Max Nordau sought the etiology of fin-de-siècle exhaustion, one of his factors was the proliferation of periodicals, and he cited the 500 percent increase between 1840 and 1890. Recent bibliographies suggest that the increase was much higher.

Wilde, who had the socialist's commitment to human possibility, had the more immediate accessibility of advertising to accomplish his personal mobility. "Advertise what you sell, not yourself, unless you are for sale," advised the American encyclopedist of advertising, the stunningly successful N. C. Fowler Jr., in *Fowler's Publicity* (1897).[9] By 1890 Wilde had advertised himself on two continents. Leaving Oxford as a Professor of Aesthetics and turning journalist to educate the "public"—itself a creation of modern advertising practices and, as we have seen in Chapter 1, a sort of objectified commodity for Wilde—he lectured on art and interior design to coal miners in Colorado.

Wilde would later write that the two great turning points of his life were when his father sent him to Oxford and when society sent him to prison; but in an acute unpublished essay A. J. A. Symons recognized the significance of Colonel Morse's sending Wilde to the United States—where the lecture, circus, Barnum's "moral" museum, and subscription publication had flourished. The precocious and romantic Oxonian, managed by a hardened publicist, came back hardened, commercial, responsible, and determined to be a dramatist.[10] Despite the ridicule it inspired, Wilde's elaborate "aesthetic" costume was not his own choice at all, but rather a costume he had contracted to wear in his commercial dealings with Morse, and it was successful. Back in England, he peddled his—and, as Whistler said, everyone else's—views on art in the provinces. However romantic or revolutionary his theories of art, the romantic artist, as Yeats said of him, had entered a commercial area. Hence the flurry of essays, dedications to potential patrons, reviews, and letters to editors.

It was in fact journalistic hostility toward the socially mobile self-advertiser that led to the controversy over *The Picture of Dorian Gray*, and it was with the reception of the novel that Wilde paid for his attacks on journalists in his literary and political theory. But both sides in the debate were so caught up in the opaque images of advertising that both presented contradictions—contradictions clearly related to an age more materialistic than its participants could admit.

Wilde insisted on the "moral" of the story, a constant moral throughout his prose fiction: that an exclusive preoccupation with the physical and material surfaces of life would result in the attrition of human creativity. But simultaneously his prose insisted on ornate description of material conditions and an obsession with physical beauty. Indeed, to a great extent *Dorian Gray* is about *spectators*, from spectators of the beauty of others such as Basil of Dorian's or Dorian of Sybil Vane's to "spectators of life," as Wilde called Wotton. Similarly, critics of what was considered Wilde's aristocratic pose and immorality could not see the moral of the novel because of their own preoccupation with its physical and material representations. Both Wilde and his critics argued for spirit; both sides' energy was directed toward externals. Both sides were situated in the context of public images and self-advertisement: the journalists posing as the gentlemen guardians of public morality, Wilde advertising himself as the subtle dandy-artist of higher morality, thinking himself within the Symbolist ranks that Arthur Symons called the "revolt against exteriority, against rhetoric, [and] against a materialistic tradition."[11]

The press's vicious attacks on *The Picture of Dorian Gray* in many ways duplicated *Fraser's Magazine*'s attacks on dandiacal literature a half-century earlier, but by 1891 the periodical arena was even more brutal in its competition to construct and undo public identities. Wilde coolly denied to an editor that he was indefatigable in his public appreciation of his own work, since of the 216 reviews he had read of *Dorian Gray* he had taken public notice of only three. Although his critics' ostensible concern was with the book's potentially "immoral" influence, its author's assertive familiarity with an aristocratic mode of life accounted for most of the journalistic hostility. Like the new commodities, the author's image seemed to imply a mode of living which "in reality" he did not enjoy. So once again, the gentlemen, with their self-image of sincerity and particular kinds of morals, battled with the dandy and his particular kind of manners.

According to a typical aesthetic reaction against middle-class materialism, Wilde divided the world of *Dorian Gray* between the upper and lower classes exclusively. He respectively associated these with Lord Henry Wotton and with Dorian's connections to the East End (the home of the Vanes) and quayside establishments of questionable services. Since it appeared unlikely that he had much authority for speaking of either, middle-class journalists numbered him among "simpleton poseurs . . . who know nothing of the life which they affect to have explored."[12] Such "posing" was judged even more reprehensible because, as all of his biographers concur, by 1890 rumors had begun to surface of his participation in homosexual circles in London. Journalists like W. E. Henley, who felt responsible in the tradition of *Fraser's* for upholding "public morality," transferred their hostility from the opportunistic and mildly ill-reputed author to his book.

The best way to demonstrate this prejudice against Wilde the dandy and social butterfly is to compare the reviews of *Dorian Gray* with those of his other prose fiction, his fairy tales and short stories, which did not provoke a scandal. Although Wilde's novel and stories were consistent in both themes and style, the first was excoriated on all accounts while the second were praised for both their "morality" and their literary craft. The only explanation for the reviewers' contradictory reaction is that the novel, unlike the stories, removed art from the locales and sentiments of middle-class life. Before examining the historical conflict of images, I want to consider these textual differences. In doing so, I hope to demonstrate that the decadence of *Dorian Gray* lay in what the novel *did not* include and was therefore external to the text.

Wilde wrote to the editor of the *St. James's Gazette* that the "moral" of *Dorian Gray* was that the unyielding perspectives of the three major characters reduced them to incomplete human beings, almost, we might say, to caricatures.[13] The artist Basil Hallward worshipped physical beauty far too much; Dorian abandoned himself to sensation and pleasure; Wotton sought only to be a spectator of life. In Wilde's stories, composed during the same period as *Dorian Gray*, the same "moral" consistently surfaces. Hallward's kind of materialism is supplanted by Christian love; mysterious, unnamed sins either are treated satirically or are condemned; Wotton's epigrammatic style is treated as shallow. Wilde's critics, on the other hand, could not see Wilde's consistency because the novel presented the moral in an "aesthetic" and aristocratic environment whereas the stories presented it in bourgeois households or fairyland.

When the novel was published in the American periodical *Lippincott's Monthly Magazine* in 1890, the few favorable reviewers found the characters "abnormal." Ethical and mystical journals like the *Christian Leader*, the *Christian World*, and *Light* focused on Wilde's "psychological explorations" of these characters and were willing to discern the moral Wilde derived from them.[14] The much greater number of negative reviewers transferred the epithets they applied to the "abnormal" characters onto the book and Wilde himself. The *Athenaeum* called the book "unmanly, sickening, vicious (although not exactly what is called 'improper'), and tedious."[15] The *St. James's Gazette* found it "mawkish and nauseous . . . tedious and stupid," and sneered at Wilde's idle, "effeminate" characters who "fill up the intervals of talk by plucking daisies and playing with them, and sometimes by drinking 'something with strawberry in it.'"[16] The *Daily Chronicle* discerned immorality in Wotton's (and by extension, the book's) appeal to cure the soul by the senses, and accused Wilde of self-advertisement:

Dulness and dirt are the chief feature of *Lippincott's* this month. The element in it that is unclean, though undeniably amusing, is furnished by Mr Oscar Wilde's story of "The Picture of Dorian Gray." It is a tale spawned from the leprous literature of the French *Décadents*—a poisonous book, the atmosphere of which is heavy with the mephitic odours of moral and spiritual putrefaction—a gloating study of the mental and physical corruption of a fresh, fair and golden youth, which might be horrible and fascinating but for its effeminate frivolity, its studied insincerity, its theatrical cynicism, its tawdry mysticism, its flippant philosophising, and the contaminating trail of garish vulgarity which is over all Mr Wilde's elaborate Wardour Street aestheticism and obtrusively cheap scholarship.[17]

The *Scots Observer*, edited by Wilde's one-time friend the moral crusader W. E. Henley, called the book "nasty" and ran a review that provoked a two-month running controversy on the relevance of moral concerns to artworks:

Why go grubbing in muck heaps? The world is fair, and the proportion of healthy-minded men and honest women to those that are foul, fallen, or unnatural is great. Mr Oscar Wilde has again been writing stuff that were better unwritten; and while "The Picture of Dorian Gray," which he contributes to *Lippincott's*, is ingenious, interesting, full of cleverness, and plainly the work of a man of letters, it is false art—for its interest is medico-legal; it is false to human nature—for its hero is a devil; it is false to morality—for it is not made sufficiently clear that the writer does not prefer a course of unnatural iniquity to a life of cleanliness, health, and sanity. The story—which deals with matters only fitted for the Criminal Investigation Department or a hearing *in camera*—is discreditable alike to author and editor. Mr Wilde has brains, and art, and style; but if he can write for none but outlawed noblemen and perverted telegraph-boys, the sooner he takes to tailoring (or some other decent trade) the better for his own reputation and the public morals.[18]

One is struck by the profusion of such terms as "unclean," "effeminate frivolity," "studied insincerity," "theatrical," "Wardour Street aestheticism," "obtrusively cheap scholarship," "vulgarity," "unnatural," "false," and "perverted": an odd mixture of the rumors of Wilde's homosexuality and of the more overt criticism of Wilde as social poseur and self-advertiser. Although the suggestion was couched in terms applying to the text, the reviews seemed to say that Wilde did not know his place, or—amounting to the same thing—that he did know his place and it was not that of a middle-class gentleman. Between "outlawed noblemen and perverted telegraph-boys," the upper and lower classes, the press discerned no place for itself.

Dandies and Gentlemen

It goes without saying today that the reviewers' insinuations of Wilde's homosexual practices had a basis. On the other hand, their basis was certainly not evident in the text of *Dorian Gray*, in which, with the exception of murder, the protagonist's "sins" are never named and are only briefly alluded to. Wilde had, in fact, been associated with an unabashedly homosexual and pornographic novel. In 1890 he brought the manuscript of *Teleny: A Physiological Romance of Today* to Charles Hirsch's bookshop on Coventry Street and requested that it be passed on to a friend who would call for it.[19] The friend called, took it away, and returned it to be picked up by another friend. The process was repeated several times by several friends until Wilde retrieved the manuscript. In 1893 Leonard Smithers altered the text by transposing the setting from London to Paris "so as not to shock the national *amour propre* of his English subscribers" and published 200 copies with the subtitle "The Reverse of the Medal." Gay Sunshine Press has only recently (1984) reissued the unexpurgated English edition, and excerpts from the 1893 edition, describing what the police called homosexual "liaisons" on the quayside and luxuriously exotic rooms and suppers amid which artists and affluent men perform spectacular sexual acrobatics, are included in Brian Reade's anthology of homosexual literature, *Sexual Heretics*.[20]

But although Wilde handled the manuscript whose consumption was so covert, and in spite of a recent Parisian foreword that attributes the work entirely to Wilde, it is fairly certain that he was neither the author nor a major collaborating author of this anonymous work. The most that can be said about its relation to *Dorian Gray* is that Dorian's haunts and pleasures, particularly in chapter 11, share an ambience with the luxurious settings of *Teleny*, and that Dorian, too, walks down by the river. In any case, whether or not readers of *Teleny* saw hints of it in *Dorian Gray*, in 1891 *Teleny* was known to only a few. And in their suspicions of immorality the reviewers cited only Dorian, whose sole explicit sins were murder and callousness; whereas the figure that homosexual readers sympathized with was probably Hallward. With his long-suffering, platonic love, the artist was much more characteristic of the period's homosexual literature. In *Teleny*, the protagonist, a pianist, ultimately commits suicide.

As Wilde said in his explication of *Dorian's Gray*'s moral, the crimes in the novel were the characters' exclusive preoccupations with the physical and material aspects of life. The result of the crimes was that Hallward lost his model and his life, Wotton saw his friends and family disgraced and was left without an audience for his pratings, and Dorian's "soul" was transferred and confined to the material image, the horrible, brittle picture. The reviewers saw the wrong sins and failed altogether to see the retribution. Rather than responding to their implicit allegations concerning his own "sins," Wilde turned the tables on his critics in a feat of condescension and self-promotion.

First, he published "A Preface to 'Dorian Gray'" in the *Fortnightly Review* (1 March 1891), including among his maxims on art the dicta "Those who find ugly meanings in beautiful things are corrupt without being charming"; "Those who go beneath the surface do so at their peril"; "The highest as the lowest form of criticism is a mode of autobiography"; and "It is the spectator, and not life, that art really mirrors." This and several other maxims in the Preface were consistent with *Intentions* in that they shifted the focus from the work to the spectator. The Preface said, in effect, what Wilde had written of *Dorian Gray* earlier: "What Dorian Gray's sins are no one knows. He who finds them has brought them."[21] In a letter to the *Scots Observer* he was able to support this statement by describing the reviews: the journals concerned with ethics discerned the moral, the journal of mystics discerned its spiritual import, the journals of British hypocrisy discerned its sinfulness.[22]

Second, Wilde made some minor deletions in the *Lippincott's* version and added six new chapters for the book form, published in April 1891. The deletions were few, primarily individual sentences and fragments, but their force was to make Hallward more pathetically enthralled with Dorian, to make Wotton more deeply sad in the silences between his epigrams, and to make Dorian's ostracism only slightly more complete.[23] Third, Wilde formulated the laissez-faire policy toward artists included in "The Soul of Man," and continued to advertise himself in his archly arrogant letters to editors—in which he repeated the "moral" of *Dorian Gray* and lamented that "the prurient" could not see it.[24]

Thus the novel did double duty in that it conceded to two distinct audiences—much as the two prose styles discussed in Chapter 1 were directed to two audiences. Members of the homosexual community could read *Dorian Gray* sympathetically, for characters like Hallward were a staple of their literature. (Writers like Marc-André Raffalovich, intimate friend of the visual inspiration of Dorian, John Gray, tirelessly proposed a connection between artistic genius and homosexuality. Even the name "Dorian" bore its significance for some as the classical term by which polemicists for the amendment of homosexual laws designated their noble ancestors in ancient Greece.[25]) On the other hand, because of the story's obliqueness regarding Dorian's sins and, especially, its entirely moralistic conclusions, journalists could only hint at their suspicions concerning Wilde.

However, Wilde's suspected homosexuality was but secondarily related to the general disapprobation of *Dorian Gray*. The short stories were well received although they included similar innuendos, particularly *A House of Pomegranates*. The reviewers' tone reflected not Wilde's innuendos but whether his settings were aristocratic and aesthetic or bourgeois, idyllic, and pastoral.

Up to our present day, critics have been unable to reconcile the stories' Christian, socialist, and pastoral themes with the themes they discerned in the novel.[26] When the first collected edition of Wilde's works was published in 1908, reviewers began to contrast the stories and *Dorian Gray* as if the latter marked a sort of demise on Wilde's part. The *Times*'s review, attributed to Arthur Symons, stated: "Only three years after ['Lord Arthur Savile's Crime'] came 'The Picture of Dorian Gray'—a withering comment on the lack of conviction and of a standard in art and life in one who would teach, or even amuse, his fellows. In that horrible book all the imagination, the power, the ingenuity of the short stories, are perverted to deplorable uses."[27] F. G. Bettany wrote in the *Sunday Times*: "Compared with ['The Happy Prince,' 'The Birthday of the Infanta,' and 'The Young King'], 'Dorian Grey' [sic] is but a *tour de force* in morbidity, interesting mainly because it gave a forecast to some extent of Oscar Wilde's own eclipse."[28] Yet although *The Happy Prince and Other Tales* (1888) was published before *Dorian Gray*, the other two collections, *Lord Arthur Savile's Crime and Other Stories* (1891) and *A House of Pomegranates* (1891), were published later. Therefore, Wilde's "lack of conviction and of a standard" or "forecast" of his "eclipse" cannot be so easily dated according to divisions in his work.

In fact, when the prose collections were first published, the reviews were overwhelmingly favorable. The *Athenaeum* and the *Saturday Review* praised *The Happy Prince* as comparable to Hans Andersen's fairy tales, with the added attraction of contemporary satire.[29] The *Universal Review* praised the stories' morals, poetic feeling, and literary craft.[30] Even after *Dorian Gray*, the *Athenaeum* recommended *Lord Arthur Savile's Crime* for reading aloud—whose title story is but a satiric version of the novel—and the American journal the *Nation* approved of its "agreeable satire" on the British upper classes.[31] *A House of Pomegranates* suffered some criticism for its "wordy descriptions," "fleshly style," and "glut of description and epithet," but the same reviewers nonetheless commended the tales' "beauty," "force," and "poetry."[32] Although they had received Wilde's extravagant descriptions of the stunner Dorian with disapproval, reviewers were noticeably appreciative of his descriptions of a red-haired witch in a green cap and of a mermaid with a pearl-and-silver tail. In the *New Review*, George Saintsbury commends "The Fisherman and His Soul" as "what seems to me the best thing Mr. Wilde has yet done."[33] This was regarding a story with more purple prose and unnamed sins than even *Dorian Gray*.

The only difference between the stories and the novel is the novel's aristocratic setting, its removal of art from middle-class life. The stories, on the other hand, reek of middle-class virtue and sentimentality. The swallow in "The Happy Prince" launches into luscious descriptions of Egypt, comparable to chapter 11 of *Dorian Gray*, but here the Happy Prince cuts him off and tells him to take the Prince's jewels to the poor of the city. In "The Nightingale and the Rose," the student of philosophy quips aesthetic maxims while the bird dies of love, much like Harry Wotton and Basil Hallward. The Miller in "The Devoted Friend" bestows his sententiae on amicability to the kind friend he is exploiting. "Lots of people act well," he says, "but very few people talk well, which shows that talking is much the more difficult thing of the two, and much the finer thing also"—a claim very like Wotton's position that "I never quarrel with actions. My one quarrel is with words. . . . The man who could call a spade a spade should be compelled to use one." The views of the "Remarkable Rocket" parody Wotton's egotism and aestheticism.

In *Lord Arthur Savile's Crime*, Wilde demystifies the suspenseful air of crime surrounding Dorian by satirically inverting the themes of the novel, reinserting art into life. In "The Sphinx Without a Secret," the mysteriousness of Dorian's sins becomes a harmless, bored woman's desire for excitement. In "Lord Arthur Savile's Crime," a cheiromantist (palm reader) is to Savile what Wotton is to Dorian: he foresees for him a future of illicit actions. Yet unlike Dorian, who cannot just act but refers himself to a work of art as conscience, Savile simply commits the murder and marries the girl (named, in fact, Sybil Merton: Sybil Vane plus Hettie Merton, the two women Dorian sacrificed). That is, Savile is a practical man of action and common sense, so he kills the cheiromantist and puts an end to his crisis of conscience. The effete, aristocratic Dorian, on the other hand, permits Wotton to dominate him. Similarly, in "The Canterville Ghost," the specter of a sixteenth-century uxoricide, obsessed with his aristocratic roles of shame and sin, is frustrated by the pragmatism of a modern American family.

In *A House of Pomegranates*, the worship of materialism is described in a style as overblown as that of chapter 11 in *Dorian Gray*; and, as in the novel, the worship of physical beauty is moralized. Like Dorian, the young king is the object of rumors due to his obsessive love of exotic materials. Bithynia, known during the time of the Roman empire for its homosexual practices, is significant as the homeland of the beloveds of Julius Caesar, Hadrian, and Elagabalus (all names which surface in *Dorian Gray*):

> Many curious stories were related about him at this period. . . . He had been seen, so the tale ran, pressing his warm lips to the marble brow of an antique statue that had been discovered in the bed of the river on the occasion of the building of the stone bridge, and was inscribed with the name of the Bithynian slave of Hadrian. He had passed a whole night in noting the effect of the moonlight on a silver image of Endymion.
>
> All rare and costly materials had certainly a great fascination for him, and in his eagerness to procure them he had sent away many merchants, some to traffic for amber with the rough fisher-folk of the north seas, some to Egypt to look for that curious green turquoise which is found only in the tombs of kings, and is said to possess magical properties, some to Persia for silken carpets and painted pottery, and others to India to buy gauze and stained ivory, moonstones and bracelets of jade, sandal-wood and blue enamel and shawls of fine wool.

But the young king gives up such treasures and is finally crowned in the church by God's sunlight.

In "The Birthday of the Infanta," all those who are physically beautiful are cruel, like Dorian, and the reader's sympathies are with the dwarf, who looks into the mirror and hates his image as much as Dorian loved his portrait. In "The Fisherman and His Soul," the fisherman sells his soul for love. Like Dorian's soul in the portrait, the banished spirit wanders through exotic backgrounds committing unnamed sins. Like Dorian and his portrait, the story concludes with the fisherman's soul and body reunited in death. The "Star-Child," like Dorian, is so enamored of his own beauty that he utters an irrevocable wish to distance himself from ugliness. He says to his plain mother: "Thou art too foul to look at, and rather would I kiss the adder or the toad than thee." Like Dorian's portrait, the Star-Child's physical aspect is condemned to bear the burden of his wish: he takes on the appearance of the toad as to his face, and the scales of the adder as to his body. The Star-Child learns generosity through extreme acts of penance and reverts to his original comeliness before he dies, just as Dorian's portrait regains its youthful aspect when he dies.

Thus in the stories Wilde represents the same themes as in the novel, but in *Dorian Gray* these are dictated as elements of aristocratic and artistic or bohemian life. In the stories, either conflicts are resolved by men of action, rather than idle lovers of beauty, or they involve only harmless water rats and rockets. When a young, pastoral king languishes amidst tapestries and repents, his story bears a "pretty morality"; when the same lush prose describes a contemporary aristocrat in a setting reminiscent of French *décadence*, his story is "poisonous."

With *Dorian Gray*, which seemed to smack too much of art for art's sake, the reviewers felt that Wilde violated the social function of art—that is, to present the normative values of society, to present the middle class. In exclusively representing the part of society that he did—idle aristocrats and romantic artists—Wilde offended an ethic of industry and productivity. He seemed to expose himself as a presumptuous social climber who penetrated aristocratic circles with offensive ease. In addition, his indefatigable self-advertisement was simply not acceptable behavior for a gentleman, much in the same way that his and Harry Wotton's lounging on sofas was not the acceptable carriage of gentlemen. The author's decadence lay in his unwillingness to capitulate to the image of the gentleman. *Dorian Gray*'s decadence lay in its distance from and rejection of middle-class life. This, not stylistics, is how decadence in British literature should be understood.[34]

Yet there is one other related aspect of the novel that is decadent: it was not only dandiacal, it was "feminine" in a sense not intended by the press's use of that term. Here is a brief excerpt from a long passage in the most notoriously decadent chapter of the novel. In chapter 11, Dorian reads "a fascinating book"—generally accepted as Huysmans's *A Rebours* although Wilde's typewritten copy for *Lippincott's* originally named the text "*Le Secret de Raoul* par Catulle Sarrazin."[35] In a passage modeled on the *ubi sunt* formula, Dorian contrasts his face, now a timeless work of art, with the ephemerality of material things, in this case legendary works of embroidery:

Where was the great crocus-coloured robe, on which the gods fought against the giants, that had been worked by brown girls for the pleasure of Athena? Where the huge velarium that Nero had stretched across the Colosseum at Rome, that Titan sail of purple on which was represented the starry sky, and Apollo driving a chariot drawn by white gilt-reined steeds? He longed to see the curious table-napkins wrought for the Priest of the Sun, on which were displayed all the dainties and viands that could be wanted for a feast; the mortuary cloth of King Chilperic, with its three hundred golden bees; the fantastic robes that excited the indignation of the Bishop of Pontus, and were figured with "lions, panthers, bears, dogs, forests, rocks, hunters—all, in fact, that a painter can copy from nature." . . . Catherine de' Medici had a mourning-bed made for her of black velvet powdered with crescents and suns.

Wilde lifted this passage almost verbatim from his review of Alan Cole's translation of Lefébure's *History of Embroidery and Lace* in the *Woman's World* of November 1888.[36] The title of the review, 21 pages in length, is "A Fascinating Book." In addition to its "decadent" descriptions of lace as sensational history opposed to Dorian's modern (that is, historyless) face, the review includes most of Wilde's opinions about art.

During his brief editorship of the *Woman's World* (November 1887 to July 1889) Wilde reviewed, favorably, dozens of examples of what he called after George Trevelyan the "art-literature" of the day—novels narrating "the workings of the artist soul . . . in which the creation of a picture forms the dominant motif"—all written by women.[37] He also reviewed dozens of "psychological" novels by women, all concerned with the effects of "sin" on personality. And contributors supplied the magazine with numerous poems and plays on sin, as well as many articles on tapestry, lace, embroidery, and jewelry, all bearing the rich "decadent" style of chapter 11 in *Dorian Gray*. Indeed, such works, and lighter works reminiscent of the society and wit of Harry Wotton, appear to have made up a consistent diet for the readers of the *Woman's World*, readers whom Wilde cultivated as women of "culture and position."[38]

Just as Wilde had dedicated his stories and tales to women of Society who would thereby ensure his reputation, he constructed the narrative of *Dorian Gray* from the standard elements of a certain genre of upper-class women's literature: art, psychology, sin, and luxury. These elements often combined to form a particularly modern problem: the relation of influence and history to present action. This was certainly the Modern Woman's problem, and in this as well as in its thematic components, the novel was indeed "effeminate." The outcry against Wildean decadence on the part of gentlemen journalists was in part an outcry against the male author who won the support of Society—an institution managed by women—by writing a book that would appeal to women. Through his experience of advertising women's books, Wilde learned the tricks that would make his own book, and himself, such a dear commodity. After Harry Wotton's dialogues, he was barraged with invitations to dinner parties.

At least with *Dorian Gray*, it is probable that the much-touted decadence was no more an attribute or style of the work or author than that the book was "really about the jealousy and pain, the fear and guilt of being a homosexual,"[39] or than that it was, as in one modern psychological critic's sensational and superstitious view, Wilde's "presentiment of what the gods within had in store for him."[40] For from such claims it would follow that the ladies and gentlemen who contributed to the *Woman's World* and who published the novels, poems, and plays read by women were also homosexual and decadent. That they wrote about sin and corruption underneath beautiful surfaces (that is, about one popular, Jekyll-and-Hyde notion of psychology) and that Wilde, as editor, selected their works, was a product of another much publicized phenomenon: current speculations in sociology and psychology, the former a science premised on social disharmony and the latter at that time primarily employed in the service of legislators. But if decadence is a tag referring to the relation between artist or work and society rather than a proper style, what precisely constitutes the critical social relations? Here we must situate the dandy, the gentleman, and, at least in relation to them, the woman, and determine the extent to which these images were also constructed by the press. For, again, the absence of middle-class life in the novel was Wilde's response to this historical situation, and the novel's scandal was the press's counter to the Wildean move.

When Wilde returned in December 1882 from his year-long tour in the U.S., he abruptly abandoned his commercial "aesthetic" costume for the conservative dress of the gentleman and limited his extravagance to the symbolic green carnation buttonhole. In this transformation he had done no more than had Disraeli when he doffed his lace, velvet, and jewelry for the black suit more suitable for Queen Victoria and Parliament and no less than had Dickens, who, in reverse order, affected in middle age the sky-blue overcoat with red cuffs, as one contemporary called it, "a gay costume—theatrical in style rather than literary."[41] With respect to the visible world for which the Victorians existed, Wilde made the respectable sartorial choice of non-working-class men: to appear as a gentleman, an image largely dominated by Victorian black, in a manner that had been perfected by a dandy.

The silver-fork novels about the original dandies and the fiction, nonfiction, and public school memoirs about the gentleman indicate that these two traditions implied social philosophies as well as rules of attire. In *The Dandy: Brummell to Beerbohm*, Ellen Moers sees the dandies' self-proclaimed superiorities and credo of idleness and irresponsibility as intentional affronts to the middle class, with its virtues of equality, energy, and responsibility. However, apostles of dandyism like Bulwer Lytton claimed that it was precisely the exposure of dandies by dandies that allowed the middle-class virtues to triumph: the dandies, both literary and real, were protean figures whose political shifts were as subtle as they were consistently progressive. Politically they appealed, at different times and in different countries, to both the reactionary and the revolutionary: to the reactionary through their refinement and to the revolutionary through their independence. George Bryan Brummell, for example, the son of an ambitious valet, retained the title of "Mr." all his life, yet he came to dominate Regency society. As Moers puts it, the dandy's levity conflicted with the heavy middle-class "earnestness."

If we contrast the middle-class importance of being earnest with the dandy Pelham's assertion in Bulwer Lytton's novel *Pelham*, we can easily see Wilde's affinities with the dandiacal tradition. Chez Lady Roseville, Pelham distinguishes himself from the "serious" members of the company:

> As for me, I entered more into conversation at Lady Roseville's than I usually do elsewhere; being, according to my favourite philosophy, gay on the serious, and serious on the gay; and, perhaps, this is a juster method of treating the two than would be readily imagined: for things which are usually treated with importance, are, for the most part, deserving of ridicule; and those which we receive as trifles, swell themselves into a consequence we little dreamt of, before they depart.[42]

On the other hand, if the dandy was Exclusive (the Regency's term for its own society), the gentleman, despite his nominal virtues of equality, energy, and responsibility, was perhaps not less so.

To clarify these terms, to situate Wilde among dandies and gentlemen, and to understand the problem of earnestness, or sincerity, in the nineteenth century, it is worthwhile to begin with Brummell, the "pure form" of dandyism. Although he produced nothing more for posterity than a cut of coat and neckcloth, Brummell, Byron declared, was one of the three greatest men of the nineteenth century. (Napoleon and Byron himself were the others.) Brummell could even still attract the attention of Bloomsbury when Virginia Woolf was composing *The Common Reader*.[43]

Brummell interested Byron for his revolutionary status as an insolent parvenu who subjugated princes and dominated British high society. He also suffered a tragic, but proud and stoical, exile, not unlike Napoleon's and Byron's. In the conclusion to the first biography of Brummell, Capt. William Jesse cites the words of Cecil Danby, the protagonist of *Cecil; or the Adventures of a Coxcomb* (1841), Catherine Gore's "autobiographical" novel of the Regency. "Our grandnephews," said Cecil, "will behold in George Brummell a great reformer; a man who dared to be cleanly in the dirtiest of times; a man who compelled gentlemen to quit the coach-box and assume a place in their own carriage; a man who induced the ingenuous youth of Britain to prove their valour otherwise than by thrashing superannuated watchmen; a man, in short, who will survive for posterity as Charlemagne of the great empire of Clubs."[44] The fashion historian James Laver appropriates for Brummell Wilde's claim for himself in *De Profundis*, that he stood in a "symbolic relation to his age":

> Perhaps we shall best understand the importance of Brummell if we realize that the revolution he symbolized was essentially a *conspiracy* against aristocracy.... Brummell saw instinctively that the day of aristocracy was over and that the day of gentility had arrived. There were to be no more peers wearing their orders proudly on their embroidered coats, but only gentlemen in plain cloth and immaculate linen. There were to be no more beplumed and gold-laced *tricornes*, but only well-brushed top hats. The top hat was indeed a symbol of the new dispensation. On this flat but exalted plateau, it seemed to say, all gentlemen are equal, even if one of them is called George, Prince of Wales, and the other is called George Brummell. Indeed there was nothing to distinguish them except that Brummell's cravat was more carefully tied and his coat better fitting.[45]

But although Byron and many later writers, particularly in France, saw Brummell as the protagonist in a social revolution, the Victorians themselves had a more ambivalent attitude toward the dandy who was a "natural" aristocrat and arose during the French Revolution, when the aristocracy was most threatened. Captain Jesse's *Life of Beau Brummell* (1844) was compiled from Brummell's notebooks and correspondence, from pestering all those who had known Brummell, and from a brief meeting with the exiled Beau in Caen in 1832, eight years before the latter's death. Although composed of mostly secondhand evidence, this first biography is still considered by historians the most valuable. Jesse himself was one of the aging Regency "bucks," or military dandies, who turned litterateur when aging bucks could no longer dominate the gambling houses, and when even second-generation dandies like Count D'Orsay could hardly live in peace off the magnanimity of the rich and nouveau riche. Partly fascinated by Brummell's legendary power, Jesse yet mocked his cowardice and impeccability and made of his two-volume life a Victorian morality tale.

Jesse's ambivalence toward Brummell's refinement and power on the one hand, and his "effeminacy" and "idleness" (terms, as we have seen, applied to Wilde's personal style) on the other was mapped in the structure of the *Life*. In the first volume, Jesse delights in the pages of Society poetry and anecdotes of Brummell's friends. In the second, a heavy moralism pervades the Beau's grotesque decline.[46] This ambivalence would be taken up in Victorian letters from Bulwer Lytton's novels to those of Dickens and from the society journals read by the Exclusives to the antidandiacal journalism of Carlyle and Thackeray in *Fraser's Magazine*. Jesse's first volume bears a surfeit of anecdotes of Brummell's "wit," a wit primarily associated with insolence and the ability to "cut" members of the nobility; of the sort that produced the legends of the Prince Regent, later George IV, admiringly taking notes while Brummell performed his toilette; of the latter's command, "Wales, ring the bell"; and finally of the Regent's stiff back when he overheard himself pointedly referred to as the "fat friend" of Brummell's friend. The second volume bears the moral of the story.

Brummell not only surveyed the Dandy Ball with a critical eye, but more importantly he was one of the chief attractions at Watier's fashionable gambling club, where he won and lost in a day as much as £26,000, only slightly less than his patrimony. The aftereffects of Bonaparte's fall, the great influx of foreigners and of manly Guardsmen coming home from the field ready for entertainment, contributed to the fall of Brummell. Insolvent, pressed by, among others, the notorious loan shark "Dick the Dandy Killer," Brummell left England for France in 1816. Politics again frustrated him when a titular Consulate preferred to him at Caen was abolished through Palmerston, probably to conserve funds for military occupation of Central Asia. His fat king and erstwhile friend George IV had dropped him for his insolence and himself been replaced by *Fraser's* "manly" King William IV, whose coronation was by contrast so economical that it was called in the press "a half-crownation."[47]

Brummell was thus abandoned to cheaper hotels and to trailing his proud and still impeccably dressed bleeding heart across Caen, while he corresponded with more affluent friends at the seaside. Unable to forbear multiple changes of clothing, snuffboxes, and buhl furniture, he was arrested for the debt of 15,000 francs and imprisoned for three months. In prison he made the acquaintance of the French peasant Pierre Rivière, who had slaughtered his mother, sister, and brother, and has been recently resurrected by Michel Foucault and his students. Not having Wilde's sympathy for those who kill the things they love, Brummell referred to Rivière as "le cannibal" and did not foresee that both he and Rivière would die within a year of one another, Brummell tended by the Soeurs de Charité at the Bon Sauveur asylum for the insane and Rivière having been observed by its assistant head physician. The democracy that Byron thought Brummell heralded did not in 1830 include the lower and criminal classes as it would by the end of the century in Wilde's *Ballad of Reading Gaol*.

Returned from prison and placed on a strict budget and limited contributions from friends, Brummell metaphorically died the day he could no longer afford to have his immaculate cambric neckcloths washed and starched. He symbolically replaced them with limp, mournful, black silk handkerchiefs. By 1838, he was completely imbecile, a victim of paralysis. The man who had replaced the court foppery of the 1770's and 1780's macaronis with a sedate and immaculate version of the country gentleman's dress, who had been known as the cleanest man in Europe, was evicted from a second-rate hotel to the Bon Sauveur because, as the proprietors said, living as he was on a straw bed amidst grease and excrement, they simply "could not keep him *clean*."[48]

From Brummell's life—in narrative structure remarkably like biographies of Wilde and, like Wilde's life, determined by dramatic fluctuations in his socioeconomic status—Jesse concludes that Brummell's fundamental misapprehension was in overlooking the fact that he could not match his purse to those of the circle he joined. Not being rich, Jesse moralizes, Brummell ought to have been "sensible"—although such a notion would have made Brummell a Jesse rather than a Brummell:

But, whatever were his powers of pleasing or of ridicule, he was totally deficient in the judgment requisite to make the position he obtained by these means of any solid advantage to him; and in spite of his intimacies with great people, he did not accomplish either of the principal objects of a sensible man's life, especially in these very hard times: he neither managed to marry well, nor to get a place—he did not even keep his own.[49]

In concluding his résumé of what Catherine Gore, the last of the Regency-inspired fashionable novelists, called "the gilded not the golden age," Jesse lists others like Brummell who, in Gore's words, "promoted the greatest happiness of the smallest number" and, in his own phrase, "finished their careers in bankruptcy of health, fortune, and peace of mind." But Jesse's moral goes one step further, to contrast the "folly" of Brummell with the "vulgar and worthless portion of fashionable society in the present."[50] And in Jesse's contrast we can see the romanticization of the Beau as part of a "natural aristocracy" that would give him his revolutionary status in an increasingly vulgarized society and that much later would make him the prototype of Wilde's dandy Lord Goring, who was idle and trivial but not corrupt and vicious:

Let us recollect, however, that Brummell wore the bells of folly rather than the brand of vice; that he was neither a drunkard nor a sensualist. . . . He had no striking virtues, and lived for the enjoyment of the passing hour; yet in this respect he was no exception to those who constituted the world of fashion in his day, or do so in the present: there were, and are, thousands like him, neither better nor worse as to principles or feelings, but far inferior both in manners and tastes.[51]

This nostalgia for the Beau, or the Beautiful, would rise again in the 1890's defense of Aestheticism. But long before that, the legendary figure of Brummell inspired the fashionable novels of the 1820's and 1830's.

With his "puffs and puffery"—or advertising—the publisher Henry Colburn was to the fashionable novelists what Leonard Smithers was to the decadents. And the same criticism that William Hazlitt and J. G. Lockhart levelled against the dandy school is to this day a dominant criticism of the decadent literature of the 1890's. Hazlitt called the novels of fashion "the most mechanical and shallow of all schools"; they indicated fashion, indeed, but not how characters felt. The dandy school gave images (of elegance, fashion, and wealth) to make people envious, rather than to supply "us with intellectual resources to counterbalance immediate privations." In a more Coleridgean vein, Lockhart wrote that, lacking "the high faculties of imagination," the dandy school could not achieve an "artist-like unity of form and purpose."[52] Later, 1890's critics like Arthur Symons, Richard Le Gallienne, Lionel Johnson, and Havelock Ellis distinguished decadent literature from "great," or "vital," literature by its break with organic form and, following Pater, by its personal impressions and images which had in themselves no shape.[53]

But although literary critics wanted more purposeful books to educate society, criticism of Colburn and his successor Richard Bentley was due more to the ungentlemanly advertising of literature in their own columns than to the self-advertisement of fictive dandies in their books. Colburn first brought out Robert Plumer Ward's *Tremaine; or, the Man of Refinement* (1825), then rapidly followed it with Thomas Henry Lister's *Granby* (1826), Disraeli's *Vivian Grey* (1826), Bulwer Lytton's *Pelham* (1828) and *The Last Days of Pompeii* (1834), all of which contain Brummell types or pseudonymous characterizations of Brummell. And the journals owned by Colburn—the *New Monthly Magazine, United Service Journal, Court Journal, Sunday Times,* and *Literary Gazette* (of which Colburn maintained part ownership and control)—ran column after column of "puffery," amounting to an expenditure of as high as £9,000 per year.

Like the 1890's attacks on advertisers in life and art, the influential gentlemanly journals of the 1820's and 1830's, like *Fraser's*, the *Athenaeum*, and the *Edinburgh Review*, attacked the publicists who recommended literature in the same column as boot blacking and soap. By 1843, the *Edinburgh Review* was devoting space to a lengthy history of advertising and lamenting that "the grand principle of modern existence is notoriety. Hardly a second-rate Dandy can start for the moors or a retired slopseller leave London for Margate without announcing the 'fashionable movement' in the morning papers."[54] By 1843, that is, the connection between dandyism and advertising—or what we shall call the commodification of the dandy—had been established in the antidandiacal, or gentlemanly, press.

In the preface to the second edition of *Pelham*, the most popular novel since Scott's *Waverley* and the most influential of Colburn's fashionable novels, Bulwer Lytton emphasizes his ambivalent attitude toward the dandy, describing his hero as a study in contradictions—the sort of contradictions that would be the defining characteristic of dandies through the 1890's:

I have drawn for the hero of my Work, such a person as seemed to me best fitted to retail the opinions and customs of the class and age to which he belongs; a personal combination of antitheses—a fop and a philosopher, a voluptuary and a moralist—a trifler in appearance, but rather one to whom trifles are instructive, than one to whom trifles are natural . . . accustomed to draw sage conclusions from the follies he adopts, and while professing himself a votary of Pleasure, in reality a disciple of Wisdom.[55]

Henry Pelham is in fact a poseur in a society of poseurs, although he frequently exposes and belittles the general posturing. Acting the fop in Paris and London—"*retailing* the opinions and customs" of others—he meticulously calculates his social advantage and political preferment. Unlike Brummell, he ultimately marries well and keeps his place. Like Wilde, he wittily inverts common language and lives dialectically, "a personal combination of antitheses," as he mounts the social ladder. He also deconstructs the essentialism of Victorian sincerity well before the Victorians tried to recuperate it. Pelham not only writes his notorious maxims for the dandy's dress, but he is obsessed with all costume, even going so far as to be dressed as a common clergyman by the ingenious master of disguise and thief Job Jonson in order to penetrate a criminal hideaway in the East End. Yet in Bulwer Lytton, no doubt, "criminal" remains a marked term in ways that it does not in Dorian's excursions to the East End. Bulwer Lytton's practice of retailing social goods in the service of social climbing is not yet the wholesale destruction of essence to which modern advertising practices contributed in Wilde's time.

In *The Last Days of Pompeii*, Bulwer Lytton understood the power of masks in a society in transition well enough to portray the decline of Regency England in the guise of ancient Rome. He portrayed it so well in fact that ten years later Jesse would begin the *Life* of Brummell with an allusion to the erstwhile dandies of Rome after "corruption had stamped the character of her citizens with effeminacy and voluptuousness" and two volumes later would conclude with a description of an "emasculated" Marquis of Brummell's set whose life could be illustrated by "the licentious frescoes of Pompeii."[56]

The Last Days was published four years after the death of George IV and during the same year that the more superstitious English were amazed by the fire that had, prophetically it must have seemed, caused greater destruction to the House of Lords than Commons. The first chapter, "The Two Gentlemen of Pompeii," begins with descriptions of effeminate coxcombs, portly merchants, society dinners, gambling and greed: a scenario intended to be familiar to Bulwer Lytton's readers. Before the luxurious Pompeiians are buried beneath the lava of Vesuvius, Bulwer Lytton combines elements of the fashionable novel with the historical novel in the manner of Scott. He describes at great length the furniture in the houses of Pompeii, and Glaucus's house is compared to that of "a single man in Mayfair." Patricians lament "the good old days of the Republic" when slaves and butlers entertained their masters by being eaten alive by lions and lampreys. In the forum lawyers are "active, chattering, joking, and punning, as you may find them at this day in Westminster." Suspect priests discourse upon the "two stages of sanctity": faith for the vulgar, and delusion and natural science for the power-hungry sage. Christianity among the pagans surfaces as the religion of the sinful, with the nineteenth-century admiration of the noble penitent. Bulwer Lytton even goes so far as to encourage the penitence of his contemporaries, for at the Pompeiians' most morally reprehensible moments he is sure to add an authorial reminder to the effect that they are "like us."

In addition to these common images and tropes of a declining Regency and an emerging Victoriana, Bulwer Lytton gave to France, via Pompeii, one of the first images of the decadent dandy, who would eventually return to England in the 1890's. The pagan-erotic poems interspersed throughout the first volume of *Pompeii* culminate in the figure of Arbaces, whose dark and decadent mansion supplies images of sphinxes, strange gods, and orgies. It was the French—for example Huysmans with his purely "mental" Des Esseintes—who took the sex out of decadence; and the British 1890's put it back. Naturally superior in intelligence and intensity of passion to the effete coxcombs and the portly merchants of Pompeii, Arbaces, the last descendant of a great house of fallen Egypt, mocks his vulgar conquerors and lives apart. Sensual and intellectual, the marginal priest of Isis wears away his body with "perverse" passions and his mind with inquiry into mysteries physical and metaphysical. As Bulwer Lytton's novels became popular in both England and France, Arbaces, like Melmoth, stood for the type of the marginal, ennui-consumed dandy.

Bulwer Lytton was able, like his character Pelham, to masquerade as a dandy until he took up the cause of the Reform Bill, at which point he criticized Regency decadence in the pages of *Pompeii*. In the progressive *England and the English*, published by Bentley in 1833, Bulwer Lytton claimed that "from the institution of clubs will be dated a vast social revolution," and he incorporated Brummell's clubs into a socialist scheme to unify families, provide education for children, and offer attention during illness. But this liberal time would not come until the British shed "that commercial jealousy of approbation which makes us so proverbially like to have a *home of our own*."[57] To achieve a new national identity, the British would have to shed traditional material symbols of identity and, like the dandy, play new roles. Similarly, Bulwer Lytton praised the fashionable novelists, modestly excluding his earlier self, for producing the greatest effect on the political spirit of their generation: "without any other merit, [they] unconsciously exposed the falsehood, the hypocrisy, the arrogant and vulgar insolence of patrician life. . . . The Utilitarians railed against them, and they were effecting with unspeakable rapidity the very purpose the Utilitarians desired."[58] Thus for Bulwer Lytton the fashionable novel paved the way for Reform and the social and industrial novel of the 1840's in the same way that Wilde's perspectives as a dandy pointed toward "The Soul of Man Under Socialism."

Disraeli, too, was able to masquerade as an Exclusive until he made enough of a name for himself to enter Parliament. (In *The Best Circles: Society Etiquette and the Season*, social historian Leonore Davidoff cites the period's formula that Parliament was the "greatest club of all."[59]) In the fictional vehicles *Coningsby* (1844) and *Sybil; or the Two Nations* (1845), the political equivalents of Bulwer Lytton's *Pompeii*, Disraeli argued for Tory Democracy as a way to unify the rich and the poor. But just twenty years prior to these he had published *Vivian Grey*, the story of a feverish, maneuvering parvenu in aristocratic circles.

From the time that Colburn's first "puff" for the anonymous novel came out on April Fool's Day 1826, the way was set for Disraeli's celebrity. Initially reviewers recommended the book for its representations of "nearly all the individuals at present figuring in fashionable society." By June, however, the truth was out that the fashionable author was an imposter who had no firsthand experience of the society he wrote of, and Disraeli was roundly abused for lying. "The 'circumcised,'" wrote one reviewer, "must have strange notions of common honesty," insinuating that Disraeli had probably purloined the diary of a real Exclusive.[60]

Nonetheless, the novel was successful and, with the added attraction of his romantic-exotic appearance and outrageous clothes, Disraeli began his social ascent, imitating his protagonist in *Vivian Grey* as Bulwer Lytton had imitated his Pelham. Of his life imitating his art, Disraeli wrote presciently in his diary of 1833:

I am only truly great in action. If ever I am placed in a truly eminent position I shall prove this. I could rule the House of Commons, although there would be a great prejudice against me at first. It is the most jealous assembly in the world. The fixed character of our aristocratic institutions renders a career difficult. Poetry is the safety valve of my passions, but I wish to *act* what I write.[61]

What Catherine Gore said of Brummell applies perhaps even more to Disraeli: "he was a nobody, who had made himself somebody, and gave the law to everybody." The dandy's versatility and adaptability—even then, as often as not, called "posturing"—were the key to his mobility. He infiltrates society with minimal repression, for, after all, he is "only posing."

This kind of mobility through posturing provoked not only overt censure, but also a more ambivalent dissatisfaction and frustration among gentlefolk. If, as Moers says, there was much personal envy and malice in Carlyle and Thackeray's respective attacks on fashionable novelists, the most interesting ambivalence toward dandyism was contained in the marginal men of the middle-class novels. These images of unhappy men would be of great significance to the 1890's, and they include the cynical-gentle characters in Jane Austen, the dissatisfied Heathcliffe in Emily Brontë, Grandcourt and Deronda in George Eliot's *Daniel Deronda*, and many more. For our purposes Dickens should serve as the acknowledged spokesperson of middle-class domesticity, whose mid-life transformation in attire represented a disturbing transformation in character and a resultant affinity with the cynical side of dandyism.

It is commonly believed that the English decadence of the 1890's, as represented by Dorian Gray, or Harry Wotton, or even Salome, with her sensuality and cynical attitude toward superiors, was a diluted importation from the French. Balzac, Barbey, and Baudelaire did indeed develop philosophies of *dandysme*, but these philosophies were derived from such books as Jesse's, Bulwer Lytton's, and Disraeli's. Dandyism survived in

Dandies and Gentlemen

England in another form: the Arbaces figure in *The Last Days of Pompeii*, so close in sympathy to Huysmans's Des Esseintes, is also the type of the cold, acutely cynical and hostile marginal men of Dickens's novels.

These gray men, as Moers calls them, such as Richard Carstone (*Bleak House*), James Harthouse (*Hard Times*), Henry Gowan (*Little Dorrit*), Sydney Carton (*A Tale of Two Cities*), and Eugene Wrayburn (*Our Mutual Friend*) are the strangers in Dickens's novels, who can be assimilated neither among the foolish bourgeois, nor among the obvious villains, nor into the saccharine domestic havens of the heroines. If one could imagine Pip's life after the end of *Great Expectations*, one might see this version of the marginal man, apart from, but cynically observant of, the general stream of middle-class life. These characters, in a little-noticed way, are indeed like Des Esseintes, who, in the tradition of Anglomania, plans to escape from his ennui through a trip to England but, getting no farther than an English restaurant at the Channel, finds that all he needs to know of England are the caricatures he meets there. So Dickens's own greatest power of portrayal is probably in these dissatisfied gray men, who do not fall into the grotesque caricatures of his Cheeryble Brothers and Merdles.

Moers also discerns another source for these gray men in Dickens's own unconventional life. One might say that he chose art over middle-class life when he abandoned wife, children, and respectability and turned to an actress, Ellen Ternan, and to the relatively lax, careless, and idle Wilkie Collins. Proposing a tour to Collins in 1857, he wrote, "We want something for Household Words, and I want to escape from myself. For when I do start up and stare myself seedily in the face . . . my blankness is inconceivable—indescribable—my misery amazing."[62] To cover up the blankness, Dickens assumed the mask, literally acting in the theaters and reading from parts in his own works. It is significant that the friend he turned to most often in this later, nihilistic stage of his life was the dramatist and playwright Collins.

The product of the tour with Collins was "The Lazy Tour of Two Idle Apprentices," published in *Household Words*. Here Dickens characterized himself as "Francis Goodchild" and Collins as "Thomas Idle." The good child's description of Idle has much in it that Wilde's detractors would later say of him: "Thomas Idle . . . an idler of the unmixed Irish or Neopolitan type; a passive idler, a born-and-bred idler, a consistent idler, who practised what he would have preached if he had not been too idle to preach; a one entire and perfect chrysolite of idleness." From Richard Carstone and Sydney Carton to Wilkie Collins and the older Dickens it is but a small step to the disillusion, the impotence, and the fatalism of the tragic generation.

The French, however, intervened between the dissatisfied-bourgeois version of the dandy and the shelter of art and aestheticism of the 1890's. French Anglomania resulted in a theorized dandy, one whose defense against the accusations of artificiality and superficiality was a more thorough critique of bourgeois values than the maneuvering of Brummell and D'Orsay or the marginality of Dickens's characters. The French made *dandysme* a movement and made it accessible to anyone who had the education to understand it. They did for dandies, that is, what the public schools did for gentlemen.

As *Fraser's* published its first attacks on the dandies, Honoré de Balzac, a young journalist who dressed like the young Disraeli to get into fashionable society, published the "Traité de la vie élégante" (1830) in the Parisian journal *La Mode*. Contrary to his own practice—Balzac called his astonishing dress "une réclame," as Wilde would later call his "aesthetic" costume a self-advertisement—Balzac chose the subdued refinement and simplicity of "Brummel" as the model for a new "moral superiority."[63]

By taking Brummell as a revolutionary figure, Balzac intended to derive for post-revolutionary France a new "natural aristocracy." He had no hope that it would be egalitarian, for by the very nature of their work laborers would not be able to participate in the "elegant life." The essay simply proposed guidelines for artists and others of sufficient leisure as to the external mannerisms that would indicate their superiority, a superiority that Balzac called "moral." Similarly, the historical improvement of the world could be read in costume: "Since costume is the most energetic of all symbols, the revolution was also a question of fashion, a debate between silk and muslin"; and "grooming is a society's expression. . . . To explain the long queue of the Franks, the tonsure of monks, the shaved head of the serf, the wigs of Popocambou, the aristocratic powder and the puddingbasins of 1790, would this not be to recount the principal revolutions of our country?"[64]

Although Moers discerns no irony here, it seems wiser to read the essay as a satire, albeit a satire opportunely making the best of the overdetermined. Balzac's maxims for the elegant life are no more than the mannerisms of the dandy, and it is clear that he saw them establishing a regime as arbitrary and as powerful as those that were attacked in the traditional discourses concerning clothing, like Juvenal's, Montaigne's, and Swift's. Balzac knew that beneath the clothing and manners more serious things were at fault; and by overvaluing the former he satirically highlighted the latter. Thus he replaced religion by manners and style. Like Arnold later with poetry, Balzac hoped that the "dogma" he espoused would take the place of obsolescent religion. In his comfort and correctness, the elegant man had "la grâce suffisante." In his amicability and adaptability, he had "la grâce essentielle." And in his natural sense of equilibrium and contentment, he had "la grâce divine et concomitante."[65]

No matter how much Balzac insisted that the new, superior man was independent of false superiority, like that bestowed by birth and wealth, no matter how many of his aphorisms emphasized that he "does not submit to laws, he imposes them," the essay's 53 maxims prescribe a very rigid hierarchy, with plenty of room for falling. The first part of the essay is much like Wilde's "Soul of Man" in its emphasis on individuality and on the artist as a model of the free agent: the artist is the exception among workers. Laborers, bureaucrats, and superior officers "are like steam-engines; regimented by work they are stamped in the same mold and have no individuality." The dandy-artist, on the other hand, defensively becomes the bestower of value where value need not imply production: it is sufficient that he mirror negatively the hopeless reification of others' lives. Like Wilde's artist, he is "an exception: his idleness is work, and his work is repose: he is elegant and negligent by turns; he assumes at his pleasure the laborer's smock or the tails of the man of fashion."[66]

Since the elegant life is "the art of animating repose," the artist who also practices the 53 maxims is the type of elegant man. But unlike Wilde's projected society of artists in "The Soul of Man," Balzac's utopia is stifling. It consists of an exclusive society with the trappings of elegance, a rhetoric that makes an announced "spirit" material, and a new system of laws, containing half a hundred maxims, that serves to constrict rather than liberate. In Balzac were the seeds of an idea that Wilde would play with in *Dorian Gray* and that would surface throughout the dandy postures of the British 1890's: that the dandy-artist's leisure was a form of critique. Yet in Balzac the leisure forms are reified, as Dorian Gray's would be, as Des Esseintes's would be, by the brittle materialism of a post-revolutionary age.

Because Balzac's essay attempted an idealization of the artistic life to counter bourgeois mediocrity but still relied on a hierarchical, exclusionary model deriving from the idea of aristocracy (whether natural or traditional), and because it was situated in the context of the dandiacal journal *La Mode*, it could serve as both satire on existing social conditions and as the manifesto of an artistic community. *Du Dandysme et de George Brum-*

mell, by the Anglophile Barbey d'Aurevilly, could not be misconstrued and was taken as the definitive word on a peculiarity of the English social system. Barbey's essay, published in 1844 after the author had consulted with Jesse and made a serious study of both fictional and nonfictional representations of dandyism and the Regency, unraveled the complex social issues involved in Balzac's treatise, located *dandysme* historically, and predicted its place in the future.

Dandyism, writes Barbey, arises in contradictions, specifically in the antagonism of the stability, puritanism, and propriety of "the richest society in the world" and the boredom that ensues upon their establishment.[67] The practice of poets on fixed incomes publishing volumes in honor of the established Church of England, and of a "young queen who affects conjugal bliss as Elizabeth affected virginity," signified for Barbey a society overburdened by habit and cant.[68] The suppression of creative fantasy had resulted in a society of drudges. Unlike Balzac, Barbey does not write of the real drudges, who have made England the richest society in the world, but rather, like Wilde in his critical dialogues and *De Profundis*, of the degree of conformity among even the leisured classes of society.

Barbey implies that the formulaic rules of high society are its counterpart to the necessary regimentation of the lower classes. The dandy is a sort of pro-tem loan for the cost of luxury: he accepts for his own benefit and others' amusement the materialism of his affluent society at the same time that he superciliously mocks the tedious stability of its participants. Through the voice of the old man in *News from Nowhere*, Morris relegated nineteenth-century graduates (like Wilde) of Oxford and Cambridge to a similar position, and he blamed them for their commerciality:

[The universities] (and especially Oxford) were the breeding places of a peculiar class of parasites, who called themselves cultivated people; they were indeed cynical enough, as the so-called educated classes of the day generally were; but they affected an exaggeration of cynicism in order that they might be thought knowing and worldly-wise. The rich middle classes (they had no relation with the working classes) treated them with the kind of contemptuous toleration with which a mediaeval baron treated his jester. . . . They were laughed at, despised—and paid. Which last was what they aimed at.[69]

Applying to Brummell an adage in *Pelham*, "he displeased too generally not to be sought after," Barbey likens society's worship of the dandy to "the wish to be beaten of powerful and licentious women."[70]

"For Dandies, as for women, to *seem* is to *be*," wrote Barbey; "these stoics of the boudoir drink their own blood under their mask and remain masked."[71] Later Shaw would write of Eleanora Duse's Magda—in Sudermann's *Heimat*, about, as Shaw said, "the revolt of the modern woman against the ideal of home which exacts the sacrifice of her whole life to its care"—"Every woman who sees Duse play Magda feels that Duse is acting and speaking for her and for all women as they are hardly able to speak and act for themselves." On the problem that actresses faced he wrote that "most educated woman have been trained to fight against emotional expression because it is a mode of self-betrayal."[72] In a society dominated by businessmen, the dandy and the woman wrap themselves up like products and sell themselves. (Such, of course, was at least the partial function of Balzac's treatise.) Having nothing else, they live by wits alone. In a society of serious hypocrites, their hyperbolic artificiality is a consoling diversion. They are the fools to the players.

Yet dandiacal and feminine "vanity"—a key word for Barbey, with no pejorative connotations—is the sole manifestation of an urge for community in a rapaciously competitive society. Dandiacal and feminine power lies in its vanity, defined as its "anxious research for another's approval," that "amiable impulse of the human heart to seek the approbation of others."[73] Thus the relation between dandies (or women) and society is symbiotic—for a time. Because society is bored, it permits itself to be amused; because society is competitive, it deserts the dandy and the woman when they are vulnerable. Any number of events can expose their vulnerability: in Brummell's case it was poverty. The dandy's sociability and consequent social power combined with his vulnerability make up Barbey's metaphor of him as "the hermaphrodite of History."[74]

Barbey's functional equivalence dandy/woman is insightful for its clarification of the social and economic appurtenances of dandyism. When Barbey's friend Charles Baudelaire published "The Painter of Modern Life" (1863), his section on "The Dandy" directly preceded that on "Woman." Baudelaire does not explicitly connect dandies and women, but he does attribute to them similar qualities expressed by similar imagery. Dandyism is a "cult of the self" arising from "the burning need to create for oneself a personal originality." Although Baudelaire writes, like Barbey, with a metaphysical vocabulary, he goes on to suggest the social and economic bases of what becomes in effect a commercial exploitation, or commodification, of the self:

Dandyism appears above all in periods of transition, when democracy is not yet all-powerful, and aristocracy is only just beginning to totter and fall. In the disorder of these times, certain men who are socially, politically and financially ill at ease, but are all rich in native energy, may conceive the idea of establishing a new kind of aristocracy . . . based . . . on the divine gifts which work and money are unable to bestow. . . . Dandyism is a sunset; like the declining daystar, it is glorious, without heat and full of melancholy. But alas, the rising tide of democracy, which invades and levels everything, is daily overwhelming these last representatives of human pride.[75]

Baudelaire sees the dandy as an auracular artwork, in Benjamin's terms, facing the onslaught of mass society. Like most representations of late-Victorian dandies, Baudelaire's is from the lost province of connoisseurship, rooted in history and his "unique existence at the place where he happens to be": he cannot be created, evolved, or duplicated in a day.[76] The passage suggests the contours of the best social analysis of British dandyism, especially the dandyism of the 1890's. Like Baudelaire's "Woman," the British dandy wears the mask, or the "maquillage," as self-advertisement. Until the rising tide of democracy cuts off the patronage of the dandy and contributes to the economic independence of women, they use artifice to "produce" something more uncommon than the debased productions of industrial labor and inherited wealth. Although Balzac, Barbey, and Baudelaire explicitly pose the dandy as liberator, as the new source of human superiority, implicit in their essays is a more chilling framework for the dandy: having discerned the commercialism of his society, he offers himself as a product, he sells his aura.

To escape such an appalling conclusion, the later Baudelaire reconceived the dandy as pure, ethereal intellect and in doing so fixed the divergent and predominant type of French *dandysme*. The gross commerciality suggested by his earlier analysis he henceforth attributed to women, their maquillage, and their base seductive bodies. It was, indeed, woman's "materialism," her pliant, productive body that turned Baudelaire entirely against her in the revealing, if repellent, *Mon coeur mis à nu*. Here woman is only a body, and Baudelaire describes love with her in the economic metaphor of prostitution: "Women cannot distinguish between soul and body," whereas "the dandy creates a more and more perceptible divorce between the spirit and the brute . . . the more a man cultivates the arts, the less often he gets an erection. . . . Only the brute gets really good erections, and fucking is the lyricism of the people." Like aestheticism, Baudelaire's dandyism was divorced from life. When he writes of George Sand, on the other hand, she represents both "slut" and the masses.[77] Although Wilde did not fall into the contradictions or meanspiritedness of Baudelaire, in Chapter 4 we shall see more of this hystericization, as Foucault calls it, of women's bodies:

women were basely materialist and unworthy of the "intellectual" love of men.

Later, in *Zuleika Dobson* (1911), Max Beerbohm would somewhat anticlimactically oppose the woman to the dandy. In the most absurd case of mimetic desire in literature, the entire undergraduate class at Oxford commits mass suicide for one beautiful woman who makes her living as a very poor magician. The foil to Zuleika Dobson, daughter of a circus rider and herself a traveling public performer, is the dandiacal Duke, a work of art with an aura, meaningless outside of his particular history, an original, unreplaceable, and clearly Beerbohm's imaginative center in the text. In longing to reproduce the Duke's inimitable heroic action, hundreds of undergraduates copy it to their demise. The Duke's history—his genealogy takes two pages to trace—is opposed to Zuleika's journalese: a mobile magic act accompanied by advertising slogans. Against the Duke's accumulated knowledge, acknowledged with every prize in Oxford, Zuleika stacks her library: a Bradshaw covered in semi-precious stones and an A.B.C. Guide. The end of *Zuleika Dobson* shows Zuleika timing the trains to Cambridge with a "thought about the power of example," or duplication. In the fallen world dominated by the sham Zuleika, the Duke leaps from a height "on the peak of dandyism . . . on the brink of eternity." The image is from *Melmoth the Wanderer*, perhaps the greatest of the metaphysical-male treatments of dandyism. Zuleika became the type of the superstar-actress.

As the dandy spiritualized, he took upon himself a host of problems. As in Barbey's metaphor and Wilde's recycled language, the cynical dandy continually recirculated his own blood as his sole nourishment and, like the aristocrat, consequently faced the probability of anemia. With respect to belief, in an age of little faith but much cant and hypocrisy—in an advertising age—dandies are the anorexics of the soul. The essential properties of soul wither in mass consumerist society, so Dorian Gray was told to cure the soul with—what else in the society of the spectacle?—the senses.

Whereas Baudelaire found it easier to hate half of humankind than to accept that artists of all sexes were marginal in a consumerist society and that aristocracies were dying, the 1890's dandies Wilde and Whistler accepted the commercialism that artists were forced to adopt if they wanted to participate in life. In an age of debased production, their commercial products were nothing less than themselves. Whistler's attacks on Wilde, through letters to editors of popular journals, for *stealing* his lines and ideas, and Wilde's responses may serve as a cogent illustration. Whistler published a letter in the *World* (17 November 1886) to the Committee of the National Art Exhibition lamenting Wilde's exploitation of the currency of language: "What has Oscar in common with Art? except that he dines at our tables and picks from our platters the plums for the pudding he peddles in the provinces. Oscar—the amiable, irresponsible, esurient Oscar—with no more sense of a picture than of the fit of a coat, has the courage of the opinions of others."[78]

Unlike the aristocratic dandy Baudelaire, Whistler fought coteries with coteries; he recognized the institutional status of the art world and recommended that Wilde keep outside of "the radius." In *Truth* (2 January 1890), he flatly called Wilde a plagiarist and noted that "in America he may, under the 'Law of '84,' . . . be criminally prosecuted, incarcerated, and made to pick oakum, as he has hitherto picked brains—and pockets!" Wilde responded (*Truth*, 9 January 1890) that the only thoroughly original ideas he had ever heard Whistler express had reference to Whistler's own superiority over painters greater than himself.

Such verbal performances and self-promotions in the press make no pretence to Baudelaire's misplaced and burning need to create for oneself a personal originality; rather, the Wilde and Whistler exchanges function as personal advertisements in the open market of the press. This commercial age was probably the only one in which Wilde's exclusion of Judas Iscariot from the great suicides of history could really come off as humorous: "Oh, Judas! I don't count him. After all he was merely a *nouveau riche*." In fact, after his downfall Wilde was even less concerned to produce the illusive auracular and original artwork: in his late letters he would repeatedly sell one copyright to many buyers. This practical exposure of art as commodity effectively bears the same radical value as the satire on the bourgeois art world in "Pen, Pencil, and Poison."

If we look at the figures of dandyism from Brummell, Disraeli, and Balzac (who paid his debts to real tailors, bootmakers, and glovemakers by advertising their names, addresses, and merits in his fiction) to Dickens, it seems somewhat disingenuous to treat, as Moers does, the 1890's form of dandyism as debased and insincere; for to contrast Baudelaire's dandy with Wilde and Whistler is merely to contrast the disaffected and self-indulgent with the democratic and demystified. Benjamin thought that the auracular artwork, the "quality" bourgeois art to be contemplated and possessed, would be devalued in the age of mechanical reproduction, and that this change could be democratizing and liberating—as Gramsci said, "a policy of quality almost always determines its opposite: dis-qualified quantity"— or it could be a tool of fascism or mass control.[79] Baudelaire simply lamented the loss of privatized art and the elevated artist.

Dandies and Gentlemen

By the 1890's the necessary commercialism of the artist was explicit and accepted. Lillie Langtry, actress and companion of the Prince of Wales, was the first to sell soap with her photograph, in the 1890's. With such competition, the last of the male dandies could hardly pretend to more auspicious principles. Men and women alike, as the pages of the *Woman's World* indicate, were selling their images. Max Beerbohm satirized the collapse of all industry but this in the *Yellow Book*'s "A Defense of Cosmetics." While Douglas dragged Wilde to the casino in Monte Carlo and Wilde's biographer Frank Harris bought a hotel there, Beerbohm compared his own age to Brummell's: gambling and artifice (rouge) were the marks of a complicated age; as women began to paint, they would lose their ability to work.[80] Wilde's radicalism lay in his rendering ironic the commercial image of dandy-artist and his using it dialectically to subvert the image of the bourgeois gentleman, as he did in the debate over *The Picture of Dorian Gray*.

Before leaving the image of the dandy, however, we should briefly note one of its last manifestations in Wilde's spectacular life. Only when he was no longer a sellable commodity did he assume, at intervals, Baudelaire's image of the dandy: this image functioned well in the only situations it could do so—in prison and in exile. In assuming his last mask, the name Sebastian Melmoth—Sebastian probably from St. Sebastian and Melmoth from his grand-uncle's *Melmoth the Wanderer*—Wilde assumed the mantle of dandyism in the high tragic mode.

The original Melmoth himself, whose story never ends and whose "sin"—that is, his precise compact with A Certain Person—is never told, became for the Romantics and Victorians an image of the most sublime (that is, Byronic) form of dandyism: omniscient intelligence, great power, deepest cynicism, extreme emotion, and extreme marginality. Maturin emphasized the latter characteristic metaphorically in the book's conclusion. After a futile search through space and time to find someone to take his place, someone, that is, to trade his soul for illimitable power and wealth, Melmoth's mortal self commits suicide and his soul is condemned to leading the planets through eternity. His divorce from life and the world is irrevocable and eternal. His last intelligible words supply the image of Baudelaire's declining daystar, glorious, without heat, and full of melancholy: "When a meteor blazes in your atmosphere—when a comet pursues its burning path towards the sun—look up, and perhaps you may think of the spirit condemned to guide the blazing and erratic orb."[81]

Melmoth the Wanderer was published in Edinburgh and London in 1820. Its eccentric author, whom some called a "dandy," the Irish Protestant cleric and nationalist Charles Robert Maturin, had been advanced by Walter Scott and Byron from his earliest drama *Bertram* and had had dealings with the publisher Colburn through his earliest novels.[82] Readers of the seemingly interminable and unclassifiable novel know that its plot cannot be communicated to the uninitiated. In Dublin in 1816, a student, John Melmoth, attends a miserly uncle, who forthwith dies in an avaricious delirium. The tale then wanders alogically, atemporally, atopically, from theaters in London during the reign of Charles II, Jesuit convents in Spain during the Inquisition, and pagan islands in the Indian Sea, to nineteenth-century Germany and England. All of the narratives, each spoken by a different character, converge through their representations of Melmoth, who has played a part in all their lives, while he intermittently appears as a narrator in the larger structure. The story haunted not only the later novelists in the Gothic tradition, but also the exponents and metaphysicians of dandyism, from Bulwer Lytton's Arbaces with his basilisk's eye and immense wealth to Oscar Wilde bankrupt in Paris.

In "Melmoth Converted" (1835), Balzac converts all the magic and grandeur of Maturin's Melmoth into the cash flow of contemporary Paris, addressing the story to "our civilization which, since 1815, has replaced honor as a principle of action by wealth."[83] Melmoth became the type who sneered at the petty commercialism of modern times. Like Captain Jesse, Balzac's protagonist Castanier is an ex-dragoon who since 1813 had been employed in civilian capacity. Having abandoned an insipid wife, Castanier embezzles 500,000 francs from the Parisian bank that employs him as cashier, in order to meet the whimsical demands of his mistress. Just as he is about to be apprehended, he meets Melmoth and chooses to take his place. (Here Melmoth is finally allowed to die, repentant and converted: satanic affluence and power having left him bored, he turns to the insatiability of religious desire.)

Now possessing Melmoth's power, the cashier too is consumed with ennui and turns to the stock exchange as the most likely place to find a victim sufficiently desperate to become his successor in Melmoth's pact. A series of bankrupts sell their interest in paradise for diminishing amounts until a house painter, who does not know what to do with the investment once he has made it, sells it for 10,000 francs to a clerk who wastes the devil's power in a twelve-day orgy with a prostitute. He dies from an overdose of quicksilver, and thus, writes Balzac, "was the extraordinary power acquired by the discovery of the Irishman, the offspring of the reverent Mathurin [sic], destroyed." Whereas the taste of power and wealth had left

Melmoth so insatiable as to turn to religious desire, his nineteenth-century successors in the pact never elevate themselves above petty materialism.

Balzac's "The Elixir of Long Life" (1830), in which Melmoth had also appeared, travestied religious conversion from the perspective of one who chose to believe in God solely because the devil was heir apparent to a contemptibly debased world, a view that would seem to be applicable to the conversions of the 1890's. Balzac had chosen Don Juan Belvidero to exemplify the evils of inheritance:

> When you reach Don Juan's refined parricide, try to guess how, under almost identical circumstances, the honest folk would behave, who, in the nine-teenth century, take an annuity on the strength of a chronic catarrh, or those who let a house to an old woman for the rest of her days? Would they try to bring their tenants to life? I should be very glad if sworn weighers of consciences would examine the question of what similarity there can possibly be between Don Juan and those fathers who give their children in marriage because of hopes.[84]

After denying his father the rejuvenating elixir, Don Juan keeps it for himself, inherits a vast estate, and becomes the perfect type of Maturin's Melmoth, differing only in scale from Dorian Gray:

> Renouncing the idea of a better world, he did not bare his head at the mention of a name, and looked upon the stone saints in the churches simply as works of art. Moreover, being familiar with the machinery of human society, he never jostled prejudices too rudely, because he was not so powerful as the executioner; but he circumvented social laws with the grace and wit so well depicted. . . . He was, in truth, the perfect type of Molière's *Don Juan*, of Goethe's *Faust*, of Byron's *Manfred*, and of Maturin's *Melmoth*. Colossal images drawn by the most colossal geniuses of Europe. . . . He mocked at everything. His life was one long mockery, which embraced men, things, institutions, ideas.[85]

So the possibility of infinite inheritance creates infinite ambition and cynicism. Balzac's Don Juan, unlike Maturin's Melmoth, does not die leading the planets, or even in a feudal duel with a stone; rather his end is that of a debased and partial man. The elixir revives him only as to one arm and his head, whereupon a greedy priest arrogates said members to the status of a miracle for the greater glory of the Church and greater income and promotion of its ministers. Amid such petty materialism, "the perfect type" of Melmoth in the nineteenth century severs its head from its dead body, proclaiming God and repudiating a fallen world.

This image of a debased and partial man applies to the great but extraordinarily vulnerable financier Augustus Melmotte in Trollope's *The Way We Live Now* (1875). Called by the novel's primary gentleman "a sign of the degeneracy of the age," the financier remains the opaque and imaginative center of the text, determining by his spectacular rise and fall the fates of the characters. Yet Melmotte himself is silent, inarticulate among Trollope's brilliant dialogues, almost without content. Representing the pure form of the power of credit to transform human lives, he retains a mysterious power, even when he all too humanly fails to trust his stock and prematurely commits suicide. Like Baudelaire's socially, politically, and financially ill-at-ease men with reserves of native energy, Melmotte the wandering Jew, son of an Irish coiner in New York, rises to untold wealth and the seat for Westminster. Corporate center of "the way we live now," hosting huge balls where his guests will not speak to him, Melmotte retains a social and emotional marginality in respectable society that allies him with dandies who entertained without belonging. As the narrator remarks of a world powerless to be born without him, "the world was more than ordinarily alive because of Melmotte and his failures."

This version of Melmoth or the dandy as somewhere between God and the devil (or debased humankind) is Baudelaire's in "On the Essence of Laughter" (1885). Nominally a treatise on caricature in the plastic arts, Baudelaire's essay traces humor and caricature of the sort in Balzac and Dickens to Melmoth and marginal men—and to their contradictions:

All the miscreants of melodrama, accursed, damned and fatally marked with a grin which runs from ear to ear, are in the pure orthodoxy of laughter. Furthermore they are almost all the grand-children, legitimate or illegitimate, of the renouned wanderer Melmoth, that great satanic creation of the Reverend Maturin. What could be greater, what more mighty, relative to poor humanity, than the pale, bored figure of Melmoth? And yet he has a weak and contemptible side to him, which faces against God and against the light. See, therefore, how he laughs. . . . And this laughter is . . . the necessary resultant of his contradictory double nature, which is infinitely great in relation to man, and infinitely vile and base in relation to absolute Truth and Justice. Melmoth is a living contradiction.[86]

If, as Baudelaire says, laughter comes from a feeling of superiority, then the greatest laughter will be the laughing philosopher's, or the dandy's. The dandy is split between a common, human caricature of himself and his own superior desires: "The man who trips would be the last to laugh at his own fall, unless he happened to be a philosopher, one who had acquired by habit a power of self-division and thus of assisting as a disinterested spectator at the phenomenon of his own ego."[87] Unlike joy, which comes from a feeling of unity, "something analogous to the wagging of a dog's tail" and the thoughtless laughter of children, adult laughter is social—that is, preceded by social divisions. Baudelaire writes:

And so the laughter of children . . . is altogether different, even as a physical expression, even as a form, from the laughter of a man who attends a play, or who looks at a caricature, or from the terrible laughter of Melmoth—of Melmoth, the outcast of society, wandering some where between the last boundaries of the territory of mankind and the frontiers of the higher life . . . who . . . longs without ceasing to barter that superhuman power, which is his disaster, for the pure conscience of a simpleton, which is his envy.[88]

Within this philosophical tradition of dandies and Melmoth, Wilde composed *De Profundis* and took up his pseudonym. His comedies had always presented the class version of superiority, with their references to the lower classes (largely absent from the theater) and their in-jokes for, and complacent images of, the elite. But the contradictory elements of the plays indicated that Wilde was superior to his audience in his ability to be self-critical. In much the way Baudelaire wrote of the superior laughter of the philosopher, the disinterested spectator who laughs at his own fall, Shaw wrote that "there was more laughter between the lines of [*De Profundis*] than in a thousand farces by men of no genius";[89] and later critics have followed Arthur Symons, who wrote that in that work Wilde "was to be the writer of the play as well as the actor and spectator."[90] Moreover, in *De Profundis*'s transition from the reprobate "feasting with panthers" to the new disciple of Christ walking among children, flowers, and gentle nights hung with stars, we find the image of Melmoth who "longs without ceasing to barter that superhuman power, which is his disaster, for the pure conscience of a simpleton." In "The Essence of Laughter," Baudelaire wrote, "for the laughter of children is like the blossoming of a flower. It is . . . joy." Wilde in *De Profundis* longs for the transition from laughter to joy.

Underlying Balzac's, Baudelaire's, and Trollope's literary types is the original *Melmoth* that began with a miser's delirium; and the novel chronicles Western greed and rapacity through four centuries. This fact and the romance of the novel are in taut contradiction, much like the contradictions of its author: the Irish Protestant cleric who was also an Irish nationalist and who adored the relics of dandyism, an Irish cleric who wrote near-interminable popular romances for the British public in order to make a living in Dublin: "I cannot again appear before the public in so unseemly a character as that of a writer of romances without regretting the necessity that compels me to it. Did my profession furnish me with the means of subsistence, I should hold myself culpable indeed in having recourse to any other, but—am I allowed the choice?"[91] When he wrote *De Profundis*, and later as Sebastian Melmoth, Wilde was imprisoned, in exile, and bankrupt. This was dandyism in the high tragic mode, but it was nonetheless the mere obverse of the Society dandy: one sold himself; the other could not sell.

As early as the third decade of the nineteenth century, social and political elevation on the dandy circuit was exposed to the kind of gentlemanly censure that would fall with full weight on Wilde with the publication of *The Picture of Dorian Gray*. Moers has researched the middle-class criticism of the Count D'Orsay, Brummell's successor as arbiter elegantiarum.[92] She cites testimonies to D'Orsay's graciousness, kindness, and unusual good nature from such sources as Thackeray, Carlyle, Tennyson, Macready, and Dickens—and one can cite similar testimonies regarding Wilde from both his contemporaries and reviewers of his letters. Yet the other side of such praise was a general distrust of the dandy who seemed to win favor without hard work. In D'Orsay's case, the very fact that he so endeared himself to the Blessingtons that they literally kept him for 30 years contributed to the attacks on him by Henry Chorley, the eminent critic of the *Athenaeum*, and by his earlier friends Disraeli and Thackeray. Their betrayal was rather surprising since D'Orsay had been, with the financial help of the Blessingtons, a significant friend and patron to artists and the arts, yet his critics concluded that D'Orsay was a dandy but not industrious enough to be a gentleman. This decisive cut probably initiated the distrust of artists economically or intellectually affiliated with the upper classes that was so fatal to Wilde.

Yet the case of D'Orsay should not obscure the fact that in most cases a dandy was a stylized discontented gentleman: one could not be a dandy without having been a gentleman first. Nor did financial independence and respectability alone make a gentleman. England had a tradition of elitism, and under the new dispensation this was to be carried on by the public schools. By the 1880's, to be a gentleman one must have attended a public school (or successfully pose as having done). The public schools created the gentleman whose discontents created the late-Victorian dandy.

It is an indication of the complexity of the 1890's that the difference between Brummell and the late-Victorian dandy was the latter's internal contradictions. The late-Victorian gentleman against which he was a reaction was equally complex. What becomes clear in the voluminous historical and sociological examination of the public school gentleman in the nineteenth century—which the following discussion synthesizes—is the conflict between the code that headmasters tried to propagate through the machinery of the school—the content of the teaching, the example of masters, chapel sermons, religious observance generally—and the values implicit in the machinery or operation of the system itself. This conflict, combined with the fact that old boys themselves had dramatically conflicting estimations of the value of their education, renders the gentleman an extremely problematic category.

Perhaps because of Britain's post-war economic lag, there has been considerable, generally conservative, attention to the history and idea of the gentleman and the question of whether he can save or has destroyed Britain.[93] Martin J. Wiener has presented possibly the most extreme thesis in blaming the decline of British industry and economy on the acculturation of the middle classes to the idea of the gentleman beginning in the nineteenth century. Impressed by the national demonstrations of appreciation of the greatest of British engineers at their deaths in 1859-60—Isambard Brunel, Robert Stephenson, and Joseph Locke—Wiener traces the defection of their sons from industry and science to the public schools. These excluded curricula in business and technology but produced a consolidated elite with commercial, professional, bureaucratic, aristocratic, and gentrified roots. The insecurity of sons less enterprising than their fathers led to the tension between the machine (the fact of the industrial age) and the garden (a pastoral myth of a gentle England) and to the sons' ensconcement in Culture and, today, what we should call the educated, or upper, middle class.

A different interpretation of the British gentleman is Shirley Letwin's, in which the gentleman is a moral category that solves the romantic philosophical problem of the divided self: the gentleman has the ability to choose rightly between reason and passion. Unlike the romantic, he knows how to live in and adjust to the world with integrity, or a coherent personality, which for Letwin includes the traditional qualities of courage, industry, practicality, courtesy, and truthfulness. Geoffrey Best adds to these qualities conventional morality, selflessness, self-control, independence, and responsibility, yet Best emphasizes that the ideal was loaded in the nineteenth century to support the social hierarchy, having less to do with mobility than acceptance. The society of gentlemen was in practice penetrable by personal attractiveness and/or money, as long as one or both lasted.

The ideal gentleman's courtesy, responsibility, and courage were largely formulations in a revival of chivalry. With *Fraser's* patriarchal campaign against the New Poor Law and laissez-faire economics in the 1830's, middle-class chivalry entered the scene, purging the older aristocratic ideal of its grosser elements with nineteenth-century religion. Henceforth Christian Socialists such as J. M. Ludlow, F. D. Maurice, Charles Kingsley,

Thomas Hughes, and E. V. Neale, with their emphasis on physical fitness, distinguished muscular Christians from musclemen in that the former's bodies were in the service of protecting others. The unstable integrity of body and soul, muscle and protection, or Letwin's passion and reason here may be seen in the Pre-Raphaelite Millais's ludicrous attempt at chivalric painting, *The Knight-Errant* (1870). A rather too open-countenanced knight slips up behind an utterly naked lady (facing the spectator) to push an enormous sword between the bonds of the rope tying her to the tree.

Like the knight's armor, the public school uniform was "the outward and visible sign of that uniformity of spirit of which [the school] was so proud."[94] Or such was the chivalric ideal. But Arthur Ponsonby described the height of the pattern using school photographs with a somewhat different conclusion:

The group today consist of two or three rows of boys beautifully turned out with immaculate, perfectly fitting clothing. In the football eleven each will wear a cap, shirt, shorts, stockings of precisely the same pattern. They stand and sit so that the line of the peaks of their caps, of their folded arms, of their bare knees is mathematically level. And even their faces! You can hardly tell one from another. . . . It is, without doubt, an outward and visible sign not only of the love of the appearance of smartness, but of the stereotyping and conventionalizing effect of our modern educational system. This stereotyping . . . constitutes perhaps the strongest indictment that has to be brought against our Public Schools.[95]

According to T. W. Bamford, from about 1870 there was a subtle but organized drive by authority to sublimate the boy's self to a team. Clearly this kind of uniformity was propitious for the military, and indeed the armed forces represented the most popular occupation of boys from both the nine major boarding schools of the Clarendon Commission and the new foundations.

If the esprit de corps fostered by public school games, clubs, and the monitorial system (prefect, head boys, fagging) supported the British military, the boys themselves often questioned whether it was equally compatible with the Christian virtues that were also the putative mark of the gentleman. On the one hand, the boys defended the less privileged, as in missions to the East End to improve the condition of the poor; on the other, the public school was an elite "world in itself, self-centred, self-satisfied,"[96] considerably differentiated from the world it protected. Many boys who had done well in school were terrified at the anonymity they feared upon leaving it. "Only forty-eight hours now between me and insignificance," Alfred Lyttleton said shortly before his last day at Eton.[97] In his autobiography, Bertrand Russell recounts the moment when he perceived the extent to which the competitive ethos had conflicted with Christian love. While self-absorbedly looking on as Evelyn Whitehead suffers a severe heart attack, Russell muses: "She seemed cut off from everyone by walls of agony. . . . Within five minutes I went through some such reflections as the following; the loneliness of the human soul is unendurable; nothing can penetrate it except the highest intensity of the sort of love that religious teachers have preached; whatever does not spring from this motive is harmful, or at best useless; it follows that war is wrong, that a public school education is abominable. . . ."[98] In *A Georgian Childhood* Cyril Connolly estimates the (and his) public school education as responsible for the "permanent adolescence" of the British ruling class. The schoolboys' triumphs and failures are so intense as to dominate their lives and arrest their development, and the result is that "the greater part of [this class] remains adolescent, school-minded, self-conscious, cowardly, sentimental, and in the last analysis, homosexual."[99]

The tensions between Christian virtues and competition can be multiplied. In the nineteenth century, Bamford points out, the great headmasters were renowned floggers, and headboys and prefects often took over such responsibilities. The lists of punishments whose abuses are abundantly chronicled include flogging, lines, fagging (the indenture of younger to older boys), indulgence of bright and pretty boys simultaneously with strictness toward unremarkable and plain ones, and codes of discretion that put great and often life-long strain on boys. Phyllis Grosskurth has written of the wrenching case of J. A. Symonds and his headmaster C. J. Vaughan at Harrow. Aware at Harrow of his own homoeroticism, Symonds brooded over his knowledge that Vaughan had had an affair with a friend, who was flaunting Vaughan's letters. At Oxford, Symonds finally revealed the story to a don, who encouraged him to tell his father. The senior Symonds not only succeeded in forcing Vaughan to resign but threatened exposure if Vaughan were ever to accept any important ecclesiastical post, and he continued to hound him throughout his life.

The system fostered peculiar moral dilemmas for society in general as well as for the boys, and these social dilemmas suggest the late-Victorian crisis of the male that divided upper-class men between dandies and gentlemen. During the 1880's, public school immorality (boyhood sexual activity) was a major topic in the press, and by 1900 intense friendships between boys and between boys and masters were suspect. The schools themselves admitted the probability of moral contamination, and parents were aware of this. They were also aware of the unsanitary conditions that led to near endemic epidemics of scarlet fever, cholera, and diphtheria, and of cruelty amounting frequently to sadism on the parts of masters and prefects. Even granting that suffering, as in the military, can be a considerable force for bonding, sensitive and less successful boys clearly suffered to such a degree that it is fair to ask why the number of public schools grew from the nine studied by the Clarendon Commission in 1861-64[100] to—depending upon the compiler—short-lists of 30 to 60 and long-lists of up to 104 in the 1890's.

J. R. de S. Honey offers five possible reasons for this increase and for parents' seemingly—for us today—bizarre complaisance. Each of his reasons can be seen to correspond with a calculated image of class or gender, and I interpret them here accordingly. Students of gender studies should also notice that, in the strategies employed in the public schools, the emphasis on gender construction of the British male cannot be overemphasized, from the removal of the boy from the domestic matrix to the assumption of his role in the Empire.

First, the growth of the Empire provided an influx of officers' sons who needed to be educated at home if they were to maintain a right perspective on Britain's superiority to its colonies. Second, upwardly mobile parents wanted to protect boys from servants and girls, association with whom could jeopardize their chances for advancement. Third, the much-valued manliness could hardly be instilled at home, an environment dominated by women and children. Fourth, in addition to a conspicuous education in the classics, boys at public school learned standard English pronunciation, the most immediate index of upper-class status and itself the product of the public school system. And fifth, since women in upwardly mobile families were increasingly expected to devote more time to society functions, sending off at least some portion of their large Victorian families was desirable.

Clearly class mobility, class solidarity, and gender differentiation underlie the growth of the public schools as a social force. And it is significant that this growth was at the expense of that other most sentimentalized of Victorian institutions, the family. The attachment to an educational community to which the memoirs of Old Etonians, Wykehamists, and Harrovians attest is in fact an indication that after 1880, when public school status alone provided the education the professions demanded, the schools competed with the family as the major social force, or, in Althusser, ideological state apparatus. Wilde's chaotic domestic affairs, one might say,

Dandies and Gentlemen

evolved from this conflict, just as Dorian was forced to choose between a loving, maternal Sibyl Vane and a male-bonded Harry Wotton.

Public school gentlemen alone could—and probably did (see Appendix B)—engineer Wilde's downfall, but they probably would not have done if the press had not already turned the public against him. The instability of the Liberal government in 1895 made a public scandal risky, and the public knew that, according to its standards, Wilde was not a proper gentleman. Therefore, when Queensberry threatened to expose Wilde's connections if Wilde were not convicted, the public school gentlemen in the government sided with the public against Wilde, who had by then become something of an embarrassment anyway.

Turning from the public school's ideal of the gentleman to the popular image, we find that for the majority of Victorians the figure of the gentleman was scarcely less theatrical—or less publicized—than that of the dandy. Although etiquette books probably do not reflect actual behavior, they can reveal the construction of a popular image of manliness. In the cult of personality in which he lived, it was this image of manliness that Wilde affronted. This is what is entailed in saying, after reading newspaper accounts of his trials, that it was the middle-class press that convicted him. (Sexual politics is examined more fully in Chapter 4; the outcry against *Dorian Gray* was merely the tip of the iceberg.)

However much a public school could stress morality over manners, those outside of the radius found that manners helped. According to historian of manners Michael Curtin, the gentleman and lady as popularly conceived in nineteenth-century etiquette books reconciled style to substance and manners to morality. But the etiquette of the gentleman was not merely the negation of the dandy's pose and frippery: it was a new pose of its own. Curtin has well described how the desired "natural" grace of the gentleman was a product of vigilant—again, almost military—training and labor; how, for example, the posture that signified the "easy style" of a moral man was somewhat more than second nature. The author of *True Politeness* (1853) advised "a method of bending the arms, so that they may repose a little forward, and so as to admit of the hands being easily clasped: one leg should be straight,—the knee of the other slightly bent out; the body erect; the neck in its place; the head poised freely, without stiffness; and the countenance expressing mildness and candour."[101] Obviously the image of Wilde immortalized by journalists in America and later by Chesterton "lolling like an elegant leviathan on a sofa . . . [talking] between the whiffs of a scented cigarette"[102] was, to a gentleman of the above frame of mind, against nature.

Wilde also broke the rules of tact in conversation, the goals of which, again, were a sort of community- or team-think. The clever, epigrammatic performances in silver-fork novels and *Dorian Gray* were eschewed as vulgar displays of individual talent. One should be, said *The Glass of Fashion* (1881), "a talker who talks not to display his wit or accomplishments, but to promote the comfort of the company in which he finds himself." One did not "discourage" others by being brilliant, or express disbelief at a fantastic account, or indicate boredom during oft-repeated anecdotes, or bore others with tales of travel or of one's children; and a gentleman, instructed *Family Etiquette* (1875), "starts no subject . . . that can be displeasing to any person present."[103]

Curtin suggests that the apparent democratic code of the etiquette books was in practice a new exclusionary tactic, designed by and for the middle classes. The formal regulations governing introductions, for example, were intended to ensure the exclusion of undesirable acquaintances. Here, the honor of a gentleman, British "reserve," and privacy—one conjures up four men standing in a small room respectively absorbed in scrutinizing a timepiece, a corner, a prospect through the window, and a newspaper, each seemingly unaware of the others—all conspired against friendliness, tolerance, and familiarity. As Curtin says, "the general rule was simple and comprehensive: without an introduction, there should be no conversation."[104] For his part, the introducer was personally responsible for certifying the respectability of both parties being introduced. To further safeguard women and social superiors, there was a "right of recognition" allowing them the option to acknowledge the acquaintance or not at later meetings. If they chose no acknowledgment, the second party was expected to suppress its attentions.

One can hardly accept the defense of Wilde one occasionally reads, that his egalitarian principles were demonstrated by his sexual relations with lower-class boys, for, as d'Arch Smith says, the Prince and the Pauper arrangement of the time (upper-class man and lower-class boy) was seldom, if ever, reversed: lower-class men did not accompany the sons of privilege. Yet even his friend Frank Harris was galled to find Wilde acknowledging him while in the presence of two boys who "looked like grooms" in the Café Royal; and Shaw lamented that Wilde was "utterly without that fortifying body of acquaintance among plain men in which a man must move as himself a plain man, and be Smith and Jones and Wilde and Shaw and

Dandies and Gentlemen

Harris instead of Bosie and Robbie and Oscar and Mister. This is the sort of folly that . . . lasted long enough to prevent Oscar laying any solid social foundations."[105] In Best's catalog of the absolutely standard hallmarks of respectability one can see how Wilde defied the public. Respectable people did not behave "wildly"; they maintained a decorous (not brilliant or purple) speech and bearing (no aesthetic costumes); and they never did or said anything in the presence of persons of the lower classes (such as young male prostitutes) which might offer encouragement or excuse for ill conduct.

The rules for tact, privacy, reserve, the institution of calling cards and "at-homes"—everything that had to do with public conduct—reflected the growing concern after the 1880's for middle- and upper-class women who were beginning to go out in public without chaperonage. However much late Victorians tried to deny it, the home-as-haven idea so heavily expressed in the middle-class novels and so conspicuously absent in *Dorian Gray* was, by the 1890's, more art than life. The etiquette books, with their elaborate instructions for calling, teas, afternoons in the park, and the like, indicate that the majority of middle-class women in fact wanted to imitate the aristocracy, who allegedly did more sociable things during the day—the sort of things, for example, that Wilde's comedies showed them doing. Davidoff contends that the home, for the rising middle and upper classes, was the base of social functions, not domestic intimacy, and that the homemaker was predominantly a social organizer. (Such priorities affected even the plans of the domicile: elaborate entrance hall, drawing and dining rooms, with the family's quarters cramped and crowded off-scene in the back.)

In 1846 the American ambassador's wife wrote home that "The subjects of conversation among women are more general than with us, and they are much more cultivated than our women as a body . . . they never sew, or attend as we do, to domestic affairs and so live for social life and understand it better." In 1870, M. Taylor, a writer on women's affairs, endorsed this view: "As her means increase every wife transfers every household duty involving labour to other hands. As soon as she is able to afford it she hires a washer-woman occasionally, then a charwoman, then a cook and housemaid, a nurse or two, a governess, a lady's maid, a housekeeper—and no blame attaches to any step of her progress, unless the payment is beyond her means." "Indeed," Davidoff adds, "it was her duty to free herself for a higher [that is, the social] sphere."[106] In this respect too the Wildes were not quite typical: many of Constance Wilde's guests wrote later of their surprise at the presence of the two young Wilde boys at social gatherings.

While American women observed that their British sisters ran their domiciles like states, Wilde advocated that the state should be run like a family. In the *Woman's World* (May 1889), he reviewed David Ritchie's arguments on the future of women in politics in *Darwinism and Politics*. He praised Ritchie, who rebutted Herbert Spencer's position in *Sociology* that women, if admitted to political life, might do mischief by introducing the ethics of the family into the state: "If something is right in a family, it is difficult to see why it is, therefore, without any further reason, wrong in the State," wrote Wilde. "If the participation of women in politics means that as a good family educates all its members, so must a good State, what better issue could there be? The family ideal of the State may be difficult of attainment, but as an ideal it is better than the policemen theory. It would mean the moralisation of politics. The cultivation of separate sorts of virtues and separate ideals of duty in men and women has led to the whole social fabric being weaker and unhealthier than it need be."

It was just such healthy and effeminate ideas that affected Wilde's status among gentlemen. The publication of *The Picture of Dorian Gray* exploded the conflicts of roles that Brummell had generated, that the public schools had fostered, and that the press had popularized; what was called decadent and unhealthy was finally dandiacal and feminine. This indicates a crisis in the 1890's of the male on all levels—economic, political, social, psychological, as producer, as power, as role, as lover.

Both gentlemen and dandies had their advocates in the popular press; each side claimed superior morality and elegance. The preoccupation with the definition and construction of the gentleman did not substantially differ from a similar preoccupation with the definition and construction of the dandy: both were commodified in the cult of personality. The gentleman was the magnum opus of the middle class, and the dandy was the repressed unconscious of mass society. An ambitious system generates its own criticism; the dandy showed the gentleman what he had sacrificed: eccentricity, beauty, camaraderie, a natural aristocracy. "Art" was the magical, fetishized term dandies deployed to replace the losses of the age of mechanical reproduction—mechanical in advertising practices as well as in the production of the public-school-stamped boy.

Contrary to Wilde's famous formula—"Basil Hallward is what I think I am: Lord Henry is what the world thinks of me: Dorian what I would like to be—in other ages, perhaps"[107]—he was really Sibyl Vane, the actor who could play any part. For judging by Wilde's romantic tradition, as well as the role-playing proposed in "The Portrait of Mr. W. H.," Sibyl Vane embodied Wilde's ideal—until she thought to give it all up for a part in a middle-class marriage. For that Wilde killed her. Yet after the conflict over *Dorian Gray*, he took up the role he denied her and escorted Constance to his very successful domestic comedies. As Maurice Saillet said of Antonin Artaud, Wilde also escaped from his own performance by means of the theater.[108]

3

Comedy and Consumers

> The theatre is really important. . . . It is as important as the Church was in the Middle Ages and much more important than the Church was in London in [the 1890's]. A theatre to me is a place "where two or three are gathered together." The apostolic succession from Eschylus to myself is as serious and as continuously inspired as that younger institution, the apostolic succession of the Christian Church. . . . Churchgoing in London has been largely replaced by playgoing.
>
> Shaw, *Our Theatres in the Nineties*

> There is no doubt that these glimpses of expensive receptions in Park Lane, with the servants announcing titles *ad libitum*, are enormously attractive to social outsiders (say ninety-nine hundredths of us).
>
> Shaw, Review of *An Ideal Husband*

Roman spectacle: Oscar Wilde and Marcus Aurelius, 1900.

*I*N HENRY JAMES'S *Tragic Muse* (1890), written at the beginning of James's siege on the theater, a cultured diplomat inquires of an Oscar Wilde figure whether he "believed in the theatre." The aesthete Gabriel Nash responds that "it's a commercial and social convenience which may be infinitely worked." Nash goes on to analyze "the essentially brutal nature of the modern audience" as

the *omnium gatherum* of the population of a big commercial city, at the hour of the day when their taste is at its lowest, flocking out of hideous hotels and restaurants, gorged with food, stultified with buying and selling and with all the other sordid speculations of the day, squeezed together in a sweltering mass, disappointed in their seats, timing the author, timing the actor, wishing to get their money back on the spot, before eleven o'clock. . . . One of [the dramatist's] principal canons is that he must enable his spectators to catch the suburban trains, which stop at 11.30.[1]

Due to the nature of modern audiences, Nash observes, modern drama must remain infinitely crude compared to the art of the novelist, an art that registers the "reflective and complicated and diffuse" nature of modern society.

This reflectiveness, complication, and diffuseness—otherwise known as psychological realism—was, of course, part of what Henry Arthur Jones termed the "Renascence of the English Drama" in the decade 1885-95, the period that included much of the work of Jones and Arthur Pinero, as well as the beginnings of Shaw's work, and that is generally felt to have been influenced by Ibsen. Psychological realism, which in the drama frequently included sensitive moral issues, typically irritated the press and put examiners of plays in a dilemma: the press dominated public opinion, and licensers were reluctant to offend the public, even when an examiner personally approved of a play.[2] The Shelley Society was founded in 1886 so that masterpieces banned by the Lord Chamberlain's office (like Shelley's *Cenci*) could be given professional, if private, performance, and J. T. Grein founded the Independent Theatre Society for the performance of prohibited or commercially risky plays like Ibsen's *Ghosts* and Wilde's *Salome*. But because theater managements were fearful of official reprisal, finding theaters for performance of unlicensed plays was nearly impossible. The audience at *The Cenci* on 7 May 1886 included such established artists as Robert Browning and George Meredith, and Grein's *Ghosts* (13 March 1891) stimulated such public interest that Grein received 3,000 applications for tickets and membership in the Society. Nevertheless, the reaction of the press to both performances—with the exception of William Archer—was predictably hostile. Like *Dorian Gray*, *Ghosts* was reviewed as having predominantly medical interest, a "morbid," "sickening dissection of corrupt humanity," a "hideous nightmare," "a putrid drama the details of which cannot appear with any propriety in any column save those of a medical journal."[3]

In fact, it was one of Wilde's scenarios, described to George Alexander in 1894 as *Mr. and Mrs. Daventry*, completed by Frank Harris, and produced in 1900, that led to public strain between the increasingly reactionary press and increasingly liberal censors.[4] Wilde wanted no concessions to the public. As he had written to Alexander, he wanted *"the sheer passion of love to dominate everything. No morbid self-sacrifice. No renunciation. A sheer flame of love between a man and a woman."*[5]

The play presented exactly that. A man of fashion and rank marries a sweet country girl who is ignorant of fashionable life. He grows bored with her and invites a fin-de-siècle crowd to their country estate. There he instructs her to flirt, and he makes love to another woman within her hearing. The wife protects her husband and the other woman from the latter's enraged spouse, but then determinedly leaves her husband. The repentant Daventry attempts to win her back, but in the meantime she and one of his friends have fallen in love. She lives with this other man and becomes pregnant. She informs her husband of her condition just before he and her lover are to duel, and he forthwith shoots himself. Rather than feel guilt, the lovers embrace at the close of the play with hope, devotion, and considerable sexual energy, regardless of the pregnancy and the dead husband.

Having just bought the Palace Hotel in Monte Carlo, Harris set the suicide scene in a suite there and used the play as free advertisement. After Clement Scott complained, the Lord Chamberlain's Office demanded that Harris delete certain explicit dialogue, like "adultery with home comforts." Although the critics deplored the "sofa scene," in which Daventry made love to Lady Langham in the hearing of his wife, as "as near to indecent as anything we remember on the contemporary stage" (*Times*, 26 October 1900)—despite Wilde's having confessed that he took the scene from Sheridan—the play ran for more than 100 performances. The examiners' dilemma—to try to appease the press yet still license plays they thought worthwhile—continued even after 1907, when 71 playwrights signed a letter to the *Times* for the abolition of dramatic censorship.

But if Wilde's plot was as radical as those of the best problem plays, it was not widely recognized as Wilde's and the dialogue was Harris's. In the plays over which Wilde did maintain control, his comedies, psychological realism has been the measure that he apparently did not meet, and this failure has been attributed to his commercial pandering to the public.[6] (Wilde's immediate and favorable effect on his audience is legendary: in both "Elizabethan Classicists" and his preface to the *Poetical Works of Lionel Johnson*, Ezra Pound insisted that "multitudinous seas incarnadine" at one time "caused as much thrill as any epigram in *Lady Windermere's Fan* or *The Importance of Being Earnest*.") The positive view of such a failure is that, in contrast to James's contempt for the audience, Wilde enjoyed the social "spectacle." If James sat in his box and derisively predicted the audience's approbation of plays he did not admire (he was too nervous to attend his own premiere of *Guy Domville*), Wilde sauntered onto the stage with a cigarette and good-naturedly ridiculed everybody's performance.

In opting for Art, James composed a costume drama of a young aristocrat's dilemma in 1780 between the continuation of his family line and his ordination as a Catholic priest.[7] ("If it is real to Mr. James," Shaw wrote of the play's rather rarefied themes, "it must be real to others.") In plays set in the present in England, Wilde worked (as Nash would say) on the audience.

Both thematically and dynamically Wilde's plays relentlessly dissolved the distinctions between art and life. They failed to differentiate the artifice of Society and politics from art; Wilde commended the audience on its performance mirroring the stage; and all—actors, author, and audience—consumed the conspicuous images offered by the play. The comedies negated art's independence from life and recalled the drama's original function in social ritual and cohesion. Such a dynamic can be called a form of psychological realism, but it is a form of the psychology of a spectacular society. I reserve discussion of *Salome* for Chapter 4: here I am concerned with Wilde's comedies, which culminate in the formal relation of *The Importance of Being Earnest* to its audience and which reflect a primitive case of what Debord calls the spectacle, "the existing order's uninterrupted discourse about itself, the self-portrait of power."[8]

Wilde subtly manipulated the most temperamental of audiences, made up of high Society and middle-class reviewers. By means of the conflicting elements in his plays prior to *The Importance of Being Earnest*—for example, social satire and melodramatic sentimentality, his unstinting criticism of upper-class affluence and his equally strong fascination with the props and property of fashionable life (the paradoxical position of the traditional dandy)—he registered the reflectiveness, complication, and diffuseness of modern Society.[9] His dramatis personae either were readily identified as contemporary types by his audience or represented an older, and by 1890 relatively ineffectual, nobility and gentry at whom the new administrative and enterprising classes could laugh, even while they prided themselves on having usurped their power.[10] In both cases, the audience sentimentally identified with the characters. On the other hand, the reviewers, who in many cases enlisted their sympathy with labor rather than administration or enterprise, identified Wilde's characters with the new upper classes; thus they frequently attacked his plays, or less frequently interpreted them as satires on Society. The sentimental/satiric interpretability functioned politically for the audience. The sentimental interpretation allowed Society to love the playwright who mocked it, and the cynical or satiric interpretation allowed the reviewers to see that his sentimentality was merely a form of ingratiation. We have seen similar double tactics in the simultaneously moralized and eroticized *Dorian Gray* and in Wilde's critical and seductive criticism. With his plays he was no less aware of the complexity of his audiences and the certainty of their public response.

Although the hundreds of reviews of Wilde's comedies before *Earnest* in both London and provincial papers present a great diversity of opinion, the majority of reviewers concurred that Society would love the plays but "the serious people who populate London," as H. G. Wells called them in the *Pall Mall Gazette* (15 February 1895), would not. The most astute reviewers discerned that Wilde's motivation for the sentimental plot and apparently contradictory profusion of epigram amounted to a simple awareness of the particular constitution of the audience: "As long as the pits of our theatres are filled with one kind of audience and the galleries with another, plays must exist to please both. There is a *Family Herald* sort of audience in the upper regions of the theatre, that asks for the triumph of virtue and the humiliation of vice, and cares nothing for art, and wit, and true comedy and Mr. Wilde flings the two or three bits of clap-trap in his play to the 'Gods'" (*Black and White*, 6 May 1893). The *Freemason* (20 April 1893) explained why Society was pleased: "[*A Woman of No Importance*] literally bristles with the smartest epigrams, and is just the sort of play for the Haymarket Theatre, as that house is chiefly an expensive seated one, and the stalls and dress circle are crammed, and will be all the London season at every performance, for 'A Woman of No Importance' is exactly the piece Society (spelt with a big S) people love to listen to. If they see themselves satirised, what care they so long as they are amused, and that we can vouch they will be to their heart's content."

The first-night audiences who frequented George Alexander's St. James's and Beerbohm Tree's Theatre Royal, Haymarket—the two theaters that initially monopolized Wilde's comedies—and whose approval guaranteed the prolonged runs of Wilde's plays, included little more than the 1890's version of social Exclusives. Since the 1860's, music halls had been drawing the lower classes from the theaters, leaving room for smaller, discriminating audiences. The St. James's and Haymarket were the most distinguished theaters of the 1890's.[11] In his *Haymarket: Theatre of Perfection*, theater historian W. Macqueen-Pope writes of the Haymarket and its audience:

Under Tree, the Haymarket became the smartest theatre in London in every sense of the word. It was not only the so-called "Smart Set" who went there, for the theatre became the centre of the social world of London. . . . His audiences were as brilliant as his plays. . . . He counted amongst his supporters all the great ones of the land. The front rank of art, literature, science, the law, medicine and politics, even the Church itself, all came to a Tree premiere—only he never called it that. No cameras flashed, no gossip-writers strained their eyes and ears. . . . There was dignity, wealth, solidarity and substance. . . . There were silks, satins and jewels. . . . There was no pushing and shoving, but good manners and deference to the ladies; no cloud of cigarette smoke, no shrill laughter. . . . The theatre was an aristocrat, and the audiences of the Haymarket, under Tree, were aristocratic playgoers from the gallery downwards. It is something that will never again be seen.[12]

Of the St. James's, Macqueen-Pope writes in *St. James's: Theatre of Distinction*, "Elegant and rich people filled the stalls, the dress circle and the two boxes. People of substance but less social standing booked for the upper circle, and the rest of the playgoers made for the pit and the gallery."[13] The prices were from one to four guineas for boxes, 10s. 6d. for stalls, 7s. and 5s. for dress circle, 3s. for upper boxes, 2s. for the pit, 1s. for the gallery. Seats could be booked by letter, telegram, or telephone, and evening dress was required for admission. "One of the most elegant audiences that ever gathered at a West End premiere received [*Lady Windermere's Fan*] with enthusiasm," writes Macqueen-Pope. "Soon, the first-night flutter filled the town, extended to its suburbs and far beyond."[14]

Beatrice Webb wrote that in the 1890's London Society included a mixed bag representing the governing class. With the Court, Cabinet and ex-Cabinet, financiers, and "the racing set," she included the better known artists and reviewers who habitually entertained these groups.[15] Because *A Woman of No Importance* followed Wilde's first major success, *Lady Windermere's Fan*, it drew the sort of crowd (in the sort of attire) that kept Society columnists scribbling for months. Max Beerbohm wrote that "all the politicians were there."[16] The first-night audience included "the arts, literature, law, and politics" (*Stage*, 20 April 1893) and, we might add, science. Beerbohm named the elements of the spectacular Society: Arthur Balfour, Joseph Chamberlain, Lord Battersea, the Randolph Churchills, Sir Edward Clarke, Shaw-Lefevre, Baron de Rothschild, Lord Wolverton, Henry Wyndham, George Lewis, Sir Spenser Wells, Burne-Jones, Conan Doyle, Richard Le Gallienne; and "Henry Rochefort stood for France." The Prince of Wales attended a few nights later, and the costume on stage and off filled the women's columns in subsequent weeks. The reviews indicate that the grandeur of the audience was to be matched in theater history only by that of the audience at *The Importance of Being Earnest*.

Florence Alexander described the opulent but *intime* atmosphere of those first nights as "great events," the technical arrangement of which she supervised personally, "sick with anxiety," down to the color-coordinating of set and costume and the arranging of flowers: "Our firstnights . . . were like brilliant parties. Everybody knew everybody, everybody put on their best clothes, everybody wished us success."[17] In *The Plays of Oscar Wilde*, Alan Bird describes the mirror of their own luxury that such audiences saw in Wilde's comedies, and the identification that public figures like the Prince Regent and his mistresses could feel with Wilde's characters. Of the intimacy that the host Mrs. Alexander recalled, Bird writes: "The rapport between management and all sections of the audience also extended to the actors and to the playwrights. . . . Wilde was able to play the parts of host and master magician at the same time. . . . His appearance on the stage, at the end of the play, with a cigarette in his hand, was perfectly appropriate: he was in his own drawing-room, a situation only possible in the reformed and renovated theatres of the 1890's."[18] As recently as 1976, Martin Green associated this image of an exclusive Society and its trappings with Wilde's comedies when he wrote that for him entering Cambridge on a Butler Scholarship "was to feel every nerve of self-consciousness as unwelcomely stimulated as if I'd walked on to a stage set for *Lady Windermere's Fan*."[19]

If Wilde turned the theater into a drawing room, his plays turned the audience into consumers. The plays worked like fetishes for members of the audience who identified with Society. They followed the characters in imputing to artificial objects or imaginary constructs strange properties. These properties consisted in the objects' or constructs' imputed ability to fulfill wishes. In "The Decay of Lying," Wilde could see the West's fetishism of Eastern ways and peoples in British orientalism and *japonisme*. Because he was a typical Victorian poseur, he was well acquainted with what in "The Soul of Man Under Socialism" he called "the things and symbols of things" to which people attached great value. In his plays, his understanding of fetishism was theatrical rather than theoretical. He supplied the one fetish for the audience that would distract it enough to allow his criticisms: an overvalued and exceedingly powerful image of itself. Since Brummell, this had been the dandies' stratagem: to stylize Society; to so refine that style personally as to put its bearers to shame; and then to be of two minds regarding that style and that Society. Wilde presented on a small scale what Debord calls the spectacle as a self-portrait of power, in which one part of the world represents itself to the world and is superior to it. It is allied to commodity fetishism and occurs, says Debord, "the moment when the commodity has attained the total occupation of social life."[20] It is a presentation of a Society for whom all wishes come true.

The next generation, of Artaud and the Alfred Jarry Theater (1926-30), would theorize a critical spectacular drama as theater of cruelty. At the end of this chapter I shall return to Artaud and the ways in which Wildean theater differs from his; clearly the historical expansion of mass imperial society is responsible for some significant developments. Here, however, I emphasize the similarities, in order to frame the following discussion of *The Importance of Being Earnest* and its antecedents in the Wildean corpus.

In "The Alchemical Theater" Artaud compared theater to alchemy: they were both virtual arts that did not carry their ends in themselves; far from being an auracular object of contemplation, the drama was to be "an intentional provocation" to its "double," the audience.[21] In theater of cruelty the focus shifts from spectacle to spectator, from the production to consumption of the work.

In so formulating the drama, Artaud attempted to situate it in mass society. The referent of bourgeois art, or psychological realism, was the interiority of the few, and it fostered either an exclusive or a complacent relation with its audience; it was addressed to the understanding. This bourgeois privatization, Artaud felt, was obsolescent in a world of mass control and mass violence. The new theater offered undeceptive violence and was addressed to the only faculties not benumbed by the modern world: it would be a sensational drama, addressed to the senses. (To cure the soul with the senses, said Dorian Gray.) Similarly, *Earnest* is not addressed to the understanding but to the senses. It reflects, not violence, but the breakdown of human community through commodity fetishism.

Obviously, *The Conquest of Mexico*—as described in the Theater of Cruelty's "Second Manifesto," with its exposure of "the ever active fatuousness of Europe"[22]—was intended to provoke the audience on a scale well beyond the modest goals of Wilde's Society drama. Whereas Artaud wanted to display and provoke modern society into self-hatred or humiliation, Wilde simply displayed it, with a critique inherent in the play. Yet in its specific attacks on the consciences of middle-class audiences, the Alfred Jarry Theater of Cruelty barely did more than make explicit what Wilde had dramatized for Society and an aspiring bourgeoisie.

For example, in *Victor, or the Children Are in Power*, Artaud and Roger Vitrac practiced mental cruelty on middle-class audiences. In a 48-page brochure entitled *The Alfred Jarry Theater and Public Hostility* (1930), *Victor* was advertised as "a middle-class play in three acts by Roger Vitrac. This play, lyrical at times, ironic, even outspoken at others, was aimed at the middle-class family unit. It featured adultery, incest, scatology, anger, Surrealist poetry, patriotism, madness, shame and death."[23] Unlike *The Importance of Being Earnest*, which also, as critics have recognized, satirizes every institution the British held sacred—family, politics, work, education, marriage, truth, colonialism, religion, friendship, feminine modesty, science, statistics, romantic love, and others—at the conclusion of *Victor*, a sort of comic version of the Little Father Time story in *Jude the Obscure*, the characters are not even left alive.

Wilde's theater used techniques similar to Artaud's, and the ways in which both fetishized the audience or public may be seen as a logical product of mass consumerist society; their statements and manifestos parody the advertiser's cynical inclusion of the public. In making the audience "an integral part of our efforts" (1926 Manifesto),[24] Artaud extended the "stage" to include the entire auditorium. He described the mise-en-scène as "the visual and plastic materialization of speech, the language of everything that can be said and signified upon a stage independently of speech, everything that finds its expression in space, or that can be affected or disintegrated by it" ("The Oriental and Occidental Theater").[25] In *Earnest* the stage was a continuation of the audience; but, again as in Artaud, the actors/characters were not.

Artaud felt that traditional sympathetic identification lulled the senses of the spectator, so he rehearsed his actors in de-identification, or ultra-stylized, jerky, and exaggerated moves, stripping the action of any naturalism. As Victor Corti put it, "all theater's traditional and well-loved tricks were amplified (sometimes coming dangerously close to parody) until stage illusion was shattered, the reality of the plays then standing out as naked as those puppets which featured in its productions."[26] This exactly describes the unnaturalism of *Earnest*. Artaud's gigantic puppets were, like the name of his theater, adapted from a play almost exactly contemporary with Wilde's, Alfred Jarry's *Ubu Roi* (1896), whose stage illusion also shattered to expose what Cyril Connolly saw as a prophecy, "the Santa Claus of the Atomic Age."[27] Wilde was allied to Jarry through more than mutual friends and directors like Lugné-Poe, who produced *Salome*. His audience identified with the spectacle, de-identified with the characters, and called his actors "puppets." His theater parodied theater and thus revealed the reality of the plays.

The Importance of Being Earnest operates on three levels: the superiority of author to audience, the mutuality of audience and stage image (mimesis, or mise-en-scène in Artaud's sense), and the audience's superiority to the farce. The material images on stage are a direct mimesis of the audience, its mirror image: an idle, luxuried community in an opulent environment of props and costumes. The play's dialogue, however, includes the author's trenchant criticisms of the audience; on this level, the author is greater than the audience. The lowest level consists of farcical action, an indication of the author's lunacy, and this has the effect of canceling the author's superior status as a critic. The absurdity of the action allows the audience to label it farce, implying that its marvelous triviality has the sole purpose of inciting laughter, while the audience simultaneously extricates itself from the charges leveled against it. If the author is critical of the audience, his play's absurd action permits the audience to be superior to him. While the social criticism and farcical action effectively cancel each other out, the audience receives reinforcement from its own dominant and fetishized image on stage.

This dominant image includes another mimetic aspect, and this was the source of the play's overwhelming success: the representation of the Society for whom all wishes come true. The audience at the St. James's could make fetishes real, could spin straw into gold. Wilde exploited this representation for his own gain, even while he criticized it.

The first two acts of *Earnest* (a play in which even the punning title raises the issue of the presence or absence of the mythical "earnestness") elaborate the poses and objects by means of which the satirized upper classes fulfill their wishes. These are: the sick brother Ernest, who allows Jack to escape from his severe moral position as guardian in the country to life as a dandy in London; the invalid Bunbury, who allows Algy to escape dining with relatives (or, as Wilde elsewhere called relatives, "merely an exaggerated form of the public"); Jack's "romantic origin" in a handbag, which stirs "the deep fibres" of Gwendolen's nature; the name of "Ernest," which represents an ideal Gwendolen and Cecily have vowed to marry (when they learn that neither of their fiancés possesses the name, they break off the engagements); the young women's diaries, in which they write only imaginary events ("I never travel without my diary," says Gwendolen; "one should always have something sensational to read in the train"); and the fetish of Miss Prism's manuscript, which is perhaps the most brilliant in the play. These theatrical devices are either fetishized poses or fetishized things and ideals, whose phantasmic properties command practical results.

Miss Prism, as the play indicates, is sexually forlorn. Like her counterpart, the Reverend Canon Chasuble, D.D., the only way her sexuality surfaces is in metaphor, a release unnecessary for the other characters in the play, whose power, presumably, permits them more accessible outlets:[28] Chasuble: "Were I fortunate enough to be Miss Prism's pupil, I would hang upon her lips. [Miss Prism glares.] I spoke metaphorically.—My metaphor was drawn from bees." Miss Prism: "Maturity can always be depended on. Ripeness can be trusted. Young women are green. [Dr. Chasuble starts.] I spoke horticulturally. My metaphor was drawn from fruits." Similarly, the gaps in Miss Prism's life are revealed with comic pathos in her excessive affection for her personified handbag:

It seems to be mine. Yes, here is the injury it received through the upsetting of a Gower Street omnibus in younger and happier days. Here is the stain on the lining caused by the explosion of a temperance beverage, an incident that occurred at Leamington. And here, on the lock, are my initials. I had forgotten that in an extravagant mood I had them placed there. The bag is undoubtedly mine. I am delighted to have it restored to me. It has been a great inconvenience being without it all these years.

When it turns out that this poor woman had placed her manuscript in the pram and the baby in her handbag, we have a brilliant parody of the fetishism of manuscript-as-child of a frustrated parent that Ibsen had treated much more seriously in *Hedda Gabler*.

But where other writers, such as Ibsen, George Eliot, and Dickens, had shown the pathos and futility of fetishes, generally because within the classes they wrote about the fetishized objects were associated with dreams incapable of fulfillment, Wilde treats the effectiveness of fetishes among the upper classes. In fact, the characters in this play care little about actual material, for the appearance of material is quite enough to get by: "Algernon is an extremely, I may almost say an ostentatiously, eligible young man. He has nothing, but he looks everything. What more can one desire?" In the original four-act version, when Algernon is "attached" for an outstanding bill of £762 for eating at the Savoy, he responds to the solicitor: "Pay it? How on earth am I going to do that? You don't suppose I have got any money? How perfectly silly you are. No gentleman ever has any money." In *Earnest*, indeed, the fetishes materialize as "truth." Jack becomes Ernest, and acquires a real brother in Algy; Gwendolen marries her Ernest; Cecily's fiction in her diary materializes as a real engagement to Algernon; Miss Prism and Dr. Chasuble, whose "unpublished sermons" make him the perfect mate for the woman who has "lost" or "mislaid" her manuscript as she had lost or mislaid the baby, embrace at the end; and Lady Bracknell, who had always fetishized family, is quite satisfied with the revelation of the orphan Jack as her "natural" nephew.

It was because Wilde had so accurately assessed the exclusive value of appearances for his audience that Shaw found the play heartless and unmoving, and that other middle-class critics found it trivial (meaning superficial).[29] Contrary to the practice of psychological realism, Wilde seemed to say that internality, depth of character, and bonds of human affection were negligible in the society represented by *Earnest*, a society of spectacle only. All that mattered was the authority of the participants' poses and the glitter of their props. "Our social relations had no roots in neighborhood, in vocation, in creed, or for that matter in race," Webb wrote of Society in the 1890's, "they likened a series of moving pictures—surface impressions without depth—restlessly stimulating in their variety."[30] Even the fast, epigrammatic language of *Earnest* functions perfectly as a political tool, which, if handled properly, can manipulate others and establish one in the highest social spheres. But beyond its political force, it is a language in which it is impossible to communicate in earnest.

The characters in *Earnest* assume *all* knowledge, not only truisms but the inverse of truisms. When they invert a Victorian platitude for their own ends, they not only state the opposite of what the audience expects but they include by inference the opposite of their own inversion. Such a discourse leaves no room for interference or input from others. The expected lines are assumed in the unexpected, and their interplay is self-generating, precluding all interference from the outside, that is, from other speakers: a closed system representing an exclusive society. Wilde himself had used this verbal technique to dominate drawing-rooms. It amounts to the reification of the insurrectionary style of diversion as we have described it in the Introduction and Chapter 1, and it appears today in the work of some post-modern architects. A wit subverting sincerity can be liberating and dialectical. A whole society of wits, as in *Earnest*, renders insincerity static, a mere tool of personal power in service of the status quo. Wit, in this case, is entirely subservient to a traditional plot of marriage and money exchange.

Limited to platitudes and their inversions, the characters operate within frames of reference as static as their power is seemingly unshakable. As Barbey had written in *Of Dandyism and of George Brummell*, the "tradition" of the British upper classes was stultifying. Wilde's images of them at tea or in the garden are of mannequins fixed in their masks. Their chins, says Lady Bracknell, are "worn very high." They do not work, their play is stylized, and the comedy concludes with a "tableau" (a static image) of traditional comic marriages—perhaps the most stultifying of all bourgeois institutions. At the end of *Salome*, Herod represents a fallen image of such a stultified ruling class. As Wilde had deplored the "things and symbols of things" that fixed the parameters of upper-class life for the restrictions they imposed on their possessors, so the impotent Herod concludes that "it is not wise to find symbols in everything that one sees," and he retires to his mirror where he sees only a "mask."

Since power to some extent depends on the maintenance and conservation of its symbols, the poses and fetishes in *Earnest* symbolize power even while their static representation is inherently conservative and prevents progress. As there could be no development but the repetition of clichéd forms in *Earnest*, Wilde felt that there could be no progress for the powerful ruling classes. Even if his audience had suspected this interpretation, it would have remained undisturbed, for it was content where it was. Furthermore, the newly "arrived" in that audience could identify with images of the aristocracy they had successfully supplanted. While the 1890's gave rise to consolidated reaction against all major labor unions, including the Engineers', Miners', Dockers' and Seamen's, and Woodworkers', Wilde's conservative images and his characters' witty disparagement of the lower classes (who were not present in the theater) served as positive reinforcement of the maintenance of the old way.

If this power illustrated by preemptory speech leaves no room for progress or development, it also leaves no room for internal life and individuated character. The characters' wishes consist in the reinforcement of their poses. "What wonderfully blue eyes you have," Gwendolen informs Jack, "They are quite, quite blue. I hope you will always look at me just like that, especially when there are other people present." Cecily's diary, as its owner instructs her fiancé, "is simply a very young girl's record of her own thoughts and impressions, and consequently meant for publication. When it appears in volume form I hope you will order a copy." The needs of Wilde's characters are conditioned by the status quo. Jack desires to know the identity of his parents, not for psychological reasons, but rather because Society requires that it be known. Whereas for everybody the name of Ernest is extremely important for its portentous sound, the fact that it was the name of Algy's father is so insignificant that Algy has forgotten it. This is a more radical critique of a mass mentality than even Artaud's, for Artaud still exploited internality sufficiently to describe Vitrac's *Secrets of Love* as "an ironic play, physically staging the misgivings, dual isolation, eroticism and criminal thoughts lurking in the minds of lovers" ("The Alfred Jarry Theater and Public Hostility").[31]

Twentieth-century critics have imputed to the social poses of Bunburying a map of Wilde's alleged guilt for his own "double life." The inspiration of Bunburying may well have derived from Wilde's homosexual experience; certainly the subplot of the original version, in which Algy faces imprisonment in Holloway for debts at the Savoy and Willis's, was a self-parody of Wilde's notorious extravagance. ("Well," says Algy, "I really am not going to be imprisoned in the suburbs for having dined in the West End.") Yet *Earnest* itself represents an arena in which poses are the norm. Wilde had earned his position in a similar arena by wearing clothes that even he thought were ridiculous, sending poems to Gladstone, dedicating them to women of Society, camping on Mrs. Langtry's doorstep, performing as was expected of him at an exhausting number of homes and clubs of the affluent, and in general learning which poses would help him and which would not. If he felt guilty, it certainly was not when he bragged that he had a play "written by a butterfly for butterflies."[32]

As we might expect from the journalistic response to *Dorian Gray*, the very personal interaction between Wilde and his elite audience elicited more attacks on the author's presumptuousness. ("Mr. Wilde," a disgruntled reviewer of *A Woman of No Importance* had written in *Hearth and Home*, "is perhaps the most popular *middle-class* wit at present before the public" [5 April 1893, my italics].) This brings us to the other audience, those whom Wells called "the serious people who populate London." In *Earnest*, Wilde altogether eliminated representations of the lower classes, except, as was typical of his comedies, in the epigrams, where they were the subject of amusing commentary. The play was written for the kind of audience that frequented the St. James's. This apparent partiality for an elite audience won the contempt of the gentlemen of the press, who spoke for the serious people who populated London. The *Times*'s reviewer called the play a farce, the first vehicle sufficiently trivial for Wilde's epigrammatic style (15 February 1895). The *Athenaeum* criticized Wilde's "sheer wantonness of contempt for his public" in presenting a play with "not a gleam of sense or sanity" (23 February 1895). *Punch*, the monolith of middle-class humor, published a bogus interview with Wilde, "The O. W. Vade Mecum," which implied that the public who would follow him was beneath contempt (23 February 1895). Even Shaw, who had admired Wilde's earlier comedies, found *Earnest*, his most successful, old-fashioned in style and heartless in content. "Unless comedy touches me as well as amuses me," Shaw wrote in the *Saturday Review*, "it leaves me with a sense of having wasted my evening" (12 January 1895).

Although the upper-class audience responded wildly to *Earnest* and the middle-class journalists frowned, nonetheless—as Wells said—the play satirized the upper classes in a way that the critics might have approved.[33] It contains the same acute social criticism that pervaded Wilde's earlier work. The upper-class characters speak epigrams exposing their own faults through ironic assertion or comic inversion. Incurably imperturbable and un-self-conscious, they dominate the world by tone alone. For example, here is Gwendolen on upper-class idealism: "We live, as I hope you know, Mr. Worthing, in an age of ideals. The fact is constantly mentioned in the more expensive monthly magazines, and has reached the provincial pulpits, I am told; and my ideal has always been to love someone of the name of Ernest." Lady Bracknell on education: "Fortunately in England, at any rate, education produces no effect whatsoever. If it did, it would prove a serious danger to the upper classes, and probably lead to acts of violence in Grosvenor Square." Lady Bracknell on paternity: "To be born, or at any rate bred, in a hand-bag, whether it had handles or not, seems to me to display a contempt for the ordinary decencies of family life that reminds one of the worst excesses of the French Revolution. And I presume you know what that unfortunate movement led to?" Miss Prism on imperialism: "Cecily, you will read your Political Economy in my absence. The chapter on the Fall of the Rupee you may omit. It is somewhat too sensational." The original four-act version has an exchange between Cecily and Dr. Chasuble on economics. "I suppose you know all about the relations between Capital and Labour?" Cecily responds, "All I know about is the relations between Capital and Idleness—and that is merely from observation." And Lady Bracknell discusses thought (quite pointedly, since the statement reflects on all the preceding nonsense of the play): "Her unhappy father is, I am glad to say, under the impression that she is attending a more than usually lengthy lecture by the University Extension Scheme on the Influence of a permanent income on Thought."

The reviews of *Victor* that Artaud quotes in "The Alfred Jarry Theater and Public Hostility" could equally apply to *Earnest*: it dissected "all our existing institutions as well as the present state of middle-class society"; it was "a criticism of middle-class life and everything which is ridiculous and stupid about it: Society, the family, the Republic, the Army."[34] In allowing Society to be reinforced by its own spectacle, however, Wilde exploited the society he criticized.

The Janus faces that Wilde's three earlier comedies showed to their audiences and that have since perplexed critics map Wilde's incipient manipulation of his audience. *Lady Windermere's Fan* (1892) presented both a sentimental, moralized conclusion and exposed Society's dominant, if self-deluded, materialism. *A Woman of No Importance* (1893) caught the audience between antiquated moral values and its own differing social practice. And *An Ideal Husband* (1895) played on the audience's idealized self-images while, like the picture of Dorian Gray, these images subtly altered to show corruption. These images pleased the audience, while reviewers the morning after were left feeling degraded. These plays went hand in hand with the development of Wilde's own self-aggrandizing devices and the disapproval of his critics.

Lady Windermere's Fan, the play that established Wilde as a successful playwright, contained the same double-edged force of *Earnest*: it criticized and attracted the upper classes. When Lady Windermere gives her fan to the adventurer Mrs. Erlynne with the words "There is the same world for all of us, and good and evil, sin and innocence, go through it hand in hand," the audience wildly applauded what seemed to be a moralized conclusion to a melodrama radiant with witty lines. The moralized conclusion was particularly functional for both Wilde and his audience, for, as Bird says, "Mrs. Erlynne, like other of Wilde's female characters, had her counterpart among the mistresses and companions of the Prince of Wales; and she was by no means an improbable figure in that age of outrageous cocottes and ladies of pleasure."[35]

In *The Days I Knew*, the autobiography of Wilde's contemporary Lillie Langtry, model, actress, and mistress, Wilde offends Langtry by telling her that he modeled the part of Mrs. Erlynne on her and by asking if she will play it—if she would, one might say, make a "spectacle" of herself. Langtry, who, of course, never mentions in her autobiography that she had clandestinely borne and committed to others' care her daughter by a prince, coldly refuses the part, saying that no audience could believe that a woman of her appearance could have a twenty-year-old daughter. ("Besides, my dear Windermere," say Mrs. Erlynne, explaining why she will not acknowledge her daughter but continue to "live childless," "How on earth could I pose as a mother with a grownup daughter? Margaret is twenty-one, and I have never admitted that I am more than twenty-nine, or thirty at the most. Twenty-nine when there are pink shades, thirty when there are not.") When Wilde composed his youthfully impassioned poem "The New Helen" for Lillie Langtry and slept on her doorstep, it had the effect of opening the doors of Society for him. After *Lady Windermere's Fan* his friendship with Langtry cooled considerably. When the poet ceased to represent the Society woman as, in the poem "The New Helen," a "Lily of love, pure and inviolate!" and dramatized her on stage as a blackmailing adventurer (albeit with one dramatic show of maternal feeling), he lost a little of the favor of the Society he played to at the St. James's. To this extent at least, Clement Scott was right when he said that a self-respecting audience might have been offended by the plot (*Illustrated London News*, 27 February 1892).

On the other hand, the play's conclusion, in which the sins of Mrs. Erlynne are forgiven and Lady Windermere's moral self-righteousness is softened by understanding, permitted the audience to maintain its self-image. The play operates between these two interpretations, the cynical and the sentimental. The device of the fan, whose symbolic change of owners clinches the moral, illustrates how Wilde used what critics called his French theatricality or "kleptodramatics" to register the double interpretations. For the audience, who carried such apparatus themselves, the fan that began as a symbol of a husband's devotion comes to signify Lady Windermere's new generosity. She gives it as a gift to the woman she once thought bad, but now has forgiven and thinks good. ("A very good woman!" are the last words of the play; and Wilde's first title, abandoned before the play was produced, was *A Good Woman*.) On the other hand, in the progress of the play the fan is used symbolically to indicate the seedier side of the action.

The fan that initially represented a husband's love and birthday gift to his wife is immediately trivialized by the opportunist Darlington, who tells Lady Windermere that *he* would have carpeted the street in front of her house with flowers. Then it is contrasted with Windermere's "presents" to Mrs. Erlynne, surreptitious installments to the tune of £600, £700, and £400. Then Lady Windermere threatens to use the fan to insult the socially fallen Mrs. Erlynne. When the latter enters Lady Windermere's birthday party, the stage direction reads "Lady Windermere clutches at her fan, then lets it drop on the floor." Similarly, Darlington persuades Lady Windermere, who is hurt by her husband's attentions to the other woman, to drop her husband and stay with him. Dropping her husband's gift augurs the weak Lady Windermere's easy surrender of her husband. In Darlington's rooms, the fan is used to disgrace the woman to whom it did not belong. Then it is given away by the wife to whom it was a gift. And, finally, it is borne "out of England" altogether by Lord Augustus, whom Mrs. Erlynne marries for his money alone. In fact, the "wonderful" fan is finally borne out of England by a man who has no personal attachment to it at all. Not only is the gift of a husband's love so lightly treated, but even the wife's name on the fan has nothing in it. The play could have been called the unimportance of being Margaret, the unimportance of being Mother, or indeed the unimportance of being married.

In addition, the fan, as a symbol of a coming of age (a gift on Lady Windermere's twenty-first birthday), the purpose of which as a cultural rite is inheritance of property, is associated throughout the play with the transfer of money. It appears on the day Lady Windermere learns of her husband's presents to Mrs. Erlynne; it appears at the party where Mrs. Erlynne requests a settlement of £2,500 annually as an "additional attraction" for Lord Augustus; and, finally, it is "carried out" by Lord Augustus, who will henceforth take on the financial burden of a wife. The critics called the fan "trivial," while the audience invested it with sentiment. In the play it is associated with reputations and, like Othello's handkerchief, although useless in itself it becomes a very dear commodity.

This trite plot, in which theater's traditional and well-loved tricks (for example, "kleptodramatics") come dangerously close to parody and thus reveal in the "life" on stage the theatricality of life, is reinforced by what critics have called the "superfluous" characters in the play. In a society where love is "clutched and dropped" and transferred as easily as a fan, persons are no more than "puppets." The so-called superfluous characters have the function of showing that the Windermeres and Erlynnes are not exceptional. Besides Mrs. Erlynne and Lady Windermere, the mother and the child whom she acknowledges only insofar as she can blackmail the husband, there are two other mother-daughter or guardian-ward relationships in the play: the Duchess of Berwick and her daughter Agatha, and Lady Jedburgh and her niece Miss Graham. The Duchess's sole concern is to marry her daughter to a wealthy Australian. ("[Australia] must be so pretty with all the dear little kangaroos flying about. Agatha has found it on the map.") Agatha's "clever talk" is her mother's pride, and she is represented as an ideal daughter. Her sole conversation consists in the line, repeated throughout the play, "Yes, mamma." ("A [Victorian upper-class] girl's whole life," writes Leonore Davidoff, "was oriented to the part she had to play in this 'status theatre.' . . . Woe betide her if she ventured to say more than 'Yes' or 'No' to remarks addressed to her—as for a joke of any sort it was unthinkable! . . . A gorgon-eye would be fixed upon her, plainly intimating that she was transgressing the proprieties and freezing her to silence."[36]) Lady Jedburgh's niece has no spoken lines at all; she simply follows her aunt around the stage. Lady Windermere's son is entirely absent from the stage, and is spoken of only when she protests that her husband could not be unfaithful because their child is but six months old. Lady Windermere forgets the child throughout the action until Mrs. Erlynne reminds her of him in Darlington's rooms. These silent, manipulated, or forgotten characters in Wilde's plays will become increasingly important. They are like "the serious people who populate the city" but who do not appear in the Society of first-night audiences: we shall hear of them but will not hear them.

Against these silent, manipulated characters is the dandiacal banter that critics felt disrupted the play's serious speech, the sort of banter that Wilde perfected in *Earnest*. Yet the men's amusing club talk in Darlington's rooms (Act III) and the chatter at the party (Act II) are crystal-clear communication when compared with the irony of sincere speech and the opacity of character to character in the dramatic scenes between the main characters. A case in point is the irony of the last agon, in which Lord Windermere, who has no knowledge of his wife's attempted desertion of the preceding evening or of her mother's self-sacrifice, says contemptuously to Mrs. Erlynne, "I know you thoroughly." Darlington himself, whom even recent critics have mistakenly seen as a typical Wildean dandy, is a hypocrite: his long speeches on innocence and purity are in direct contradiction to his pouncing on his friend's wife and to his attacks on Windermere's "falsity." His foil is the real dandy in the play, Cecil Graham, who does speak like Wilde. Graham's response to Dumby, the club bore, who says "Experience is the name every one gives to their mistakes," is "One shouldn't make any." Cecil Graham, unlike Darlington, does not moralize and does not act. In a corrupt society he remains marginal. Finally, Lady Windermere's born-again speech about how her eyes have been opened is in direct contrast to the fact that she is never informed that Mrs. Erlynne is her mother, a delusion that her husband still permits. Moreover, the play is framed in gossip, which, if untrue, still threatens to destroy a marriage. The dandiacal banter functions as a relief in a society in which serious language inevitably entails deceit, self-deception, or hypocrisy. The inevitability of the plot simply indicates the overdetermined successes of a Society for whom all wishes come true.

Wilde's position was much like that of Barbey's dandy. He both entertained and attacked a consummately bored upper class—"he displeased too generally not to be sought after." Like Barbey's dandy, he was criticized by the middle classes. The *Times*'s review of the first performances of *Lady Windermere's Fan* sneered at Wilde's "adaptations of the maxims of La Rouchefoucauld and Talleyrand" and longed "for a refreshing breath of sincerity on this barren and dreary waste of epigram" (22 February 1892). Calling Wilde's upper-class characters "puppets," the reviewer credited the play with no distinctive personalities at all. Similarly, with its parody of one of the epigrammatic scenes in the play, *Punch* included a cartoon of Wilde languidly leaning on a stack of French books from which he borrowed his plots; he is dangling from a fan with strings little "puppets"; Wilde also dangles from his mouth a cigarette; and rings of smoke, bearing the gloss "puff!!! puff!! puff!," encircle his head as he presumably addresses the audience (5 March 1892). The caption, executed with *Punch*'s typical overkill, satirized Wilde's indecorous and audacious peroration to the audience at the curtain call, delivered, as it in fact was, between puffs on the scandalous cigarette.[37] In the *Illustrated London News*, Clement Scott also attacked Wilde's effrontery—which, as we shall see in Chapter 4, was considerably more than Scott imagined—from his smoking on stage to the plot itself, which portrayed a blackmailing, deserting mother. Scott felt that such a portrayal should have offended rather than amused the audience (27 February 1892). Even A. B. Walkley, with Archer one of the two most powerfully influential dramatic critics of the time, felt that the attraction of the performance was in the author's "splendid audacity," "agreeable charlatanry," and "a hundred-Barnum-power of advertisement" in changing "old customs and preventing life from being monotonous" (*Speaker*, 27 February 1892). Such an assessment is remarkably close to Barbey's analysis of the dandy, and it indicates that only half of the drama of Wildean theater was in the play itself.

Although the majority of the audience was disposed to flatter itself with the sentimental image of the upper classes on stage, the reviewers, critical of that majority, discerned Wilde's irony. This understanding, however, only served to perplex them as to Wilde's motives (and as to his success). And the perplexity continued. In a 1966 *Plays and Players* review of *Lady Windermere's Fan* at the Phoenix Theatre in London, Frank Marcus concluded, "How stupid and trivial these people are . . . and how vicious, as Wilde was soon to find out to his cost! . . . It all reminded me of a dismal television programme years ago, showing the late Sir Alfred Munnings and some of his cronies, having what they pathetically supposed to be witty afterdinner conversation. There, as here, one felt sad and sorry for these victims of self-delusion. The talk ceased and was forgotten. All that remained was stale cigar smoke and the smell of rancid champagne."[38] Although the audience at the St. James's was able to see a sentimental conclusion to the play, Wilde himself, contrary to Marcus's conclusions, was indeed aware of how trivial, vicious, and self-deluded was the Society represented by puppets who fetishized cigars and champagne. But since that Society was also powerful, he was astute enough to flatter it with a sentimental portrait.

With *A Woman of No Importance*, Wilde again presented a duplicitous dramatic scheme. Here the reviews indicate that the audience was caught between its required sympathy for a moral heroine and its own delight in a "villain" with a practical, if amoral, wit. The dramatic conflict consists in the clash of two worlds, one maintaining traditional moral values and the other modern social practice, represented by Mrs. Arbuthnot and Lord Illingworth respectively. The first act establishes the contours and characters of Illingworth's world, the social class that inhabits the country estate at Hunstanton Chase. During the play, the greatest change that these chattering aristocrats, idling on the lawn, will undergo, with perhaps the exception of Illingworth himself, is to move from the lawn to the drawing room. (Reviewers complained that there was too much talk and too little action in the first two acts, but that was precisely the point Wilde was making about the class he represented on stage: his character Hester Worsley criticized the dramatis personae on the same score that the reviewers criticized Wilde.) Act II introduces the conflict between the values of that world and the "puritan" values of the young American guest, Hester Worsley (who will be joined in her values by the "heroine," Mrs. Arbuthnot). In Act III, Illingworth's world seems to win the conflict. But Act IV initially reverses the triumph to Mrs. Arbuthnot and Hester, and then exposes neither side as triumphant: the two would seem to be mutually exclusive. Wilde's world is precisely that twilight world of modern society where puritan values and cynical actions—two equally deplorable antitheses—operate in a symbiotic relationship.

For it was precisely in the "moral triumph" of Hester, Mrs. Arbuthnot, and her son Gerald at the play's conclusion that Wilde caught the audience. Although reviewers and audience alike took Mrs. Arbuthnot's part, praising her "pathos," "dignity," and "moral" fortitude, they were drawn to the sparkling cynicism and "mature" common sense of the "villain," the blasé roué Illingworth.[39] Even American critics loved the "brilliantly cynical" Illingworth—perhaps even more so because, as a result of their attacks on the lack of action and industry on the part of Society in *Lady Windermere's Fan*, Wilde had provided them a mouthpiece in *A Woman of No Importance*, Hester Worsley. Labeled a "puritan" by the British high society of Hunstanton Chase, Hester frequently castigates her hosts for their useless lives spent in idle, abusive conversation. Americans, she tells them, act; they do not talk.[40] *Punch*, indeed, discerned the double structure of the play when it satirized "Mems. From the O. W. Uncommonplace Book" (6 May 1893). It divided the play between the latitude of the villain (his saucy epigrams) and the platitude of the heroine (her "moral sentiments to suit the bourgeois palate"). Although Mrs. Arbuthnot's was the acceptable moral code, Illingworth's practicality was much closer to the audience's own practice. (Wilde told a private audience that he had taken the last act from *The Family Herald*.[41])

Elissa S. Guralnick and Paul M. Levitt have argued that in *A Woman of No Importance* Wilde intended comparison with *The Scarlet Letter* to contrast his own hypocritical, shallow society with Hawthorne's portrayal of a society with living values.[42] It is true that names like "Hester," "Illingworth," and the "pearl of price" for the illegitimate Gerald are obviously more than coincidental. In addition, Mrs. Arbuthnot's and Hester's consistently Old Testament tone and their reiterated "no's" recall the puritan conscience and Mosaic law. When Hester rushes up to offer her millions to the mother and son for a new life in America, she sounds half like Hester

Prynne anticipating her escape to England (and half like a broken Coriolanus): "No, no; you shall not [marry Illingworth]. That would be real dishonour, the first to touch you. Leave him and come with me. There are other countries than England. . . . Oh! Other countries over sea, better, wiser, and less unjust lands. The world is very wide and very big."

Yet the play works more subtly than Guralnick and Levitt suggest; for it is clear from the reviews that however deficient Mrs. Arbuthnot and Hester seem to twentieth-century critics who compare them to the characters in Hawthorne's novel, Wilde's audience thought them true heroines, comparable to Hester Prynne. But Wilde's is not simple imitation, or quotation, of Hawthorne: he adds a twist of Debord's "diversion." While the audience was moved by and applauded the moral resoluteness of the "puritans," it was attracted to the character most like it in all but his acute social criticism and self-awareness. (When asked by a liberal M.P. about the problem of the East End, Illingworth responds like Wilde in "The Soul of Man": "It is the problem of slavery. And we are trying to solve it by amusing the slaves." He advises Gerald to study the Peerage: "It is the one book a young man about town should know thoroughly, and it is the best thing in fiction the English have ever done.")

Wilde had shown that the drama in the play was a mere relic from an age gone by and the play's attractiveness was in its representation of the social values that the audience morally repudiated—just as the audience attested to moral views that it in fact did not practice. Wilde vivisected his spectators' hypocrisy and outmoded ethics through their disapproval of Illingworth (the practical future) and their admiration of Mrs. Arbuthnot (the penitent past). It is significant that several critics saw Illingworth as authorial self-criticism; for Illingworth is a man who, despite his feelings, and because of his "role," could not change. And Wilde was well aware that while his contemporaries frequently mocked him for his idleness, lack of sincerity, idle talk, and even often impugned his morality, he was nonetheless one of their chief sources of entertainment.[43]

One might do well to give the metaphor of Society that Wilde included in the play. One of his typically wonderful offstage characters, the Dickensian Mrs. Daubeny, wife to the Archdeacon, is never present, but she is talked about throughout the play. She is the image of dissolution; organ by organ, faculty by faculty, she evidences ashes and dust. Yet she maintains appearances. She can no longer call, but "she is happiest alone." She is deaf, but she reads: "she has many resources in herself, many resources." Her eyesight is rapidly going: "but she's never morbid, never morbid."

The gout has crippled her fingers, but "she has many other amusements. She is very much interested in her own health." She has all but lost her memory, "but she finds great pleasure in recalling the events of her early childhood, great pleasure." She lives entirely on jellies, "but she is wonderfully cheerful, wonderfully cheerful. She has nothing to complain of." This woman, a legend of lost graces, is a metaphor of the audience at the Haymarket, applauding, sentimentalizing, fetishizing the old world tones and morals of the "heroine" Mrs. Arbuthnot while, underneath that moral veneer, being drawn to the social practice and scintillating wit of the villain Lord Illingworth.

An Ideal Husband was the play that James attended the night that his own ill-fated *Guy Domville* opened at the St. James's, and it was the play that, according to Leon Edel, made James realize that he and Wilde could not share the same public. It opened at the Haymarket a mere month before Alexander replaced *Guy Domville* with *Earnest*, and it contains Wilde's most direct correlation between poses, external (fetishized) objects—"the symbols of things" designating affluence—and corruption. But Wilde again straddled the fence by permitting two interpretations of the fetishized poses and objects: a sentimental interpretation for his audience and a cynical interpretation for his critics.

The sentimental interpretation may be approached through the "Triumph of Love," a spectacular tapestry that is in the background throughout the first act, decorating the walls of Sir Robert Chiltern's luxurious octagon room. At the conclusion of the act, after Gertrude Chiltern has just persuaded her husband not to submit to Mrs. Cheveley's blackmail, Chiltern, knowing that he will be ruined, sits inconsolably before the tapestry. The stage direction reads, "The only light there is comes from the great chandelier that hangs over the staircase and illumines the tapestry of the Triumph of Love." Although the triumph of his wife's love over the demands of the blackmailer may initially be taken seriously, references to artworks multiply with other import. In Act II, Mabel protests against "that dreadful statue of Achilles. Really, the things that go on in front of that work of art are quite appalling. The police should interfere." And, more significantly, Chiltern himself seems to stress the exchange-value of art when he describes his erstwhile mentor, the man to whom he had confided the government's intent to purchase Suez Canal shares:

One night after dinner at Lord Radley's the Baron began talking about success in modern life as something that one could reduce to an absolutely definite science. With that wonderfully fascinating quiet voice of his he expounded to us the most terrible of all philosophies, the philosophy of power, preached to us the most marvellous of all gospels, the gospel of gold. . . . He was living then in Park Lane, in the house Lord Woolcomb has now. I remember so well how . . . he led me through his wonderful picture gallery, showed me his tapestries, his enamels, his jewels, his carved ivories, made me wonder at the strange loveliness of the luxury in which he lived; and then told me that luxury was nothing but a background, a painted scene in a play, and that power, power over other men, power over the world, was the one thing worth having, the one supreme pleasure worth knowing, the one joy one never tired of, and that in our century only the rich possessed it.

Writing of the diverse sources of high society in the 1890's, Webb qualified her remarks, "But deep down in the unconscious herd instinct of the British governing class there *was* a test of fitness for membership of this most gigantic of all social clubs . . . *the possession of some form of power over other people*. The most obvious form of power, and the most easily measurable, was the power of wealth. . . . The dominant impulse was neither the greed of riches nor the enjoyment of luxurious living, though both these motives were present, but the desire for power."[44] The spectacle is the self-portrait of power.

That Chiltern never in fact repudiates the philosophy of power is clear in the last act, when Goring convinces Lady Chiltern that if she permits her husband to retire from public life according to her own severe moral codes she will ultimately lose his love: "Do you want to kill his love for you? . . . Women are not meant to judge us, but to forgive us when we need forgiveness. Pardon, not punishment, is their mission. Why should you scourge him with rods for a sin done in his youth, before he knew you, before he knew himself? A man's life is of more value than a woman's. It has larger issues, wider scope, greater ambitions." Goring's view is supported by Chiltern's obvious bitterness and feeling of persecution when he learns that his wife wants him to decline the Cabinet seat. Of course Gertrude does take Goring's advice and parrots his words when she rips up her husband's letter of resignation. And the play does conclude with a happily married couple and intimations that Chiltern will be Prime Minister some day. But it is indeed an ironic triumph of love that depends upon the wife's self-effacement and the husband's maintaining political power. This love is a mere background. As a work of art with an aura, it is a fraud, a frill to catch the audience.

Wilde emphasizes the point of such artful shams in his presentation of the cast of characters, who are quite openly "puppets," though well-dressed ones, and hard as statues. His stage directions for the entrance of each character are illuminating. Gertrude stands before the tapestry, "a woman of grave Greek beauty." Mrs. Marchmont and Lady Basildon make a tableau on a Louis Seize sofa: "They are types of exquisite fragility. Their affectation of manner has a delicate charm. Watteau would have loved to paint them." Lord Caversham is "a fine whig type. Rather like a portrait by Lawrence." Mabel Chiltern is "a perfect example of the English type of prettiness . . . really like a Tanagra statuette." Lady Markby has "grey hair à la marquise and good lace." Mrs. Cheveley is highly colorful and brightly plumed: "A work of art, on the whole, but showing the influence of too many schools." Sir Robert Chiltern bears the distinctive marks of a politician: "It would be inaccurate to call him picturesque. Picturesqueness cannot survive the House of Commons. But Vandyck would have liked to have painted his head." The point of such descriptions is to show an entirely artificial society, a society made up of established poses: a spectacular society.

The secondary characters need merely to maintain their poses. The first act establishes their artificiality and hypocrisy. Mrs. Marchmont and Lady Basildon "never know why" they attend all parties throughout the season, although they are "horribly tedious." They both admit to having "perfect" spouses, who also bore them. Lady Markby represents the aristocracy, which she knows to be effete and degenerate: "Dear Duchess, and how is the Duke? Brain still weak, I suppose? Well, that is only to be expected, is it not? His good father was just the same. There is nothing like race, is there?" Asked whether she is optimist or pessimist—fashionable philosophies of the day, both of them, like an interest in clairvoyance or bimetallism—Mrs. Cheveley discusses poses: "Oh, I'm neither. Optimism begins in a broad grin, and Pessimism ends with blue spectacles. Besides, they are both of them merely poses." Asked if she prefers to be natural, she responds, "Sometimes. But it is such a very difficult pose to keep up."

The butler Phipps, who, more than any other of these interchangeable figures, is a necessity and therefore a symbol of the upper classes, has effaced his personality altogether. He is the ideal form of servantness: "The distinction of Phipps is his impassivity. He has been termed by enthusiasts the Ideal Butler. The Sphinx is not so incommunicable. He is a mask with a manner. Of his intellectual or emotional life, history knows nothing. He represents the dominance of form." Having no content, no relations, no history, Phipps is reminiscent of the servants of the fashionable novels. When Pelham visits his uncle and mother at Glenmorris Castle, he scans the long line of servants arranged to greet him and reflects on "that tribe one never, indeed, considers as possessing a life separate from their services to us: beyond that purpose of existence, we know not if they exist. As Providence made the Stars for the benefit of earth, so it made servants for the use of gentlemen: and, as neither stars nor servants appear except when we want them, so I suppose they are in a sort of a suspense from being, except at those important and happy moments."[45] (In *The Tragic Muse*, James commented that a particular butler differed from his master only in "an expression": he would have been "wonderfully like [the master of the house] if he had had an expression. He did not permit himself this freedom."[46]) "Because these servants were seen as an extension of the household 'aura,'" Davidoff writes of upper-class domestic help, "they were deliberately depersonalized, hidden under standardised liveries and often called standardised names, e.g., Thomas and Susan, whatever their real names might be. . . . The analogy between a theatrical performance and Society functions is very strong. Upper servants were aware of this."[47] One might recall the manservant Lane in *The Importance of Being Earnest*, who habitually lies to protect his employer. And Wilde once dashed off frantic instructions to his producer to change the name of one of his characters: he had erroneously given a servant a gentleman's surname. This mistake could have turned the world of the play upside down and spoiled the mimesis.

In the amazing scene in which Goring complains that his buttonhole is too elaborate, making him look "almost in the prime of life," Wilde gently shows that where the members of the upper class profit from their masks and adherence to forms, Phipps has achieved form by suppressing his relations and his history:

Goring: For the future a more trivial buttonhole, Phipps, on Thursday evenings.
Phipps: I will speak to the florist, my lord. She has had a loss in her family lately, which perhaps accounts for the lack of triviality your lordship complains of in the buttonhole.
Goring: Extraordinary thing about the lower class in England—they are always losing their relations.
Phipps: Yes, my lord! They are extremely fortunate in that respect.
Goring [turns round and looks at him. Phipps remains impassive].

It is this distinction between what must be surrendered in masking, which for the upper classes is nothing but personality and for Phipps is all social relations, that goes unnoticed by the traditional critics of Wilde's "poses," who claim for him such epithets as "a mask with a manner" or an "egoist without an ego."[48] But Wilde's phrase "a mask with a manner" is not, as these critics imply, applied to dandies with power, but to butlers without it. Upper-class characters have masks because they do not need personalities; and their servants have them because they cannot afford to have personalities. Observing this distinction could substantially extend the implications of Wilde as "a mask with a manner."

In Wilde's first two plays, *Vera; or the Nihilists* (1881) and *The Duchess of Padua* (1883), there are two aristocrats among the major characters, and these are the only two who possess the conversational skills later known as Wilde's particular kind of wit. These two villainous figures, Prince Paul Maraloffski in *Vera* and the Duke in *The Duchess of Padua*, were directly opposed to Vera, the nihilist who spoke for the people, and the Duchess, who both spoke and acted like Shakespeare's Juliet. Wilde was naively sincere in his popular sentiments in these plays, and both plays were commercial and critical failures. We need only note that the nihilists in *Vera* wore masks and posed as a troupe of players. The Czar, who was assassinated by the revolutionaries, did not take masks lightly.

In *An Ideal Husband*, the dramatic action consists in the unmasking of the upper classes, showing their sham if not obliterating their power. The luxury of Chiltern's home in Grosvenor Square was founded on the swindle with Baron Arnheim. Mrs. Cheveley's diamond brooch was acquired through theft. Chiltern, "to the world, as to [his wife] . . . an ideal always," was undeniably corrupt, although he attempted to couch it in terms of a classical hero's fatal flaw: "To stake all one's life on a single moment, to risk everything on one throw, whether the stake be power or pleasure, I care not—there is no weakness in that. There is a horrible, a terrible courage. I had that courage. I sat down the same afternoon and wrote Baron Arnheim the letter this woman now holds. He made three-quarters of a million over the transaction." But the fetishized tragic-hero role is merely an example of Chiltern's self-delusion, for in the long run he is no better than the blackmailer Mrs. Cheveley. Whereas Chiltern views himself as a tragic hero caught through the machinations of an evil blackmailer, Wilde, who occasionally fancied himself as risking everything for the sake of pleasure, if not power, was constitutionally too generous and socially too aware to pretend to the double standard that concludes his play. When he refused to submit to the blackmail attempts of Allen and Clibborn, he good-naturedly gave them cab fare for their trip, saying, "I am afraid you are leading a wonderfully wicked life." The dogged Clibborn returned Wilde's letter gratis, with "There is good and bad in everyone of us." "You are a born philosopher," said Wilde as they parted.[49]

Yet H. G. Wells, like the audience, took the sentimental view of the play: that Mrs. Cheveley was rightly exposed *and* that Gertrude Chiltern rightly forgave her husband and encouraged him to accept the Cabinet position with a clear conscience. Whereas women were wrong to go to any lengths for money and power, politicians were right to do so. "The subconscious pursuit of power was manifested in a more equivocal form," Webb wrote of Society's double standard. "The conventional requirements with regard to personal morality, sexual or financial, were graded with almost meticulous exactitude to the degree of social, political or industrial power exercised by the person concerned. . . . Past iniquities of a multimillionaire, whose millions were secure, were discreetly forgotten; an honourable bankruptcy brought about by lack of knowledge or sheer ill luck led to ignoring not the sin but the sinner."[50] Like the Triumph of Love, the ideal leader was the audience's fetish. Wilde, wrote Wells, "is sloughing his epigrams slowly but surely and discovering to an appreciative world, beneath the attenuated veil of his wit, that he too has a heart." Nonetheless, Wells felt that the sentimental melodrama, "an attempt at commonplace emotions and the falling off in epigram, may be merely a cynical or satirical concession to the public taste."[51]

The actual success of the play was at least partially due to the audience's sentimental interpretations of British politics. The Prince of Wales congratulated Wilde after the performance. When the author apologized for the play's length and expressed his intention to cut it, Edward admonished him, "Pray do not take out a single word." He, of course, relied heavily for his support on the financiers Baron Hirsh and Sir Ernest Cassell, men much like Wilde's fictitious Baron Arnheim. Although the broad public was unaware of it, many members of the highest circles who attended the Haymarket were certainly aware that Disraeli had borrowed money from the Rothschilds for the government's purchase of Suez Canal shares. This intended purchase was the secret that Wilde's Chiltern had sold to Baron Arnheim, thereby making £110,000 and rising on its capital to political eminence and a life of ostentatious integrity.

The reviewers discerned this cynicism, although they credited its justification in varying degrees. William Archer acknowledged the irony of the sentimental conclusion: "The thousands have increased and multiplied; [Chiltern] is wealthy, he is respected, he is Under-Secretary for Foreign Affairs, he is married to a wife who idolises and idealises him; and, not having stolen anything more in the interim, he is inclined to agree with his wife and the world in regarding himself as the Bayard of Downing Street."[52] A. B. Walkley, more politically naive, felt that the plot was most improbable: "When Bulwer Lytton and Disraeli wrote novels picturing politics as a drawing-room game of this kind, they only distorted, not actually falsified the facts. . . . But nowadays, of course, such a picture is stark, staring nonsense" (*Speaker*, 12 January 1895). (Yet the Disraeli who wrote fashionable novels became the diplomat to make his fiction fact.) Similarly, critics in the U.S. hated the cynicism and the elite, drawing-room atmosphere of the play. (In the twentieth century, Americans came to expect this of British politics. One of the main reasons that Harold Nicolson hated the publicity of the Maclean/Burgess affair was that it "would enrage the Americans."[53]) The reviewer for the *New York Daily Tribune* excoriated Wilde's "Pelham" attitudes—"the attitude of the half-baked juvenile cynic, who knows that all women are vicious and all men corrupt, and consequently goes about with his eyes peeled and his ever-ready sneer in good working order" (13 March 1895). The *Times*'s reviewer could not understand why Wilde should allow the characters to "drop the subject in hand and score verbal excesses at each other's expense" (4 January 1895), and the *Athenaeum* felt that the (sentimental) conclusion was "wholly disproportionate to what the author holds to be the offense" (12 January 1895). Yet it was precisely the seriousness of the offense and the glittering and sentimental veneer obfuscating it to which Wilde directed the spectators' attention. (In the twentieth century, Martin Green contends in *Children of the Sun*, the glitter and sentiment *were* the defense of the dandies who were also traitors to Britain.)

In *The Tragic Muse*, James also likened politics to theater. Before giving it all up for the life of art, Nick Dormer muses on his activity in Parliament that "this was not really action at all, but only a pusillanimous imitation of it. . . . [He] acted as much as possible under the circumstances. . . ."[54] The difference between James and Wilde was that James elevated art over politics whereas Wilde saw them both as performances.

There is one character in *An Ideal Husband*, the only character that our own contemporary critics are likely to call principled, who is implicated in neither the glitter of the artistic shams nor the seriousness of the offense.[55] The American reviewer in 1895 who saw Goring as "an idiot"[56] failed to recognize that Goring's insistence on staying out of politics is a direct foil to Chiltern's corrupt luxuriousness and hypocritical idealism. This marginal man is probably the only traditional dandy that Wilde fully developed. Unlike Darlington in *Lady Windermere's Fan* and Illingworth in *A Woman of No Importance*, Goring never acts against conventional ethical standards; unlike Wotton in *Dorian Gray* he never pays a price for his marginality—except of course, like Lear's fool, the price of marginality itself. He is 34 years old and acts like an adolescent, as if youth and idleness were a defense against corruption and the stultification of occupational poses. ("I hate this affectation of youth, sir. It is a great deal too prevalent nowadays," his father tells him. "Youth isn't an affectation. Youth is an art," he responds, thus establishing a positive type of art to be distinguished from the affectations and artful poses in the play.) He may not be a fraud, like his friend Chiltern, but several times in the play it is emphasized that he does nothing, that he is, like art in the Preface to *Dorian Gray*, "quite useless." ("I am afraid I can't take him with me to Downing Street," his father says of him. "It is not the Prime Minister's day for seeing the unemployed.") But Goring, who is no more than a frill, does determine the "happy" outcome of the play by persuading Gertrude to overlook the faults of her husband. If there are alternatives in Society, they are limited to being a fraud or a frill.

Goring's function, like the tapestry's, is to be the frill that renders the fraud passable. He is the only one who is not described in his entrance as art. Yet as he stands in front of the mirror with Phipps, we see that the only reason he is not described, like the others, as a work of art is that he is all art and has no illusions about his artificiality: "Enter Lord Goring in evening dress with a buttonhole. He is wearing a silk hat and Inverness cape. White-gloved, he carries a Louis Seize cane. His are all the delicate fopperies of Fashion. One sees that he stands in immediate relation to modern life, makes it indeed, and so masters it. He is the first well-dressed philosopher in the history of thought."

The traditional dandy, of course, was the first to make dress and fashion the basis of a philosophy, of the only philosophy, in fact, that was consistent with modern, materialist life. Here, indeed, in Wilde's description of Goring we can see something of his own role. From prison Wilde wrote that he himself had "stood in symbolic relations to the art and culture of [his] age." He had set the fashions, and he had thought that he had mastered the age. In providing that age an image of its own glitter, he at least realized how a frill could decorate a fraud.

This double status of the critical yet entertaining marginal man was exactly Barbey's analysis of Brummell's character. With *Earnest* Wilde himself was the dandy, presenting a glowing image of the age while exposing its underlying ugliness. But as philosophers of dandyism know, its existence is due to certain fluxes in social economy, to conditions, like the decline of the aristocracy, in which social mobility leads to universal posing.

Being what Baudelaire called a "natural," rather than titled or financial, aristocrat, the dandy has traditionally not had the financial resources to be secure in the Society he amused and criticized for the season. Wilde was of course vulnerable in this regard: during his trials, his Society would not support him against the press and the middle-class public from which he had come.

As in the case of Brummell, Society dispensed with its dandy but retained for long after the fetishized image of Society that the dandy had made for it. Upon Wilde's arrest on 15 April 1895, his name was removed from the playbills and programs of *Earnest*. On 8 May Alexander withdrew the play, attributing a financial loss of £289 8s. 4d. to the scandal of the trials. In 1902 he revived it at the St. James's but did not make a profit. On its second revival in 1909, it made the striking profit of more than £21,000, and so was produced again in 1911 and 1913. Wilde's son, Vyvyan Holland, was considerably enriched by the copyright which Alexander bequeathed to him.[57] After the trials, *Lady Windermere's Fan* and *A Woman of No Importance* joined the risky *Salome* in the repertoire of Grein's Independent Theatre. It was left to Grein, the patron of the theater of psychological realism, to praise Wilde as a dramatist on his death in 1900 and to review very movingly a revival of *Earnest* at the Coronet in 1901.[58]

Today, since there are few conscious aristocrats among audiences, Wilde's comedies can be seen as Wells saw *Earnest*: as satires puncturing the bombast of the end of the last century. But the lack of reciprocity between audience and stage-image has deflated the force of the satire: history has replaced the spectacular forms of nineteenth-century Britain with new media. In the 1890's the actors mirrored the audience; today, having no equivalent to that audience, few actors have the imaginative grasp of its vanished power to present the play with its original force. The lines that should be uttered with imperturbable gravity are breezed through by embarrassed actors as ghosts of dead wit. Mirroring nothing, *Earnest* is trivialized. The one exception is the perfect film production of the early 1950's, with Edith Evans as Lady Bracknell.

As for the dandy himself, Wilde, like Brummell, was trapped by the fetishes, despite his knowing too well that they were fetishes. Captain Jesse wrote that Brummell had "died" when he could no longer afford to have his cambric neckcloths laundered. Wilde wrote in prison to Douglas of the symbols of their love, the amber-scented Dagonet 1880, the special *cuvée* of Perrier-Jouet, the custom-designed ruby and diamond sleevelinks from Henry Lewis. Without such props, Wilde could still criticize Society, he could write powerful and effective letters to the *Daily Chronicle* on the necessity of prison reform,[59] and he could write *The Ballad of Reading Gaol*; but he could not write drama. For the social outcast with no place on the stage, and for the bankrupt deprived of his props, the insubstantial pageant had vanished altogether. Yet his own type of psychological realism, the realism that sent an audience in pursuit of its own manufactured image, anticipated twentieth-century consumerism.

More so, finally, than did Artaud's. The theater of cruelty shared with Wilde's incipiently confrontational drama a mission of provocation (see especially the discussion of *Salome* in Chapter 4); a spectacular mise-en-scène that included the audience and that in both cases fetishized a modern consuming "public" that was, in Artaud's phrase, "an integral part of our efforts"; a technique of de-identification, as in *Earnest*, in which puppets parodied society; and an insistent and inclusive thematic critique of middle-class *mentalité*. Their goals were even similar. Artaud concluded a famous essay, "No More Masterpieces," with a cynicism worthy of Gabriel Nash describing Wilde's actual audiences: "I do not believe we have managed to revitalize the world we live in, and I do not believe it is worth the trouble of clinging to; but I do propose something to get us out of our marasmus, instead of continuing to complain about it, and about the boredom, inertia, and stupidity of everything."[60]

The differences between theater of cruelty and Wilde's theater are attributable to the influence of more traditional philosophies on Artaud, philosophies that Wilde rejected when he chose to see himself as "the first well-dressed philosopher in the history of thought," not philosopher-king but rather philosopher-consumer. Artaud's spectacles included violent, sometimes bloody, physical images of existential determinism; with the exception of *Salome*, Wilde's spectacles, like Jarry's *Ubu Roi*, showed economic and political determinism. In a brochure for the Alfred Jarry Theater's first year, Artaud warned that stage "trappings" should not turn the play into a show, but should be minimalized to suggestive abstractions "in the spirit of disturbing action," whereas Wilde encouraged the audience to consume the show of its own spectacle. Artaud wanted an integral or total theater which included dreams and dream-work, whereas Wilde drained his characters of deep psychology to show that the dominant dream of modern society was consumption and the national power to consume the world. The audience capable of that consumption was smaller in England in the 1890's, which is the major difference between Wilde and Artaud's drama—

a difference in scale that indirectly resulted in Artaud's taking exploitation as the human condition rather than as a political and economic category.

To conclude this chapter with the more local politics of Wilde's theater, with its sentimental/satiric interpretability, twentieth-century theorists of advertising have devised the tools to understand why the press was hostile and perplexed.[61] Public relations practitioners distinguish between publicity (the effort to promote one view among a "choice" of alternatives) and propaganda (the effort to enforce an either/or dichotomy). In Wilde's consistently multi-faceted works, he was a publicist: through open interpretations he appeared to give alternatives to the public. His critics, like Shaw and Wells, wanted him to be on one side or the other. Their critical techniques more often than not fell into the two-valued system of propaganda. Given their political convictions, this is not surprising. Given the demands from the press for partisanship in what was essentially a conflict between middle- and upper-class identities, it is also not surprising that Wilde, the parvenu who entertained aristocrats and parvenus, answered with paradox. The press would have its revenge in 1895, when, from Society and theatrical columns, Wilde's name began to appear in the headlines.

4

Art for Love's Sake: 'Salome' and 'Reading Gaol'

> Nothing speaks so well for the nature of man as his strong indifference to any system of rewards or punishment either heavenly or terrestrial.
> In Wilde's commonplace book of notes, kept in the 1880's

Wilde's trials and bankruptcy auction as presented in *Police News*, 1895.

UNTIL 1895 a relatively isolated art world in Britain held two views of aestheticism. For Wilde aestheticism was "a mode of acting, an attempt to realize one's own personality on some imaginative plane out of reach of the trammeling accidents and limitations of real life" ("The Portrait of Mr. W. H."). Its political goal was to enable its proponents to "know the meanings of the words, and realise them in free, beautiful lives" ("The Soul of Man Under Socialism"). For others it meant a heightened perception through the senses. This last was certainly the view held by J. A. Symonds when he wrote to members of his set describing his hypersensitivity to beauty, whether the beauty of Italian architecture, of the perfect proportions of the male form, or of male comradeship.[1] Both views resisted the Victorian values of utility, rationality, scientific factuality, and technological progress. In Wilde's trials in 1895, his perceived position as both spokesperson for art and example of sexual deviant resulted in a remarkable elision in the public domain of art and sexuality and thus in the creation of a new category of aestheticism.

As the press reported it from the trials, Wilde's life—the most prominent elements of which appeared to be young men of aristocratic and unemployed status—exhibited the same lack of conformity to middle-class norms as had *Dorian Gray*. As his works were given equal time with his sexual practices during the trial, aestheticism came to represent a distinct and private realm of art and sexuality. Wilde's trials confronted the public with an art that refused to say nothing but the truth, that refused to take its interrogation solemnly, and a sexuality outside of the rational demands of reproduction. Thus aestheticism came to mean the irrational in both productive (art) and reproductive (sexuality) realms: an indication of the art world's divorce from middle-class life.

In the art world, Wilde's homosexuality, contrary to mainstream notions of "productive" or "purposive" sexuality, likewise contributed to his particular formulation of aestheticism, including his explicit rejections of Victorian notions of the natural (as in "Nature imitates art"), of the purposive (as in his stance of idleness), and of the productive (as in "art for art's sake"). The genesis of his formulations may be traced in the homosexual literature of the period; they reached their culmination in *Salome* and *The*

Ballad of Reading Gaol. Had it been performed, a play like *Salome* would have confronted Victorian audiences with a spectacle of purposeless, "unnatural," unproductive, and uncensored art and desire. In the same lush language that had spoken all along to a community of men, *Salome* attempted to seduce a broader audience into an awareness of its suppressed longings. *The Ballad of Reading Gaol*, a tribute to that original community of men—by 1898 dispersed throughout Europe—provided the spectacle of their banishment from polite society. *Reading Gaol* provided an image of the separation of art and middle-class life, a separation enforced as much by life as by art. This chapter will trace that separation and conclude with the two works that were respectively an attempt to heal it and a monument to the failure to effect that healing.

A note of caution, however, is in order: the separation of art and illegitimate sexualities from middle-class life was neither simple nor total. When I use the term "homosexual" in this chapter I do so for the sake of brevity and with the following qualifications. Before his conviction, Wilde was a married man and father who also engaged in same-sex practices and frequented the society of men who engaged in same-sex practices. Although his imaginative life was male-centered, he materially inhabited a genuinely double life and lived before a time when sexual preference had become an identity. I shall cite evidence that a community of men engaged in homosexual practices cautiously with respect to the larger society while many of its members worked publicly for political reform. This community was coherent insofar as its members were aware of its oppression and, in some cases, repression in the larger society. Nonetheless, homosexual identity as opposed to homosexual practice is, as Foucault suggests in his *History of Sexuality*, a possibility that was only coming into being in the 1890's in England. Wilde did not, properly speaking, enjoy a gay identity.[2]

On the other hand, in addition to the identity of the oppressed, we should remember that the other consistent manifestation of this male community was an evident male consumerism, from pornography to a specialized tourism. The brave critiques of sexual oppression discussed in this chapter were to some extent already co-opted by bourgeois consumerist practices: a "life-style"—the neologism has come to represent precisely the convergence of such phenomena—of identifiable costume and predictable presents (cigarette cases, sleevelinks, etc.), holidays (in Paris, Monte Carlo, Naples, etc.), and ostentatious dining out at all hours (at the Café Royal, Willis's, Savoy, etc.). All this suggests that the "idleness" of these men was not simply a protest against an ethos of productivity or reproduction but was also another form of conspicuous consumption, in this case the consumption of time as "leisure." (For an explicit Wildean treatment of sex as commodity and commodities as sexy, see Appendix C on *A Florentine Tragedy*.) As Foucault has suggested, what could not be integrated into the circuits of production could be assimilated into the circulation of profit. This is the other side of Salome's spectacle, its integration or sameness in society, which should not be forgotten as, in this chapter, the discussion takes up difference.

Before examining the attacks on the homosexual Cause in the press, popular criminology, and even in the work of other artists (who called themselves counterdecadents), it is worth situating them in the gender confusion of the times. Like the dandies and public schoolmen treated in Chapter 2, the historical tradition of aestheticism in England was burdened with such confusion. In 1895, the members of the Rhymers Club were stunned by the craven, or commercially shrewd, defection of Wilde's erstwhile publisher John Lane.[3] Lane, the leading publisher of the early 1890's, whose firm, the Bodley Head, was known for its poetry and belles lettres, banished Aubrey Beardsley from the art editorship and pages of the year-old *Yellow Book*. When Beardsley, Max Beerbohm, Charles Conder, Joseph Conrad, Ernest Dowson, Havelock Ellis, Lionel Johnson, Bernard Shaw, and Arthur Symons linked up with Leonard Smithers in 1896, some thought that they had, like Melmoth, sold their souls to the devil. Smithers was one of what Chesterton called "the decadent publishers," who had promised to "publish anything that the others [were] afraid of." He was also, as Wilde said, "the most learned erotomaniac in Europe," loaning to young Beardsley his *Gamiani ou deux nuits d'excès* and *Priapeia*, translated in collaboration with Sir Richard Burton.[4] As in most bargains with the devil, the association with Smithers was, for a time, lucrative. The new magazine the *Savoy* and Smithers' publications more or less sustained Beardsley, Dowson, and Wilde for the few remaining years of their lives.

Sometime during the early 1890's, Madame Blavatsky told Yeats why people sold their souls to the devil: "they do it to have somebody on their side."[5] In *The Trembling of the Veil* Yeats talks about the members of the Rhymers Club, who were paralyzed (and polarized) by the moral posturing and public poetry of the middle classes. Yeats apologizes that they were poor men, but too rich in Paterian perfectionism to sell out to the vulgar demands for art. Consequently they were too poor for taking on a wife and domicile, and Yeats describes them seeking beauty in classical scholarship and Roman Catholicism. Less of a perfectionist and more ambitious,

Wilde conceded to the popular tastes and sought beauty in the members of the Rhymers Club. (Among them was John Gray, probably the visual inspiration for *Dorian Gray*, who became a priest at St. Peter's in Edinburgh—the church built for him by his friend Marc-André Raffalovich, the author of *L'Affaire Oscar Wilde* [1895] and the Catholic apologetic for homosexuality *Uranisme et unisexualité* [1896].[6] Raffalovich, a wealthy Russian Jew from Paris who converted to Catholicism in 1896, was largely responsible for Beardsley's conversion the year before he died.) Unlike the Rhymers, Yeats wrote, Wilde was a public man who needed a crowd; since the Victorian crowd, according to Yeats, lacked heroism and nobility, Wilde's talents were wasted in idle performances: "He must humour and cajole and pose, take worn-out stage situations, for he knows that he may be as romantic as he please, so long as he does not believe in his romance, and all that he may get their ears for a few strokes of contemptuous wit in which he does believe."[7]

But although Wilde's superior "true thought," as Yeats put it, may have been closer to the Rhymers' than to that of the public, there is a key difference between him and "the tragic generation": the Rhymers treated their marginality with sentiment. With the exceptions of Yeats and Beardsley, the Rhymers were for the most part Oxford men; their immediate artistic tradition included the Pre-Raphaelites and Pater. While Tennyson was composing the treacheries and betrayals of *The Idylls of the King*, the Pre-Raphaelites and their associates were eluding typical versions of Victorian domesticity and transforming the problems of their eccentric ménages in their art and poetry. They found that if one were to marry a working woman, specifically a model, she could as easily sit for one artist as another. William Morris, aware of the growing love in his house between his wife Jane and Dante Gabriel Rossetti, ran off to write *The Earthly Paradise*—in Iceland. Rossetti, in turn, kept his wife Elizabeth locked up in a decrepit house on the river and shared his income with an amiable mistress, Fanny. Meanwhile their defender, John Ruskin, was losing his wife to the renegade from the Brotherhood who had turned from Mantegna to advertising, John Millais. (With his customary oblique insight, Ruskin accused Millais's painting of infidelity.) And Swinburne, while multiplying praise upon praise of Venus in terms of classical erudition, was receiving drawings from Simeon Solomon of boys being flogged by schoolmasters and was himself habitually flagellated at a brothel in Regent's Park. Swinburne's contributions to the large body of Victorian flagellation literature, like his images of the hermaphrodite, contain the typical elements of the genre: male submissiveness and instability of identity—the direct antithesis of the gentleman's ideals of manliness, solidity, certitude of self, and singleness of purpose.[8]

Behind all these figures is the astonishingly erudite and exotically inclined Sir Richard Burton, whom the Pre-Raphaelites universally admired and whose material in his sixteen-volume translation of *The Book of the Thousand Nights and a Night* (1885) necessitated, he felt, the inclusion of a "Terminal Essay" on the history of pederasty all over the world up to the year of writing. The "Terminal Essay" was published during the same year as the passage of section xi of the Criminal Law Amendment Act, which related to the commission of homosexual practices among consenting adults in private and under which Wilde was sentenced to two years' imprisonment with hard labor. The advertisements for Burton's "Arabian Nights" emphasized that they were not for women or children and were available only by subscription; yet Swinburne publicly praised them in a poem in the *Athenaeum* on 6 February 1886 and treated Captain Burton, who resembled Errol Flynn, as a sublime Melmoth in his "Memorial Verses on the Death of Richard Burton." In one of her last letters to Smithers, Isabel Burton, who resembled the elderly Queen Victoria, prayed for her husband's tortured soul in purgatory. In an earlier letter to Smithers from the Mid-East, Burton had prayed for the poor and for women who were trapped in the purgatory of London.[9]

The Rhymers were caught between this half of their tradition and Pater. Despite the vividness of desire, often of orgiastic violence, in Pater's *Renaissance* and *Imaginary Portraits*, the Oxford don's life was so uneventful that today the thought of his biography, even after several have been written, seems excessive. His followers, on the other hand, were left to bear the implications of his prose. Although scholars today assure us that in the "Conclusion" to *The Renaissance* Pater "intended" a refined, intellectual aestheticism, the Rhymers found that to some extent it was false to pretend that the "passion" for and "impressions" of paintings in the Louvre could be restricted to museums, as if passion in life always led one way and passion in art always led nowhere.

It was probably just this sort of betrayal that led to Richard C. Jackson's celebratory poem of Pater's suppressed eroticism, "Joy Standeth on the Threshold: A Reverie of Walter Pater" (c. 1887-89),[10] and to Lionel Johnson's two vastly different tributes to Wilde. Johnson's first tribute, "In Honorem Doriani Creatorisque Eius," was in Latin, "modo modulans Romano / Laudes dignas Doriano" thanking Wilde, "qui tanta cernis," in a language worthy of his Dorian, for perceiving so much. The second, "The Destroyer of a Soul," was composed after Johnson had introduced Alfred Douglas to Wilde in 1891. Although Yeats tells us that the Rhymers were always unerringly polite, something went awry in the aftereffects of this particular introduction. The poem begins "with a necessary hate" directed toward one who has corrupted a friend with "the soul of a saint." The poem ends, "Call you this thing my friend? this nameless thing? This living body, hiding its dead soul?" Johnson had fallen in love with Douglas at Winchester.

The Rhymers' emotional crux between Paterian idealism and their own desires is apparent in their pathetically confused lives. Yeats tells us that Lionel Johnson, who lectured Dowson from the Church Fathers on chastity, was discovererd at his autopsy "never to have grown, except in the brain, after his fifteenth year." Dowson dedicated all his poems to Adelaide Foltinowicz, the teenage daughter of a restaurateur. Upon reading a newspaper account of a courageous girl's indictment of her abductor, Dowson began to fear that his intentions would be misunderstood and delayed proposing. Adelaide married someone else and died as a result of complications from an abortion in 1903.[11] In volume III of the *Yellow Book*, Dowson published a story entitled "Apple Blossom in Brittany" in which a Jamesian literary gentleman encourages the young girl he loves to enter a convent. Beardsley, whose drawings after Wilde's trial were attacked as "sexless" and "asexual," meaning too erotic, and "unclean," died penitent, "like a saint." His sister, on the other hand, who cared for him as Pater's sisters had cared for their brother, continued her career on stage long after she married in 1902.[12] Yeats himself has best described his own sexual frustrations, including his relationship to the dynamic and public figure Maud Gonne. In his draft *Autobiography* he recounts their mystical consummation, "the initiation of the spear": in a double vision Maud Gonne is "a great stone statue through which passed flame." Yeats, of course, found himself "becoming flame and mounting up through and looking out of the eyes of a great stone Minerva." Shortly after the double vision, she told Yeats that she had a horror and terror of physical love.[13]

The "tragic generation" of men were either cared for by sisters, intimidated by New Women, or like Johnson, after "four or five glasses of wine," denied "that a gelded man lost anything of intellectual power." Whereas the Victorian organization of gender deserted them in their romance and pain, Wilde was supported by a "modern" (their term) homosexual community, a community candid in its pleasures and unified in its protectiveness. Despite a critical tradition that has taken for granted a radical disjunction between Wilde's pre-prison and post-conviction work and an assumption, following Wilde's early biographers, that prison was psychologically and literarily good for Wilde, Wilde's position as a practicing homosexual leading a "double life" in society contributed to the peculiar form of witty paradoxes in the pre-prison work and to the paradoxical themes of the later material. The paradox and epigram, which criticized society by turning its own language curtly on its head, and the double-edged critical impetus of Wilde's comedies were particularly appropriate techniques for a homosexual Irishman with socialist sympathies in nineteenth-century Britain.

For the difference between the pre- and post-prison work is that at first Wilde lived the contradictions with a sense of amused and proud superiority, with the added *frisson* of danger, and that later the contradictions surfaced as an allegiance to a loved community that conflicted with an equal desire to be an accepted member of the larger society. After prison Wilde was free to love the way he wished, but for this freedom he had forfeited his social position and economic security as well as the personal affection of many former friends and his right to see his two young sons. The distinction, therefore, between the so-called "trivial" paradoxes of the pre-prison work, for which Wilde's wit was so well known, and the "profound" paradoxes of the later work, like the *felix culpa* and joy in suffering in *De Profundis*, has nothing to do with an alleged "redemption" on Wilde's part, but is rather a light versus a more solemn treatment of the politics of inside/outside social relations.[14] Although he treated it with varying degrees of levity, this political problem was a consistent one for Wilde and is a persistent element in his works. Unlike most of his confused and tragic generation, Wilde saw the problem as political and treated it as such.

During the three trials, which terminated with Wilde's and Alfred Taylor's sentencing, with the exception of one daily and one weekly journal (the *Daily Chronicle* and *Reynolds's Newspaper*), the London press was uniformly hostile to Wilde; and frequently its hostility was directed toward art, education, and "idleness" as well as toward homosexuality. After the conviction the *Daily Telegraph* wrote that "No sterner rebuke could well have been inflicted on some of the artistic tendencies of the time than the condemnation of Oscar Wilde at the Central Criminal Court. . . . The man has now suffered the penalties of his career, and may well be allowed to pass from that platform of publicity which he loved into the limbo of disrepute and oblivion which is his due. The grave of contemptuous oblivion may rest on his foolish ostentation, his empty paradoxes, his incurable vanity." Through the press, the middle class complacently chastened the "upper sections of society" in which Wilde had "enjoyed a certain popularity." The article continues, "Young men at the universities, silly women who lend an ear to any chatter which is petulant and vivacious, novelists who have sought to imitate the style of paradox and unreality, poets who have lisped the language of nerveless and effeminate libertinage—these are the persons who should ponder with themselves the doctrines and the career of the man who has now to undergo the righteous sentence of the law." The *Evening News* attacked the Aesthetic school, "a centre of intellectual corruption," and called for the corrective of public opinion to terminate the fashion of conceding immoral license to men of genius. The editor also imitated Wilde's legal prosecutors in his rebuke to the lower-class young men who had crossed the boundaries of class and intellectual pretense in their association with artists: "Light has been let in upon them now in a very decisive fashion, and we venture to hope that the conviction of Wilde for these abominable vices, which were the natural outcome of his diseased intellectual condition, will be a salutary warning to the unhealthy boys who posed as sharers of his culture." The *Echo* wrote: "The best thing for everybody now is to forget all about Oscar Wilde, his perpetual posings, his aesthetical teachings and his theatrical productions. Let him go into silence, and be heard no more."[15]

During the trials not only were Wilde's own works, particularly *The Picture of Dorian Gray* and "Phrases and Philosophies for the Use of the Young," used as evidence against him, but he was also called to answer for the alleged immorality of others' works, like "The Priest and the Acolyte," *A Rebours*, and Alfred Douglas's sonnets.[16] In the first trial, which terminated with the prosecution's admission of justified libel in order to avert Queensberry's witnesses against Wilde, the defense played to the jury with such statements as Edward Carson's insult to Wilde, "I do not profess to be an artist; and when I hear you give evidence, I am glad I am not."[17] In Carson's opening speech for the defense he emphasized the confluence of art, crime, and the lower classes in Taylor's establishment: "Taylor has in fact been the right-hand man of Mr. Wilde in all the orgies in which artists and valets have taken part." Carson mocked the highbrow artist whose standard for his readers seemed to be at odds with that for his companions: "[Wilde] took up with Charles Parker, a gentleman's servant, whose brother was a gentleman's servant; with young Alphonse Conway, who sold papers on the pier at Worthing; and with Scarfe, also a gentleman's servant.

Then his excuse was no longer that he was dwelling in regions of art but that he had such a noble, such a democratic soul [laughter in the court], that he drew no social distinctions, and that it was quite as much pleasure to have the sweeping boy from the streets to lunch or dine with him as the greatest *literateur* [sic] or artist."[18]

Throughout the second and third trials, in which Alfred Taylor was Wilde's co-defendant, the counsel for the Crown, first Charles Frederick Gill and then Frank Lockwood, the solicitor-general, attempted to get extended mileage out of Taylor's having independent means, frequently stating that his habitual mode of living was "idle" and "extravagant." In the third trial the verdict of guilty for Taylor preceded Wilde's trial but the sentencing was deferred until after the verdict on Wilde had been reached. During the cross-examination the solicitor-general asked Taylor how he had met the Parker brothers. Taylor replied that he was having a drink after the theater. "Following your usual custom of doing nothing?" Lockwood demanded. "Yes, if that's what you call doing nothing," Taylor replied.

Although the prosecution and press overgeneralized and put to execrable use their association of art and "crime," it should be noted that two of the leading artistic journals of the time had openly contributed to the pro-homosexual literature of the period. *The Artist and Journal of Home Culture*, under the editorship of Charles Kains-Jackson from 1888 through 1894, and *The Studio*, under that of his friend Joseph Gleeson White in 1893, were the vehicles of polemical and research articles on homosexuality as well as a good deal of homosexual poetry and fiction. Until 1895 contributors to these two journals formed an informal, migratory artistic coterie, first at Christchurch, then in Chiswick, then in London. At these locations visitors met other visitors of similar tastes, two of which were a love of arts and the Greek philosophical tradition of pederasty.[19] At Oxford, such grown-up journals were imitated by the undergraduate *Chameleon* and *Spirit Lamp*. On 19 November 1894 John Francis Bloxam wrote from Exeter College to Kains-Jackson that he had discussed the founding of the *Chameleon* with Wilde and George Ives at Ives's home, where Wilde promised him aphorisms.[20] Under the editorship of Alfred Douglas, the *Spirit Lamp* was advertised as for "all who are interested in modern life and the new culture"—the new culture being one coterie's term for homosexuality.

Like the prosecution and hostile press, popular criminology also linked crime and art—thereby conditioning middle-class suspicion of art and encouraging their divorce; and today it is impossible to know who took the vocabulary of disease, degeneration, and genius from whom. Several books by the Italian criminologist Cesare Lombroso (1836-1909) had been translated into English and were popular enough that in prison Wilde cited Lombroso's theories on "the intimate connection between madness and the literary and artistic temperament" in his appeal to the Home Secretary for an attenuated sentence.[21]

Lombroso's *Man of Genius*, included in the Contemporary Science Series edited by Havelock Ellis, specifically addressed itself to the connection between education, superior intelligence, art, and crime. His enumeration of symptoms of insanity reads like a checklist of the elements of Wilde's style, literary and personal: "In literature and science, a tendency to puns and plays upon words, an excessive fondness for systems, a tendency to speak of one's self, and substitute epigram for logic, an extreme predilection for the rhythm and assonances of verse in prose writing, even an exaggerated degree of originality may be considered as morbid phenomena. So also is the mania of writing in Biblical form, in detached verses, and with special favourite words, which are underlined, or repeated many times, and a certain graphic symbolism." Lombroso urged that students, and especially politicians, beware lest "geniuses" usurp power over the "true normal man, the man who works and eats." Signs of the imminence of such a crisis are the proliferation of abstract systems for social reform, systems particularly containing "declamation, assonances, paradoxes, and conceptions often original, but always incomplete and contradictory," systems, that is, which "take the place of calm reasoning based on a minute and unprejudiced study of facts."[22]

In Lombroso's *Crime: Its Causes and Remedies*, sexual crimes and crimes of fraud are "the specific crimes of advanced civilization." Regarding the former, he wrote, "It seems that the more a man's psychic activity increases, the more the number of his needs and tastes for pleasures grows, especially when his mind is not occupied with great scientific and humanitarian ideas, and when his wealth permits an over-abundant diet. Of all these, the sexual need is certainly that which is most keenly felt, and this is that which, throughout the whole animal world, is in the closest connection with the cerebral system."[23] Journalists, too, perceived the connection between sex and cerebration, not only in *The Artist* and *The Studio*, but in the traditions of Oxford. Brian Reade has traced the beginnings of the enormous increase in male romantic-erotic literature between 1850 and 1895 to the writings and all-male community of the Tractarians, particularly

Newman, his close friend Richard Hurrell Froude, and his intensely devoted Frederick William Faber.[24] The term "pervert," which, as Lombroso might have said, was a special favorite, underlined and repeated so many times in the press and popular criminology, had been once reserved for the Oxford converts to Roman Catholicism; genius, mysticism, and surreptitious sexuality formed another notorious triad in representations of colleges as well as those of monasteries and convents in gothic novels. By the 1890's, the *Spirit Lamp*, to which Wilde contributed, and the *Chameleon*, which included "The Priest and the Acolyte," the two poems by Douglas that elicited such scrutiny during the trials, and Wilde's "Phrases and Philosophies for the Use of the Young," seemed to indicate to the middle classes that the products of "genius" and "education" required some immediate control.

As preventatives of such "sexual excesses" as adultery and pederasty, Lombroso recommended greater facility of divorce and "the diffusion of prostitution in the agricultural districts, and especially in localities where there are a large number of sailors, soldiers, and laborers. It is especially necessary to make sexual intercourse accessible to all dissolute-minded young men."[25] Although Lombroso did not hesitate to suggest the indenture of women to cure the excesses of heterosexual men, he made no similar provisions for men who could not be redirected toward women. Occasional ("criminaloid") offenders needed only sustain "a conditional punishment," for once out of barracks and colleges they would revert to legitimate sexual access. "Born" offenders, on the other hand, "who manifest their evil propensities from childhood without being determined by special causes," should "be confined from their youth, for they are a source of contagion and cause a great number of occasional criminals."[26]

In addition to Lombroso's recommendations for jurists in *Crime: Its Causes and Remedies*, in the conclusion of *The Man of Genius* he set down principles of literary criticism: "What I have hitherto written may, I hope (while remaining within the limits of psychological observation), afford an experimental starting-point for a criticism of artistic and literary, sometimes also of scientific, creations." The most explicit attack on artists as criminals duly came from his pupil and friend—their books are dedicated to each other—Max Nordau. This attack was entitled *Entartung* (1893) and was translated into English as *Degeneration* in 1895. Wilde also referred to Nordau's chapter on "Oscar Wilde" in his petition to the Home Office, while Bernard Shaw, in less personal jeopardy, answered Nordau in the

American paper *Liberty* (1895) and later republished his essay for the New Age Press (1908) under the title *The Sanity of Art: An Exposure of the Current Nonsense About Artists Being Degenerate.*[27]

As Shaw succinctly put it, the message of Nordau's massive, very popular text was "that all our characteristically modern works of art are symptoms of disease in the artists, and that these diseased artists are themselves symptoms of the nervous exhaustion of the race by overwork." The point of Book 1 ("Fin-de-Siècle") of *Degeneration* was that the upper classes of European civilization were exhausted and deranged due to the rapid expansion of technology. There Nordau noted the deleterious effects of "railway spine" and "railway brain" as well as those of the press and postal systems. (Later in the book he would paradoxically argue that the symbolists' critique of science and Mallarmé's hesitancy to publish were also signs of degeneracy.) In his exposé of artists as carriers of the hereditary symptoms of the "fin-de-race" disease, Nordau not only finds all the French writers whom Arthur Symons heralded in *The Symbolist Movement in Literature* to be "imbeciles" and "idiots," but he includes chapters on Tolstoy and Wagner ("mystics" nostalgic for the "dark ages"), Whitman (a "vagabond," "reprobate rake," and "erotomaniac"), Ibsen, Wilde, and Nietzsche ("egomaniacs" who are directly contrary in their views to Nordau's ideal of "altruism"), and all French and German proponents of "realism" and "naturalism" (translated as the degenerate tendencies of "pessimism" and "obscenity").

Nordau, himself a novelist as well as a practicing physician, advocated the ordered progress of the community through the potentialities of the natural sciences. He saw the "style" and "word games" of much modern literature as elitist and detrimental to the social function of art. (His own positivist attitude toward language was indicated in his changing his name from Südfeld—southern field—to Nordau—northern meadow—when he broke from his Hungarian rabbinical family to enter the profession of journalism in Germany.[28]) Lombroso allowed that "the frequency of genius among lunatics and of madmen among men of genius explains the fact that the destiny of nations has often been in the hands of the insane; and shows how the latter have been able to contribute so much to the progress of mankind." Nordau, however, who had patience with nothing but normality and middle-class values like discipline and materialistic science, had no sympathy with any extraordinary attitudes or practices, including those of artists who felt themselves estranged from the larger work force.

Thus Nordau's critique of Wilde stems from the latter's dress and his criticism. (Wilde's literary works, says Nordau, are mere imitations of the degenerate mystics Rossetti and Swinburne.) For Nordau, Wilde's egomania is apparent in his eccentric dress, in his "hatred" of nature (so different from Nordau's organic view of humanity in the world), in his ideal of inactivity, and in his admiration of crime and "sin." The social body has a necessary duty to expel the egomaniac, and Nordau stresses that degenerates in thought are no less virulent than active degenerates. In the last chapter of his book he calls on "sane" members of society to pull in their stomachs, tighten their belts, clear their minds, and act.

Mystics, but especially ego-maniacs and filthy pseudo-realists, are enemies to society of the direst kind. Society must unconditionally defend itself against them. Whoever believes with me that society is the natural organic form of humanity, in which alone it can exist, prosper, and continue to develop itself to higher destinies; whoever looks upon civilization as a good, having value and deserving to be defended, must mercilessly crush under his thumb the anti-social vermin. To him, who with Nietzsche, is enthusiastic over the "freely-roving, lusting beast of prey," we cry, "Get you gone from civilization! . . . Our streets and our houses are not built for you; our looms have no stuffs for you; our fields are not tilled for you. All our labour is performed by men who esteem each other, have consideration for each other, mutually aid each other, and know how to curb their selfishness for the general good. There is no place among us for the lusting beast of prey; and if you dare return to us, we will pitilessly beat you to death with clubs."[29]

Here, as throughout his book, one can see why later socialists, and specifically advocates of socialist realism, could find sympathy with Nordau's views on art and society. (When Nordau died, the French Communist newspaper *Humanité* praised his "noble love for mankind" and hatred of bourgeois ideals.[30]) The apparent paradox of the bourgeois par excellence hailed as a hater of bourgeois ideals is explained by the fact that Nordau's 1895 attack on the effete upper classes with their hereditary degeneracy was later duplicated in the socialist attack on the effete, complacent bourgeoisie. Even Shaw admitted that in the course of his attack on art Nordau had incidentally said "many more true and important things than most of the counsel on the other side were capable of."[31]

After 1895 all Nordau's books as well as his activities in Paris were extensively covered by the British press. On one occasion, the entire front page of the Sunday Edition of the *Weekly Sun* reviewed *Degeneration* as book of the week (16 June 1895). The reviewer quotes Nordau at length and recommends the book with the greatest approbation "to the admiration of every honest, pure, and manly man." In a biographical sketch of Nordau on pages one and two of the *Westminster*, Wilde's biographer and devoted friend Robert Sherard interviewed Nordau, who was fulsome on his own achievements and industriousness. Since genius and disease were equated in his system, the physician was paradoxically proud that he had not healed himself: about one of his plays, *Der Krugel,* he observed that critics in Berlin "wrote that no such filth had ever been served up on the German stage before." Sherard concluded that Nordau was an example of industry, "indeed his only pleasure in life is in hard work. He has fully deserved all his success."[32]

A few critics exploited Nordau's middle-class conservatism for humorous effect. The *Daily Chronicle* (8 May 1896) cited Nordau's *Paradoxes* of 1885 to criticize his tendency toward generalization and his irritating ability to dictate on any subject whatsoever. If you know one woman, Nordau had claimed, you know them all, with but few exceptions. Be particularly wary of "the original woman," "for deviation from the type is in woman, in eighty cases out of the hundred, significant of disease." Finally even Lombroso had to criticize *Degeneration* in the pages of the *Century* for Nordau's exaggeration and misinterpretation of data. In *La Revue Blanche* (1 June 1896) Alfred Douglas lamented that "even that superior (although unconscious) humorist, Max Nordau, has great difficulty in discovering . . . symptoms of degeneracy" in Douglas's poems: "I say it with regret, for who would not wish to be a degenerate in company with Verlaine, Rossetti, Oscar Wilde and so many others?" A few weeks after Wilde left prison, a journalist in Paris asked his opinion on "Nordau's firm belief that all men of genius were mad." "I quite agree," the exile reportedly said, "with Dr. Nordau's assertion that all men of genius are insane, but Dr. Nordau forgets that all sane people are idiots."[33]

Although he could joke about Nordau, Wilde, like the most politically active among the homosexual circles, continued to be interested in the growing dissemination of sociological and criminological literature. In prison he had also requested William Douglas Morrison's *Criminology Series,* which included Lombroso's *Female Offender* and *Criminal Sociology* by Enrico Ferri, who was greatly influenced by Lombroso. Wilde had admired the prolific work on prison reform by Morrison, who was a chaplain at Wandsworth as well as a recognized criminologist, and he sent him a personal copy of *The Ballad of Reading Gaol.*

Nor were the less flamboyant scientists of the time able to ignore the work of Lombroso and Nordau. Francis Galton, who is recognized as the founder of eugenics, had published *Hereditary Genius: An Inquiry into Its Laws and Consequences* in 1869. He studied lines of descent of genius from 1660 to 1865 according to the reputations of British judges, statesmen,

Peers, commanders, literary men, men of science, poets, musicians, painters, divines, and senior classics of Cambridge; he included oarsmen and wrestlers of the north country as examples of inherited muscle and concluded with a chapter entitled "The Comparative Worth of Different Races." In his prefatory chapter to the edition of 1892, Galton acknowledged where Lombroso's, Nordau's, and his own findings converged:

> The relation between genius in its technical sense . . . and insanity had been much insisted upon by Lombroso and others, whose views of the closeness of the connection between the two are so pronounced that it would hardly be surprising if one of their more enthusiastic followers were to remark that so-and-so cannot be a genius, because he has never been mad nor is there a single lunatic in his family. I cannot go nearly so far as they, nor accept a moiety of their data. . . . Still, there is a large residuum of evidence which points to a painfully close relation between the two, and I must add that my own later observations have tended in the same direction, for I have been surprised at finding how often insanity or idiocy has appeared among the near relatives of exceptionally able men.[34]

The most disastrous abuse of such medical and psychological theorizing occurred in the notorious Pemberton-Billing libel trials of 1918. The internationally renowned dancer Maud Allan and J. T. Grein on behalf of the Independent Theatre jointly sued Noel Pemberton-Billing, a zealous, vice-crusading M.P., for publishing a libelous article on Grein's production of Wilde's *Salome*. The article, for which Pemberton-Billing took full responsibility, linked Allan, the Theatre, and its subscribers with "the Cult of the Clitoris." During the two trials, spanning three months, Pemberton-Billing conducted his own defense and called no fewer than fourteen witnesses, including Alfred Douglas, minor dramatic critics, and doctors of psychology. Pemberton-Billing justified his libel by claiming that "the exhibition of an overpowering but unnatural passion of a child of tender years for the prophet . . . culminating . . . in the presentation of a physical orgasm, is calculated to attract moral perverts who . . . seek sexual satisfaction in the watching of this exhibition by others. . . . *Salome* is calculated to do . . . harm not only to the young men and the young women, but to all who see it, by undermining them, even more than a German army itself."[35]

One Dr. Serrell Cooke, a witness for the defense and authority on psychosexual pathology, testified that *Salome* "was quite likely to light up dormant perversion in men who did not even know they possessed it, and in women." The same psychologist had become interested in the case upon reading in the press Grein's first testimony, largely in support of *Salome* as a work of art. Cooke said that he "came to the conclusion that [Grein] had some mental aberration from the peculiar way he replied to questions." (Grein's testimony exhibited shades of dandiacal wit.) It was the doctor's opinion, solicited by Pemberton-Billing's examination, that Grein should be "locked up." The dramatic critic from the *Morning Post* testified that *Salome* was "a drama of disease"; the part of the actress, "sadistic"; and that Herod was "suffering from erotomania." The judge advised that the jury take such "sworn evidence" very seriously, and the jury duly bowed to the opinions of these experts when it acquitted Pemberton-Billing.

So much for literary psychologizing. Regarding heredity, in an act of zeal and cruelty Pemberton-Billing stunned the entire courtroom by confronting Allan with newspaper clippings of her brother's execution in San Francisco for murdering two young girls. When the stricken dancer admitted the kinship, Pemberton-Billing asked her if her brother had not defiled the bodies, explaining to the objecting judge that he was trying to prove that sadism was hereditary. The case grew to outrageous proportions, including allegations of German plots that implicated Asquith and the very judge hearing the trial, and recent histories have linked it with a generals' plot to bring down Lloyd George's coalition government. (Further details are included in Appendix A.)

Unfortunately for many writers at the turn of the century, attacks on art were not perpetrated solely by megalomaniacal physicians and legislators encouraged by the press. Richard Le Gallienne, the major reader for the Bodley Head, and William Watson, a major contributor to the *Yellow Book*, called themselves counterdecadents and stolidly upheld a romantic-Victorian tradition in the face of what they considered the French-inspired impressionism of the likes of Wilde, Arthur Symons, and John Gray. The colored impressions of the so-called decadents exhibited "merely limited thinking" at best and unhealthy effeminacy at worst.[36] In his preface to Alfred Austin's *English Lyrics* (1890), Watson wrote:

> If poetry is not to sink altogether under the lethargy of an emasculate euphuism, and finally to die surfeited with unwholesome sweetmeats, crushed under a load of redundant ornament and smothered in artificial rose-leaves, the strenuous and virile temper which animates this volume must come to be more and more the temper of English song. . . . If we be wise we shall turn more and more to whatsoever singer scents his pages, not with livid and obnoxious *Fleurs du Mal*, but with the blossoms which English children gather in their aprons, and with the candid breath of our hearty English sky.

In Le Gallienne's "To the Reader" of his own *English Poems*, he emphasized, as did all the counterdecadents, the Englishness of his work and lamented that the temple of English art had become "a lazar-house of leprous men."[37] Since Le Gallienne had long befriended Wilde in his private life and had written numerous, indeed generous, appreciations of his and other "decadent" work, such rallying around the temple must be taken as less inspired by purity than politics and profit.

Only the subtlest authors could employ the decadent themes of the time and remain above suspicion. In the first entry of the first *Yellow Book*, "The Death of the Lion," Henry James included all the elements of decadence: a "fantastic book," a male narrator in love with a male literary lion, nominal sex changes in profusion, and the fall of an artist to publicity and an unworthy public. Yet the discreet James was responsible for no more than upholding the dignity of art and poking fun at authors who, like Mary Chavelita Dunne ("George Egerton"), masculinized their names so as to be better able to express the "larger view" on the New Woman and relationships between the sexes.

Amid such liberal, and illiberal, debate, several groups of men, a number of whom were included on either Nordau's or Watson's blacklist (or on both), were writing and publishing their own sexual manifestos. At the same time that Wilde was posing in the dominant society, the meaning and significance of his works and actions were interpreted differently by members of the homosexual community. As the literary skit *The Green Carnation* (1894) by Robert Hichens goes to great lengths to suggest, by putting Wilde's words in the mouth of the great aesthete Esmé Amarinth and Alfred Douglas's form and attitudes in the character of Lord Reggie Hastings, the unnatural flower that the uninitiated thought merely symbolic of an aesthetic school served also as a secret sign among men who loved men. In defending the "unnatural" flower to a lady who speaks of herself as the "superior officer" to her pubescent "soldier" son, Esmé paraphrases Wilde on the term "natural":

How I hate that word natural. . . . To me it means all that is middle-class, all that is of the essence of jingoism. . . . It might be a beautiful word, but it is the most debased coin in the currency of language. Certain things are classed as natural, and certain things are classed as unnatural—for all the people born into the world. Individualism is not allowed to enter into the matter. A child is unnatural if it hates its mother. A mother is unnatural if she does not wish to have children. A man is unnatural if he never falls in love with a woman. A boy is unnatural if he prefers looking at pictures to playing cricket, or dreaming over the white naked beauty of a Greek statue to a game of football under Rugby rules . . . [Yet] it is natural to one man to live like Charles Kingsley, to preach gentleness, and love sport; it is natural to another to dream away his life on the narrow couch of an opium den, with his head between a fellow-sinner's feet. I love what are called warped minds, and deformed natures. . . . There are only a few people in the world who dare to defy the grotesque code of rules that has been drawn up by that fashionable mother, Nature, and they defy—as many women drink, and many men are vicious—in secret, with the door locked and the key in their pockets. And what is life to them? They can always hear the footsteps of the detective in the street outside.[38]

We know that Wilde approved of *The Green Carnation*, for he advertised it in the original four-act version of *The Importance of Being Earnest*. In the search for his father's name, Jack mistakenly gives Lady Bracknell the novel rather than the *Army Lists* of the preceding 40 years, telling her to "bring [her] masculine mind to bear on this subject." True to the intentional confusion of gender roles in the quotation on the natural above, and to Lady Bracknell's "masculine" mind, Lady Bracknell responds that the "culture of exotics" in the novel seems to preclude the masculine military type: "This treatise, the 'Green Carnation,' as I see it is called, seems to be a book about the culture of exotics. It contains no reference to Generals in it."

Wilde was not the only writer of the period whose devaluation of nature (as in "nature imitates art") and the natural derived from sexual pleasures that were viewed by society as "unnatural." In his impassioned plea for the amendment of homosexual laws and the termination of social persecution of "urnings," "A Problem in Modern Ethics" (1891), J. A. Symonds, poet, literary critic, and collaborator with Havelock Ellis, repeatedly criticized the term "unnatural." It was precisely his discomfort with terms like "unnatural," "perverse," even the medical "invert" that resulted in his comically elaborate adaptations of K. H. Ulrich's categories of male sexuality: dioning, uraniaster, urning, mannling, weibling, zwischen-urning, virilized urning, uranodioning. Such a vocabulary produced rather bizarre English sentences like "Headmasters know how many Uraniasters they have dealt with, what excellent Dionings they become, and how comparatively rare, and yet how incorrigibly steadfast, are the genuine Urnings in their flock."[39] (Translation: Headmasters know how many occasional homosexuals they have dealt with, what excellent heterosexuals they become, and how comparatively rare, and yet how incorrigibly steadfast, are the genuine homosexuals in their flock.) Trying to distance himself from the prejudicial vocabulary of his times, Symonds found that his Germano-scientific vocabulary had the added advantage of distancing him from his own very anguished emotions. His multiplied, multiform vocabulary, like Wilde's epigrams and paradoxes, also sought to break down the conventional dualist vocabulary of natural/unnatural, normal/abnormal. Similarly, by 1913 Kains-Jackson was able to outline to Ross a personalized vocabulary that relieved the individual body of normative definitions altogether: "If instead of harping on the word 'abnormal' [the Psychiatry Committee of England] takes up the sound *physical* line that the normal is what to that person is normal, it will do much good."[40]

The more enthusiastic of Victorian heterosexuals also had to reconstruct nature. Although the official Victorian view of female sexuality was that it did not exist except for purposes of procreation, Victorian pornographers, who fought their own battles against current views of the natural, viewed nature from rather un-Victorian prospects. Steven Marcus uses their own clichés to describe their "representation of nature": "It is usually seen at eye-level. In the middle distance there looms a large irregular shape. On the horizon swell two immense snowy white hillocks; these are capped by great, pink, and as it were prehensile peaks or tips—as if the rosy-fingered dawn itself were playing just behind them. The landscape then undulates gently down to a broad, smooth, swelling plain, its soft rolling curves broken only in the lower center by a small volcanic crater or omphalos."[41] The essential image of nature in the pornographic utopia, says Marcus, is this immense, supine, female form. And nature thus defined exists "for the sole purpose of confirming the existence of its creator." That is, the insatiable and eternally accessible woman exists as the dominion of the fruitful, replenishing penis: an Eden of natural surplus.

As our contemporary historians of homosexuality have shown, the works of Wilde and the humiliation of Wilde that began in 1895 were watched with great, if dismayed, interest by both practicing and nonpracticing homosexuals, from the socialist Edward Carpenter living in Sheffield to J. A. Symonds.[42] Although many of these preferred the manly homoeroticism that they discerned in Whitman's poetry to what Symonds called the "morbid and perfumed" manner of *Dorian Gray*, the very absence of the name of the sins in Wilde's stories and novel indicated to some men of the "modern" same-sex preference the presence of a like mind. That is, in the absence of named sins in *Dorian Gray* and the stories, the middle-class journalists found the presence of the sin they despised and the members of the homosexual community found the presence of the sin they loved.

In other ways, too, Wilde apparently signed to fellow homosexuals. In a surprising review of Whitman's *November Boughs*, the great aesthete praised Whitman for, in effect, artlessness.[43] As Jeffrey Weeks has shown, a great appreciation of Whitman was an explicit point of contact among homosexuals like Symonds, Carpenter, George Ives, and Laurence Housman, the two latter being founders of the secret homosexual society of the 1890's, the Order of Chaeronea, as well as friends of Wilde. Symonds included in "A Problem in Modern Ethics" Whitman's indignant denial that such a construction could be put on the "comradeship" described in "Calamus"—a denial that had exceedingly frustrated Symonds. But despite Whitman, Symonds cited long passages from the poem in question as "idealistic" sanctions of homosexual love. In 1889 Wilde had discerned in Whitman's views "a largeness of vision, a healthy sanity, and a fine ethical purpose." He found the value of Whitman's work "in its prophecy not in its performance," and he heralded Whitman as a "prelude" to "a new era," "a precursor of a fresh type," a "factor in the heroic and spiritual evolution of the human being." "If poetry has passed him by," Wilde concluded, "philosophy will take note of him." Such high praise succeeded a long quotation in which Whitman states that *Leaves of Grass* "is avowedly the song of Sex, and Amativeness, and even Animality."

In like manner the homoeroticism of "The Portrait of Mr. W. H.," the references to hermaphroditism in "Pen, Pencil, and Poison," and the double life of Bunburying in *The Importance of Being Earnest* must have represented to the subculture the "posing" and "double lives" to which homosexuals were accustomed until very recently. Indeed, in an unpublished introduction to Wilde's letters to Ives, Louis Marlow, a friend of Ives, claims that Ives served as Wilde's "Bunbury" on a trip to visit a friend at Cambridge.[44] Although within the circle Ives and Kains-Jackson were looked upon as authorities to help indiscreet men out of frays, Ives himself was so discreet that after prison Wilde repeatedly rebuked him for his lack of courage. At Posillippo near Naples with Wilde, Douglas wrote to Ives parodying his mysterious epistles:

My dear G.,
 O showed me your letter. We are here at N or rather at P which is close to N. We met a charming fellow here yesterday. I wonder if you know him; his name is X and he lives at Z. He was obliged to leave R on account of a painful scandal connected with H and T. The weather here is D today but we hope it may soon be L again.
Yours in strictest privacy,
A.B.D.

A less discreet letter follows, and it concludes, doubtless to Ives's chagrin, "Oscar sends his love."[45]

 In his double life, Wilde established a balanced economy that pervaded not only his view of nature but art and production as well. Like his redefinition of the natural and the dialectics of his paradoxes, his theory of art for art's sake was linked with sexual pleasures contrary to bourgeois notions of productive or purposive sex. In two of the most controversial chapters (22 and 23) of Frank Harris's biography of Wilde, Wilde and Harris debate the merits of homosexual versus heterosexual love. Wilde's basic argument is against the unaesthetic bodies of Victorian women, particularly when they are pregnant, and the fact that their function as producers of children has wrenched from women the possibility of so-called nonpurposive, that is merely pleasurable, passion; just as domestic servitude had deprived women of the opportunity to pursue merely pleasing intellectual study. This argument is so typical of the defenses of homosexuality in the period's literature, and so contrived a justification of sexual desire, that Harris's account need not be particularly credited. Yet the components, sex for sex's sake and intellectual study for its own sake, are entirely consistent with Wilde's view of art for art's sake. As in Nordau's projected expulsion of the lustful beast and Lombroso's herding of prostitutes to save society from dissolute-minded young men, the Victorians advocated sexuality for the state at the expense of the citizen's sexual freedom and pleasure. This sexuality for the state, in combination with the likes of Nordau's prescriptive views of art for society, made up an ethos of productivity for art and sexuality. And this ethos was directly contrary to art for art's sake and "nonpurposive" sex.

In fact, both sides of the Victorian debate on sex proffered implicit or explicit economic metaphors or theories of "production." Although today Marcus's primitive psychoanalytic framework for interpreting Victorian pornography is increasingly dubious and his Freudian attitude toward his material and sex in general is needlessly grim and depressing, he is nonetheless correct to discern that the official Victorian papers on sexuality calculated the expense of spirit on an economic model of scarcity.[46] Against this model, in which an ounce of semen meant more to a man's health and well-being than forty of blood, pornography—as we have seen in *Teleny*—presented worlds of infinite resources, both economic and sexual. Similarly, we need not read the eleven volumes of *My Secret Life* (c. 1890) to know that the anonymous author's emotional distance from his women partners was due to the Victorian economic and class structure that turned women into commodities: for woman-as-commodity is a figure pervading even the most respectable Victorian novels. And of course Victorian pornography itself is dominated by a kind of (male) consumerism.

Art for Love's Sake

That good women were no more than the means of reproduction was not only Wilde's alleged complaint to Harris but also the source of the antifeminist thread running through the polemical homosexual literature of the period. Foucault has posited this "hysterization of women's bodies" in the course of the eighteenth and nineteenth centuries, and we saw an example of it in Chapter 2 in Baudelaire's treatment of George Sand. Foucault describes the process in terms of sexual politics:

A hysterization of women's bodies: a threefold process whereby the feminine body was analyzed—qualified and disqualified—as being thoroughly saturated with sexuality; whereby it was integrated into the sphere of medical practices, by reason of a pathology intrinsic to it; whereby, finally, it was placed in organic communication with the social body (whose regulated fecundity it was supposed to ensure), the family space (of which it had to be a substantial and functional element), and the life of children (which it produced and had to guarantee, by virtue of a biologico-moral responsibility lasting through the entire period of the children's education); the Mother, with her negative image of "nervous woman," constituted the most visible form of this hysterization.[47]

In "The New Chivalry" (from *The Artist*, April 1894), Kains-Jackson argues that now that England is militarily stable, she need not concern herself with population; real "civilization" may consequently and finally flower under the "new chivalry" of more spiritual, more intellectual male love.[48] Part of the reason, of course, that love between males was more spiritual and more intellectual was that in many cases it was unconsummated. Many homosexual men of the time were so accustomed to frustration, through their own reticence or others', that they habitually valued contemplation (e.g., of the beloved) above activity, which was often associated with sex with a woman. Symonds wrote to his sister in disillusionment the morning after his wedding night. He had hoped that marriage would save him from his illicit desires. It did not. "So action is always less essential than contemplation," he writes. "But after it is done, a sense of inadequacy and incompleteness, proceeding from the contrast between the deed meditated and the deed accomplished, springs up."[49] Although Wilde was not one to be reticent, his comic insistence upon "the importance of doing nothing" may well have a similar source.

Certainly the association of activity and sex with women was as common in homosexual literature as that between material production and sex with women. In *Homogenic Love* (1894), even the mild, socialist Edward Carpenter says: "It may indeed be doubted whether the higher heroic and spiritual life of a nation is ever quite possible without the sanction of this attachment [that is, "Dorian" or homosexual love] in its institutions; and it is not unlikely that the markedly materialistic and commercial character of the last age of European civilized life is largely to be connected with the fact that the *only* form of love and love-union that is recognized has been one founded on the quite necessary but comparatively materialistic basis of matrimonial sex-intercourse and child-breeding."[50] And Marc-André Raffalovich's poem "Put on That Languor" contrasts the affectation of idleness characterizing some of the homosexuals of the time with the industrious activity of a materialistic age.[51] A later Uranian poet went so far as to claim that a boy lover was more economical than heterosexual procreation: for a boy could satisfy both sexual desire and a desire for children.[52]

From the argument that women were biologically materialist, it followed in the minds of such poets that women were industrious, and they were consequently lumped together with the distasteful aspects of an artificial industrial age. With them could thus be contrasted the beautiful young boy in nature or sport, as "Philebus" (John Leslie Barford) contrasted them in his pretty *Young Things*:

> Is it unnat'ral that I should joy
>   To join in the heart of natural things?
> To run and swim and ride with you, my boy?
>   To feel the thrill that sweating effort brings?
> To watch with envious love your limbs' display?
>   Or should I chase some chocolate-chewing girl?
> Pass in a cinema a sunny day
>   And nightly in a dusty dance-hall whirl?

That girls must be held in contempt for chewing chocolate is, however, forgotten in *Fantasies*, when a boy offers Philebus a morsel and the poet poignantly takes it all:

> If a boy all suddenly thrust in *your* hand
> Some chocolate, *you* would laugh
> And, failing entirely to understand
> His meaning, would give him half.
> Though loudly I laughed, yet a tear I hid,
> As *I* took the lot from the funny kid.

In the long run the sharpest among the proponents of these anti-action and anti-materialist arguments and metaphors were troubled by the contradiction that although the bodies of women were gross and produced gross, material fruits, the bodies of men and boys were themselves just as material. With the exception of one petition to the Home Office from prison, in which Wilde humbly repents and excuses his "vice" as "madness" (an obvious pose for obvious reasons), he insisted to the last that he did "not hold with the British view of morals that sets Messalina above Sporus";[53] yet in his post-conviction letters he does frequently regret his earlier "materialism." When homosexuals sought to defend themselves by way of critiques of materialism and consumerism they were caught in the most serious and pervasive contradiction of the age.

Here it need only be noted that in the rather extensive homosexual literature of the century—fiction, poetry, and polemic—a tradition Wilde participated in to a limited degree but knew fully, one finds some shame, more social persecution, but for the most part candor and affection on the parts of the writers. The tradition predominantly includes, that is, exactly what we might expect: a love literature for and about men, ranging from the idealistic and chivalric to the openly sexual. There is, for example, a quite distinct genre of encomia on boys bathing. It was probably the extent of this literature, and the support of the community that produced it, that saved its members from the overwhelming guilt that the larger society expected of them. Homosexuals who felt guilt were probably too fearful to publish or to participate in the community in the first place.

Although 1895 began an enforced hiatus, unpublished correspondence of the early 1890's proves the community's political and polemical solidarity. In September 1893 the young Alfred Douglas very enthusiastically praised Kains-Jackson's "New Chivalry."[54] Answering a letter in which Kains-Jackson had criticized Wilde and his "jeweled" prose style, Douglas defended his friend and concluded, "Perhaps nobody knows as I do what he [i.e., Wilde] has done for the 'new culture,' the people he has pulled out of the fire, and 'seen through' things not only with money, but by sticking to them when other people wouldn't speak to them." Through his 1890's correspondence Douglas consistently agitated for homosexual rights and penal reform. He had tactfully done so in the pages of the *Spirit Lamp*. In an editorial "Memoriam" for Symonds, Douglas lamented that Symonds had died before completing his political and literary work: "there were chains he might have loosened, and burdens he might have lifted; chains on the limbs of lovers and burdens on the wings of poets."[55]

Douglas's largely suppressed and very forthright articles of outrage after Wilde's imprisonment, however much he falsified and repudiated them in his later Catholic and celibate life, remain testimony to the courage and precocity that Wilde must have loved in him. (These later writings receive comment in Appendix B.) In November 1894 Douglas wrote Ives concerning a suicide reported in the paper of an unnamed man of social position who had been charged with assault on one or more boys. Douglas wanted a full-scale scandal so as to educate the public and prevent cause for any more suicides. He also begged Ives to publicize in this connection an earlier death of an Oxford history professor under similar circumstances. In November 1894 Douglas wrote to Kains-Jackson asking legal advice or practical help for a man called Bernard awaiting trial for a similar offense. In April 1895, he scrawled distraught letters to Ives and Kains-Jackson for some help for Wilde. "Do you know no strong fearless man who will stand up?" he asked. Ives and Kains-Jackson did not, but there were a few. James H. Wilson, a Quaker, had written articles in *Reynolds's* on the blackmail industry of male prostitutes and reform of the law of 1885, and he wanted to publish attacks on the authorities during Wilde's trials throughout July-October 1895. Ross and More Adey, however, prevented him, feeling that such publicity would harm Wilde.

Yet until 1895 Wilde seems to have been amused by his ability to pose and pass, and consequently to get the best of both worlds. Take, for example, a real incident involving the green carnation. In *Salome*, the daughter of Herodias promised a young captain who was loved by a page a "little green flower" on the condition that he release to her John the Baptist. During Wilde's lifetime and in later criticism, this particular green flower, the green carnation, has been taken as a symbol of the aesthetic movement. It has been interpreted as a symbol of dandyism or decadence, of the triumph of the artificial over Nature and things called "natural." In W. Graham Robertson's account of the premiere of *Lady Windermere's Fan*, he discussed Wilde's plan for the flower, a plan that would turn the audience itself into an object of artifice, that would make the audience play a role, replete with props, in the theater—even though only an initiated few would be aware of the precise nature of the role. Wilde requested that Robertson wear a green carnation at the premiere and that he persuade as many men as he could to do likewise. Many others, Wilde told him, had already promised to do so. It would "annoy the public," Wilde said. "But why annoy the public?" Robertson asked. Wilde responded: "It likes to be annoyed. A young man on the stage will wear a green carnation; people will stare at it and wonder. Then they will look round the house and see every here and there more and more little specks of mystic green. 'This must be some secret symbol,' they will say. 'What on earth can it mean?'" "And what does it mean?" said Robertson. "Nothing whatever," said Wilde, "but that is just what nobody will guess."[56]

Wilde was disingenuous here, for although most English were unaware

Upon publication of Alfred Douglas's *Oscar Wilde and Myself*, 1914.

of it, he, like Robert Hichens, knew that the distinctive green carnation was the emblem worn by homosexuals in Paris.[57] By encouraging members of the audience to wear the flower, Wilde not only made them part of the performance, forcing them to regard themselves, but he also created an amusing drama for his own entertainment. If he was compelled to double as heterosexual, he had the pleasure at the premiere of watching straight men unwittingly bearing the emblem of homosexuality. When he strolled onto the stage with a cigarette and casually remarked upon the role of the audience in the performance—"I congratulate you on the *great* success of your performance"—he did not, of course, explain the particular joke that had contributed to his enjoyment of the show.

Such, then, was the social climate in which Wilde led his double life, and such was his attitude toward it. Two of his works directly and indirectly deal with his attitudes toward the body and toward the larger society that limited the body's activities. *Salome* was written in France just prior to the events (1892-93) for which Wilde was indicted three years later, that is, for his relations with young men, many of whom were associated with Alfred Taylor's rooms on Little College and Chapel Streets. *The Ballad of Reading Gaol* was composed in 1897, just after Wilde's release from prison. *Salome* liberates and communicates physical desire; *Reading Gaol*, on the other hand, portrays the confinement and punishment of the bodies of men who are almost exclusively characterized as lovers.

With *Salome*, Wilde expected, in a more forthright manner than with the trick of the green carnation, to confront Victorian audiences with their own sexuality. In the work that he felt was his best illustration of art for art's sake, through the figure of Salome, he portrayed sex for sex's sake, without purpose or production. Within the play, Salome subverts the laws and authority of the Tetrarch and the Kingdom. If she succeeds on stage, she makes the audience uncomfortable and subverts the laws of the theater. Yet literary—unlike dramatic—critics have largely avoided the subversive themes of the play through criticism that either seeks authorial forefathers or focuses on psychoanalysis of Wilde. The first of these two critical traditions more often than not concurs with one of the first reviews of the book: that "*Salome* is the daughter of too many fathers. She is the victim of heredity" (*Pall Mall Gazette*, 27 February 1893). The second tradition has read the play entirely from the male characters' points of view, imputing to Wilde internal landscapes of voyeurism, castration fears, and sadomasochism. The emphasis there has been on the viewpoint of male characters, rather than on sadomasochism in the terms of some of our own contemporary discussions—as ritual exchanges of power—which may well be more appropriate.[58]

Yet when Wilde himself imagined his play on stage, he envisioned a synaesthetic picture, appealing to the aural, visual, and olfactory faculties, and emphasizing Salome's effect on the audience. Salome's words were "like music"; he first wanted her to be costumed in shades of yellow, then in gold or silver, then green like a lizard, then as unadorned as Victorian stages would permit; he wanted braziers of perfume wafting scented clouds before spectacular sets. Before the British censor intervened, he and Sarah Bernhardt planned how best to affect the audience. He consistently stressed that Salome, rather than Herodias, Herod, or Iokanaan, was to be the focus for the audience.[59] And this emphasis would result in the audience's unavoidable focus on itself.

Art for Love's Sake

In fact, howsoever Wilde's comedies finally work with the audience, *Salome* is the only one of his plays that seems as if it could have been constructed on the models articulated by Artaud in the "First Manifesto" of the Theater of Cruelty:

Every spectacle will contain a physical and objective element, perceptible to all. Cries, groans, apparitions, surprises, theatricalities of all kinds, magic beauty of costumes taken from certain ritual models; resplendent lighting, incantational beauty of voices, the charms of harmony, rare notes of music, colors of objects, physical rhythm of movements whose crescendo and decrescendo will accord exactly with the pulsation of movements familiar to everyone, concrete appearances of new and surprising objects, masks, effigies yards high, sudden changes of light, the physical action of light which arouses sensations of heat and cold, etc.[60]

Salome's words were "like music," Wilde wrote, a repetitive, obsessive melody. "It is not a question of suppressing the spoken language, but of giving words approximately the importance they have in dreams," wrote Artaud. And his collapsing of the stage into the auditorium seems a perfect metaphorical or psychological description of *Salome*:

THE STAGE—THE AUDITORIUM: We abolish the stage and the auditorium and replace them by a single site, without partition or barrier of any kind, which will become the theater of the action. A direct communication will be re-established between the spectator and the spectacle, between the actor and the spectator, from the fact that the spectator, placed in the middle of the action, is engulfed and physically affected by it.

Moreover, the fatal human determinism—as Artaud says, "sometimes bloody"—of the relation between the sexual and social in Wilde's play is consistent with Artaud's notion of the inescapable cruelty of modern life. To suffer this effect in the dynamic of the play is to go beyond both traditional literary psychologizing of Herod, Iokanaan, or Wilde and histories of literary and visual representations of the figure of Salome.

It is Salome's peculiar distinctions that bring such anarchy to Herod's kingdom. Unlike the Salome of the Gospels, Wilde's dancer is not a pawn for her mother's political maneuvering. "I cannot conceive of a Salome," Wilde reportedly told Gomez Carrillo, "who is unconscious of what she does, a Salome who is but a silent and passive instrument." Others in the play wait passively for signs and symbols: Herodias's page sees ill omens in the moon; the young Syrian captain watches Salome; Herod fears meteorological signs and the Baptist's prophecies; the soldiers watch the face of Herod; and the Jews, Nazarenes, and Romans watch for the Messias and Caesar. Yet Salome, self-absorbedly confident, attends to nothing but her own desires. When she looks at the moon, she sees only an image of herself: "She is cold and chaste. I am sure she is a virgin. . . . She has never abandoned herself to men, like other goddesses." Salome does not depend on others to make meanings for her (she is not an ideological pawn), so she cannot be fooled by court politics. She scorns the soldiers' caution, saying immediately that the Tetrarch fears Iokanaan; similarly, she knows, contrary to the soldiers' equivocation, that her mother is the object of the prophet's curse.

Her insistent seduction of the infatuated Narraboth—"Thou wilt do this thing for me. . . . Thou knowest it. . . . I know that thou wilt do this thing"—indicates her awareness of the sexual power she will later use against Herod. Throughout her catalogue of the parts of Iokanaan's body, her metaphoric flights relentlessly appropriate the man. Her images turn negative only when he rejects her, and they end with her fixation on his nay-saying mouth. When Iokanaan will not look at her, Salome waits. She will not be insistent again until she demands her prize from Herod. Then she calls to Herodias's page, who was cheated by her of his lover Narraboth. To the page, left, like herself, unsatisfied, she gives the terrible dictum: "there are not dead men enough."

Against Salome's law, that she get what she wants, Wilde counterposes Herod's secular law and Iokanaan's divine law. About these Wilde is initially satirical. Herod is a wit who comes on stage making jokes about the "ridiculous" Stoics who slay themselves, praising Caesar for writing satires, and lamenting Narraboth's suicide in ironic terms: "His father was a king. I drave him from his kingdom. And of his mother, who was a queen, you made a slave, Herodias. So he was here as my guest, as it were." He is later reduced to an absurd indecisiveness, not knowing whether he is happy or sad, whether Salome should dance or not, whether Caesar will come or not, and whether the Baptist's prophecies should be heeded or not.

Surrounding Herod are those, like Iokanaan, who "only believe in things that one cannot see," that is, they are directly opposed to Salome, for whom the body is the soul. (Wilde said elsewhere that "those who see any difference between body and soul have neither.") The Jews and Nazarenes dispute whether the Messias has come or not, whether God is in evil as well as good, whether angels exist or not, and whether the Messias was last seen in Samaria or Jerusalem. Throughout these quibblings, the effect of which is comic, Iokanaan's voice from the cistern prophesies the death of Herodias and the coming of Messias bearing the fan of the Lord—prophecies which in the scope of the play are wrong in all specifics.

With her mother's sanction, Salome subverts both divine and secular law to get the body of Iokanaan. As she comes closer to her object, Wilde also has it that she accomplishes the destruction of the kingdom. Knowing that Herod's potency as Tetrarch is dependent on his keeping his word, on his ability to maintain an image of authority in the eyes of the people, Salome relentlessly pursues his oath to her. Herod is thus caught in a double bind: if he does not kill the prophet, his word will henceforth be ineffectual in the community; on the other hand, his own superstitious fear of Iokanaan's divine prophecies prevents him from killing the prophet with a clear pagan conscience. In addition, killing the prophet will cause havoc among Herod's own diverse population.

When he is finally forced to submit to the law that a king fulfill his oath, his submission includes an effective abdication of authority. When he says "Hereafter let no king swear an oath," he cuts off his office of making commitments to his people. "I will not," he says, "look at things, I will not suffer things to look at me. Put out the torches! Hide the moon! Hide the stars! Let us hide ourselves in our palace, Herodias." Thus the Tetrarch removes himself from the sight of his people and obliterates his ability to personify the law. With "It is not wise to find symbols in everything that one sees," and "Only in mirrors is it well to look, for mirrors do but show us masks," Herod repudiates the desire that comes from looking and from its inexorable result, in the play, in the fetishism of objects. But while such a move to some extent releases him from Salome's erotic power, it remains suicidal; for there can be no central authority without the visible symbol of sovereign power in the aspect of the king. In retiring to his mirror, Herod abandons his subjects to their own versions of Salome's subjectivity, thus creating a state of anarchy. One can only assume that it is his order to kill Salome (his soldiers crush her beneath their shields) that has permitted critics to see the Tetrarch as triumphant and "strong." But since her death does not alter the political impotence of his last lines, which are "Let us hide ourselves in our palace, Herodias. I begin to be afraid," we can only see Herod's triumph as fanciful.

Divine law, as well, is explicitly subverted. By consistent perversion of the language of Scripture, Wilde makes it clear that the ruling divinity of the play is sexual desire.[61] Trying to divert Salome's desire for the Baptist, Herod scandalizes the Jews by offering the dancer the veil of the sanctuary. As Salome makes lawless love to the head of Iokanaan, Herodias preempts the Father's Word from Luke 3:22 upon the descent of the Dove, "Thou art my beloved Son; in thee I am well pleased" with "I am well pleased with my daughter," fulfilling the promise and prophecy of the Word in Salome. Where Herod and Iokanaan had "heard in the air a beating of wings" and Iokanaan had foreseen the coming of Another bearing "the fan of the Lord," Salome dances with "feet like white doves" and her mother repeatedly calls for her "fan," speaking in the words of the Dove and fanning herself while Salome embraces the head. The baptism of fire that Iokanaan had prophesied is fulfilled in the fire that "did fill [Salome's] veins" and which she had communicated to Herod.[62] This Pentecostal vision of fire and doves, spoken in the new tongue of sexual love, celebrates the triumph of Salome and her mother. The feast is served on a silver charger.

Wilde's *Salome* posits the castration of the forces of law and order by the forces of illicit sexual desire. Wilde's recorded statements on the subject and Beardsley's androgynous decorations confirm that Wilde chose a girl to represent desire in order to organize a struggle against the forces of law. We have already seen the period's "hysterization," or sexualizing, of the female body: Wilde used it here for sexual politics. The language of *Salome* resembles most closely the jeweled language of Wilde's dialogues or "The Sphinx": the language that, as we have seen in Chapter 1, was employed for seduction. But here Wilde moves beyond a community of select young men to try to seduce a general audience. His statement about *Salome* in *De Profundis*, that he "took the drama, the most objective form known to art, and made it as personal a mode of expression as the lyric or the sonnet," also confirms that *Salome* was his personal fantasy of the triumph of sexual love over the repressive forces of society.[63] But the "personal mode of expression" to which Wilde refers is duplicated in the effect of Salome on audiences: she confronts them with their own desire.

Literary critics have been able to avoid this aspect of the play.[64] All reviews of performances of the play and of Richard Strauss's opera *Salome*, on the other hand, confirm that the success of the performance depends upon Salome's ability to excite the audience—as in the following two examples, both from typical audiences of Wilde's time.

The first is Max Beerbohm's review of a poor (private) performance at the Bijou Theatre in 1905. Beerbohm first complains that the head was obviously cardboard, recognition of which spoiled the audience's illusion of Salome's real sexual desire. He insists that with Sarah Bernhardt and proper setting the play could have been superb; but in this performance the attraction of Salome was hopelessly diffused by the propriety of the

Edwardian actress: "The actress at the Bijou Theatre was just a young lady—a clever young lady, a conscientious and promising young lady. . . . To think that a young English lady in the twentieth century could have been so badly brought up as to behave in so outrageous a manner! We looked severely at her mother. Was she not ashamed? But no; not a day older nor a degree less ladylike than her daughter. . . . There was only one thing for us to do; to strike them both off our visiting-lists" (*Saturday Review*, 13 May 1905). Thus where Wilde intended that Salome—a princess, but not a lady—command the stage, actresses constricted by Edwardian carriage and costume were themselves the object of commanding censoriousness. Beerbohm's mock severity with Herodias for bringing up such an "outrageous" English young lady indicates that the depiction of Salome as an authentic demiurge was simply incompatible with the position of women in Edwardian England. To attempt such a part was merely for the unfortunate actress to be publicly rebuked for her lack of modesty.

On the other hand, a production of the Strauss opera at the Metropolitan Opera House in New York in 1907 was reviewed by Richard Aldrich as supremely successful. Preceded by sensational advertising, the opera drew a crowd "such as no previous opera [had] drawn to the Metropolitan." Aldrich described Salome's effect on the audience: "After the curtain went up on 'Salome' there was no sensation until the dance began. It was the dance that women turn away from and many of the women in the Metropolitan Opera House last night turned away from it. Very few men in the audience seemed comfortable. They twisted in their chairs, and before it was over there were numbers of them who decided to go to the corridors and smoke" (*New York Times*, 23 January 1907). Wilde had tricked an audience of heterosexual men into wearing the emblem of homosexuality. With *Salome*, a marvel of mimetic desire, he thought to involve the audience in an aura of desire.

The subsequently much maligned examiner Edward Pigott, who in 1892 refused to license the play for public performance, had predicted the response of the audience at the Met. Like Wilde, Pigott foresaw the play's effect on the British public, so while he could not in good conscience release it for the theater, he passed it on to the lively imaginations of his own private circle. His letter to Spencer Ponsonby is one of the surviving treats of censorship:

I must send you, for your *private* edification and amusement, this MS. of a 1 act piece . . . written by Oscar Wilde! It is a miracle of impudence. . . . [Salome's] love turns to fury because John will not let her kiss him *in the mouth*—and in the last scene, where she brings in his head—if you please—on a 'charger'—*she does kiss his mouth, in a paroxysm of sexual despair.*

The piece is written in French—half Biblical, half pornographic—by Oscar Wilde himself.

Imagine the average British public's reception of it.[65]

If *Salome* was the fantasy of triumphant sexual love, *The Ballad of Reading Gaol* was the triumph of the forces of law. In his subjective vision of prison as a place where lovers go when they have killed the thing they love, in his erotic images during the night as he sympathetically suffers with the condemned man, and in his outbursts against the dehumanizing forces of the Law, the narrator of *Reading Gaol* bears the stamp of Salome's subjectivity and rebelliousness. Yet Wilde's critics, who typically find his prison experience a more decisive turning point than he did, have but rarely seen the connection between the play and the poem. That is, the critical camps have largely been divided into two groups: that which, following Arthur Symons, sees Wilde's post-conviction works as expressing a new "sincerity" on his part; and that which, following W. E. Henley, sees them as merely new poses.[66]

The connection between the two works has gone unperceived in the twentieth century, although it lurked subliminally—and was considered as a negative aspect of the poem—in two of the first reviews of *Reading Gaol*. This aspect had to do with the physical images in the poem and its concern with the sufferings of the body, images and concerns which indicated to the two reviewers "softness," "hysteria," and "weakness" on the part of the author. Such intimations, one suspects, amounted to a carryover of the charge of "effeminacy" that had been raised against Wilde's earlier works. The reviewer in *The Academy* (26 February 1898) wrote that although *Reading Gaol* "was a remarkable addition to contemporary poetry," Hood's "The Dream of Eugene Aram" was the finer of the two works: "Its author had more nervous strength, was a more dexterous master of words, was superior to morbidity and hysteria." "S.G." in the *Pall Mall Gazette* (19 March 1898) was even more explicit. Estimating *Reading Gaol* as "the most remarkable poem that has appeared this year," the reviewer went on to contrast Kipling's "Danny Deever," "a conspicuously manly piece of work," with Wilde's poem, which, "with all its feverish energy," was "unmanly":

The central emotion in [*Reading Gaol*] is the physical horror of death, when death comes, not as a relief or in a whirl of excitement, but as an abrupt shock to be dreaded. That the emotion is genuine admits of no doubt; but it is one very fit to be concealed. The writer's dread of any thing that pains the body extends even after death; again and again he insists on the horror of burial in quicklime, the soft fibers of flesh being lapped about in "a sheet of living flame." If we were to judge poems by the test that Plato proposes—whether they will tend to strengthen or enervate—we should put this poem very low indeed. Yet it has beautiful work in it, and touches of a genuine and honourable sympathy for the sorrow of weak things suffering.

The sorrow of weak things suffering: Wilde, no longer an active threat to the sons of the English, could now be condescendingly pitied as the pathetically effeminate weakling. For the sympathy in his poem, and now that he had made due reparation to the British, he was given pity for his weak, "diseased" condition.

However, if we delete the smug judgment of the prisoners as "weak things," we can see that the reviewer here is on to the unique status of Wilde's poem in the genre, popular during his time, *in carcere et vinculis*. Charles Thomas Wooldridge, or "C.T.W.," the Royal Horse Guardsman to whom the poem is dedicated, was not just any murderer. In the notice of his execution, the *Reading Mercury* (10 July 1896) quoted the prison officials to the effect that he had died "truly penitent . . . without a struggle and without a word."[67] C.T.W.'s silence and passivity, which so strike the narrator of the poem, were particularly meaningful for Wilde; for C.T.W.'s crime was attributed to the weakness of loving not wisely but too well. The *Reading Mercury* states that at C.T.W.'s trial it came out that his wife had been living away from him, and that on Sunday, 29 March 1896, C.T.W. had cut her throat "in a very determined manner, she having excited his jealousy and greatly annoyed him."

It is true that in merely cutting his wife's throat in a very determined manner, C.T.W. went only half as far as Salome, who severed Iokanaan's head. But the inmate-narrator feels a fascination for C.T.W. similar to the one Wilde reportedly felt for Salome. Like Salome crushed beneath soldier's shields and C.T.W. hanged, the narrator was paying for a physical, i.e., sexual, love. As if implicitly confirming his sympathy with C.T.W., who was imprisoned first metaphorically by, and then literally for, his love, Wilde later amused Robert Ross by claiming that *"The Ballad of Reading Gaol* [did not] describe his prison life, but his life at Naples with Bosie and that all the best stanzas were the immediate result of his existence there."[68] *Reading Gaol* is about physical love. Since society is eliminated from the poem by the image of the prison walls, it only surfaces as the Law that controls the physical environment of the prison (that is, warders, physicians, chaplain—as in *Salome*, both secular and divine laws). Wilde's

Art for Love's Sake

sympathy for this environment, made up of the prisoners, has much to do with his apparent limiting of the inmates' crimes to crimes of love. The poem depicts a community of men who kill the thing they love and their banishment and divorce from society.

Thus in Part I, in which the narrator begins to take an interest in C.T.W. as the man who had to die because he had killed the thing he loved, he does not complain that the punishment is unjust, but merely points out that it is indiscriminately applied:

> Yet each man kills the thing he loves,
> By each let this be heard,
> Some do it with a bitter look,
> Some with a flattering word,
> The coward does it with a kiss,
> The brave man with a sword!

Here the narrator's self-righteous rebuke to hypocrites on the outside reminds one of Claudel's phrase cited by Sartre in his biography of Jean Genet: "the shortest path from one heart to the other is the sword."[69] The taboo against homosexual love and, as in C.T.W.'s case, against any love whose fruits were not sanctioned by the state, rendered such love destructive; just as it rendered the lovers enemies, each potentially capable of causing the social downfall of the other.[70] Therefore, the only honest love, and the most profound, would be open destruction in the face of society. We have seen similar destructiveness in Salome's love for Iokanaan. This open rebelliousness according to subjective demands is the narrator's reason for siding with C.T.W. His catalogue of crimes of love duplicates Wilde's (misguided) indictment of Douglas's hypocrisy in *De Profundis,* and the catalogue concludes with the inmates perceived as scapegoats:

> Some kill their love when they are young,
> And some when they are old;
> Some strangle with the hands of Lust,
> Some with the hands of Gold:
> The kindest use a knife, because
> The dead so soon grow cold.

(With a perverse but profound sympathy, Douglas had considered death for his imprisoned friend. He begged Ives for help: "I cannot see Oscar nor give him anything, not even some poison to kill himself with. I should be glad to hear that he is dead, and I wish he had died before this terrible thing happened."[71])

> Some love too little, some too long,
>   Some sell, and others buy:
> Some do the deed with many tears,
>   And some without a sigh:
> For each man kills the thing he loves,
>   Yet each man does not die.

In Parts II and III erotic images pervade the proposed distinctions between life on the inside and that on the outside. Outside, free persons live, love, and dance; inside, the prisoners pass each other without signing or speaking, their contact prevented by surveillance. Characteristically, the narrator thinks of shelter in "the holy night" as opposed to "the shameful day." Part III climaxes in the inmates' complete identification with C.T.W. during the night preceding his execution. But, again, the vehicle of the narrator's sympathy is a night of erotic horrors. The evil sprites he imagines, who "walk by night," are frenzied erotic images recalling the dancing figures in the earlier poem "The Harlot's House" (1885), whose stanzas describe what the lovers saw as they passed the brothel:

> Like strange mechanical grotesques,
>   Making fantastic arabesques,
> The shadows raced across the blind.
>   We watched the ghostly dancers spin,
>   To sound of horn and violin,
> Like black leaves wheeling in the wind.
>
> Like wire-pulled Automatons,
>   Slim silhouetted skeletons
> Went sidling through the slow quadrille,
>   Then took each other by the hand,
>   And danced a stately saraband;
> Their laughter echoed thin and shrill.

In his sympathy with the sins of the condemned man, the narrator sees similar phantoms cavorting in "sarabands," "masques," and "arabesques." They mock the prisoner for playing with sin "in the secret House of Shame":

> Around, around, they waltzed and wound;
>   Some wheeled in smirking pairs;
> With the mincing step of a demirep
>   Some sidled up the stairs;
> And with subtle sneer, and fawning leer,
>   Each helped us at our prayers.

As the prisoners march around the prison yard in Part IV, their isolation from the outside is symbolized by the stanzas on the naked, fettered corpse buried beneath the burning quicklime. These stanzas struck the Victorian critic as Wilde's unmanly fear of the corruption of the body after death. But, having been "hanged as a beast" and "hid in a hole," mocked by the warders for his swollen purple throat and staring eyes, the body of C.T.W., now cherished in all its degradation, is a sort of *habeas corpus* for the inmates. Just as Salome making lawless love to the head of Iokanaan, in the process making the audience uncomfortable, is a sort of *habeas corpus* for the girl who desired. The body that had sinned through love of the body is now protected by the bodies of the inmates surrounding it. And these inmates, as Wilde has presented them, were all incarcerated for loving the body.

In Part V, the poem's polemic beginning with "I know not whether Laws be right, / Or whether Laws be wrong," the narrator is ambivalent on the issue of incarceration. His allegiance to the community of prisoners, which is a real community united in work and sympathy, is counterposed with the recognition that real living can only happen on the outside and that the social goal of rehabilitation with respect to the inmates is a joke. As the hallucinations during the night had indicated, prison only exacerbated the prisoners' isolation and aggression:

> The vilest deeds like poison weeds,
>   Bloom well in prison-air;
> It is only what is good in Man
>   That wastes and withers there:
> . . . .
> Each narrow cell in which we dwell
>   Is a foul and dark latrine,
> And the fetid breath of living Death
>   Chokes up each grated screen,
> And all, but Lust, is turned to dust
>   In humanity's machine.

The choice between the humanizing community on the inside, albeit a community living in squalor, and the freedom of action on the outside cannot be resolved by the narrator. It merely becomes a division in himself, in the image of the heart breaking so that Christ may enter it. This physical heart that had to break to unite the soul and body (and that had surfaced as early as "The Fisherman and his Soul," "The Happy Prince," and "The Nightingale and the Rose") was Wilde's image of the self that had always been divided—even in its language—between the body and Society. The image of Renan's Christ, the social rebel against everything that his society thought "natural," who was exclusively the savior of the outcast and poor, concludes the poem, as it concludes *De Profundis*. And it is he who is opposed, finally, to "the man in red" on the outside "who reads the Law."

In Wilde's pre-prison works the contradictions he was living surfaced in a polished technique of epigrams and paradoxes subverting the tropes and truisms of Victorian life. He criticized current notions of purpose, production, and the natural from the point of view of one who enjoyed pleasures that were "nonpurposive," "unproductive," and "unnatural." His criticisms were witty and satiric until he went to prison; but there the genuinely paradoxical choice between an allegiance to a humane community of outcasts and a desire to be part of the world outside of the prison walls resulted in a work that was on the one hand a plea for sympathy to outcasts and for their re-entry into society, and on the other hand a personal testament to the power of sexual love, a power investing the narrator's images and his characterization of the inmates.

Salome got the body of the Baptist—or at least enough of it to satisfy her. In the fantasy her death was anticlimactic to her satisfaction. In *Reading Gaol* Wilde reaffirmed the dignity of the beloved body. So in Naples he forgot to mention the long letter he had written to Douglas, and he forgot almost everything he had written in it. He was as weary as Melmoth—a name that he assumed only when polite circumstances required it and that he repudiated every chance he could—of posing for people who sent one to prison. In Naples he stayed with the real Douglas, and he returned to Paris with her real boys and real absinthe. It was perhaps the first time he was really able to live aesthetically. He was entirely marginal, and for that reason, as Croft-Cooke says, it may have been the best time of his life.

5

'De Profundis':
An Audience of Peers

> The life of the artist should be a practical protest against the so-called decencies of life: and he can best protest by frequenting a tavern and cutting his club. In the past the artist has always been an outcast; it is only latterly he has become domesticated, and judging by results, it is clear that if Bohemianism is not a necessity it is at least an adjuvant.
>
> George Moore, *Confessions of a Young Man* (1888)

"The Apostle of the Aesthetes"; from the *Hour* cartoon supplement, 1881.

De Profundis, the title that Robert Ross added to the early editions of Wilde's very long letter to Alfred Douglas from prison, was meant to suggest to a consumerist public a revealing autobiography from the depths, as Wilde said, of a soul in pain. But the title that Wilde himself gave the letter, *Epistola: in Carcere et Vinculis*, is far more specific about the conditions in which the letter was produced, and a consideration of both prison conditions in the 1890's and prison writings in general is more relevant to the letter than are the traditional approaches to autobiography. These latter have historically resulted in the judgment that Wilde "was a poseur to the last," that is, constitutionally theatrical, or that his work is a fiction, according to however current theory construes the fictive.[1] Yet in prison Wilde lived under the contemporary regulations of solitary cellular confinement for two years; his daily routine was determined by a rigorously enforced timetable, and he was not permitted to talk. The self in his letter is a self constructed in a particular imaginative act of resistance against insanity and against the material matrix[2] of prison space and time—that is, confined, segmented space and timelessness. It is probably not too much to say that, by means of the letter, art literally saved Wilde's life.

Two expressions that Wilde applies to Douglas reflect the letter's structure: that Douglas had passed, even before they met, "from Romance to Realism"[3] and that his series of telegrams to Wilde had been a "strange mixture of romance and finance" (456). In Wilde's letter the totalizing plan to love and forgive, including the romance of Jesus Christ and art and Wilde's own future as well as his efforts toward some closure for the relationship, is disrupted repeatedly by the minute reconstruction of his "real" past as he sees it and outbursts of "real" hatred as he feels it. Romance and realism here are psychological—even survival—functions: romance dreams a future for the prisoner and resists the temporal regimentation of prison life; realism, in its patient enumeration of details, reconstructs the past obliterated by the sterile prison space. The letter's constant shifts between romance and realism, romance and details like finance, become a strategy by means of which Wilde triumphs over the threats posed to his unique "style" by the prison bureaucracy and the silence it enforced.

In this sense the letter is a complete triumph. Auden only liked the bits about Bosie and thought that the bits about Christ were tedious. Yet the wonder of the letter is that it includes both the realism of Bosie and the romance of Christ. From a world in which his guards in the infirmary were selected because they were so dull they would not laugh at his jokes and in which governors were so insensitive that they relieved him by recommending enforced gardening, in which silent, unbelievable monotony threatened insanity, Wilde remembered with all the verve of a dramatist Savoy dinners of crinkled Sicilian vine-leaves and Dagonet 1880; a *film noir* legal world where "in the ghastly glare of a bleak room you and I would sit with serious faces telling serious lies to a bald man" (493); torrid, volatile scenes in which Bosie threatened to knife him; Renan's sexy celebrity called Jesus Christ, who caused minor revolutions with a band of young men; and a 3 franc 50 c. homely *table d'hôte* with Robbie.

This chapter will concentrate on the triumph of the letter, on the way Wilde constructed a romance of past and future to combat the timeless isolation of the prison and filled it with memories to combat the insanity fostered by prison conditions under centralization. That is, I claim that the physical conditions of the prison determined the form and style of the work. Yet beyond Wilde's success in conquering the anonymity and monotony of incarceration, *De Profundis* has a special significance, for it is the only work he wrote without an audience. If there had not been an Alfred Douglas, Wilde would have had to invent one. His criticism had been written for ideal audiences he hoped to create; *Dorian Gray* had been a sort of glass in which the press saw every face but its own; his plays were for the audience who saw themselves on the stage; and *Reading Gaol* was for the prisoners and wardens to whom he sent copies. Now Wilde used Douglas to fill the place of the absent audience, writing a self-serving biography of Douglas in order to write an autobiography that explained Wilde to the world. Douglas was for Wilde the image of all unworthy audiences: once he was demystified he could be forgiven, and Wilde could go on to demystify and forgive the whole society he had played to. He could go on to freedom in Paris amid the street boys and acrobats, to acknowledge his first audience of peers: the rebels, criminals, and outcasts who had always known that a society without romance was a bleak room in which one sat with serious face telling serious lies to a bald man.

In concluding with a materialist reading of a work whose production in a solitary cell is relatively anomalous, I also want to suggest that some works resist modern consumption. *De Profundis* is yet to be digested: a letter whose isolation is extreme and whose production is intimately connected to material conditions unknown to most of us presents a truth unassimilable in the complacent consumption of commodities in mass society. Embedded in its aura *in carcere et vinculis*, it is so marginal to everyday life that Ross could only market it by cutting it to a moral tale and naming it after a Psalm; and readers of "literature" as a creation of middle-class comfort can only call it "false"—or, more sophisticatedly, "fictive." In analyzing the conditions that show the letter's engagement inside its own world and that make it opaque to academic readers, I have gratefully drawn upon numerous writings from prison (to which I have compared *De Profundis* with more profit than I could have imagined) and conversations with former prisoners and prisoners of war, whose reception of my analysis has reinforced my belief in it. The auracular prison-blue manuscript in the British Library, frayed with Wilde's nervous, punctilious revisions concerning the precise day they dined, the hour supped, and the exact cost in shillings, equally reinforces the contours of my reading.

Like others' experiences in prison, Wilde's too became part of his history and language, especially in *De Profundis* and in the collective form of *The Ballad of Reading Gaol*, to which I shall return in the conclusion of this chapter. His association with the prison did not end when he left it: he corresponded after release with inmates, prison administrators, and reformers like Michael Davitt, and he wrote letters describing prison conditions to the *Daily Chronicle*. He read the debates on penal reform while he was still imprisoned and experienced firsthand the demise of the official penal philosophy of deterrence.

Two momentous pieces of legislation had changed the character of British penal practice in the second half of the nineteenth century.[4] The first was the uniform institution of separate cellular confinement under the Prisons Act of 1865; the second, the transference of all administrative power from the justices of local boroughs and municipal corporations to the national government under the Home Secretary and his appointed Prison Commissioners under the Prisons Bill of 1876-77. The Bill had first been opposed as an almost unparalleled centralization and a slur on local government; then, when the counties were promised remuneration for cells emptied under reconsignment, it was amended by Irish members who had seen the treatment of political prisoners convicted of treason-felony. In addition, the Act of 1853 had replaced the sentence of transportation with that of penal servitude, and the Acts of 1864-65 had abolished the intermediate sentences of three and four years' penal servitude. Consequently, the sentencing alternatives in 1895 were one day to two years' imprisonment in local prisons (under which Wilde received the full two year sentence) or five years' penal servitude in convict prisons. The practical difference between the two sentences was that after the first nine months of hard labor in the cell, prisoners under penal servitude could work "in association" and could be conditionally released after serving three-fourths of their time. Under imprisonment, the prisoner would remain in solitary confinement laboring in the cell for the duration of the sentence. Because of their fear of prolonged solitude and silence, prisoners often found the longer sentence less intimidating than the shorter.

When Pope Clement XI instituted the practice of enforced silence and solitary cellular confinement at the penitentiary in Rome in 1704, the monastic discipline of meditation as a moral agent, applied to prisoners to a limited degree, was thought to be preferable to the admixture of classes of prisoners in one confined space. In Britain, the model penitentiary at Pentonville adopted the system of solitary cellular confinement when it opened in 1842 "with all the refinements of modern science." It reminded Mayhew in 1862 of the Crystal Palace. Initially enforcing eighteen months of total isolation and silence, Pentonville's administration was forced to reduce the term to nine months in 1848 due to the high rate of insanity among prisoners. By 1895, at the termination of Col. Sir Edmund Du Cane's appointment as Chairman of Commissioners of Prisons under the national system, the arguments for solitary confinement were that it would prevent prisoners from contaminating each other, that it would separate the hardened criminal from the first offender, and that a prisoner's only verbal contact would be with prison officials free from crime. The counterargument was that it in no way prepared the prisoner for his reentry to society, that it indeed frequently resulted in permanent insanity.

During his imprisonment, Wilde requested the works of the two most currently authoritative writers on the penal system and penal reform, Du Cane and William Morrison. In the period 1878-94, which the Webbs called "the Du Cane Regime," Du Cane imposed extreme uniformity on the prison system. He encouraged hard, not industrial, labor; his theory was deterrence, not rehabilitation; and he fundamentally believed that atavism was the source of most criminality. He recommended that potential criminals be incarcerated until the age of 40, as past the prime age for criminal activity; he felt that literary education (prison libraries) had not the desired effect on prisoners; and he discouraged the use of dietary increases as rewards because prison food might then exceed the habitual diets of the respectable poor on the outside and thus serve as an inducement to crime.

The requirement of silent and solitary cellular confinement under the Prisons Act of 1877, which Du Cane and the inspectors directly subordinate to him implemented, raised special problems in the employment of convicts. The Act reduced the term of compulsory hard labor from three months to one month. This meant that entirely unproductive work on the crank (a box in the cell whose crank was turned x number of revolutions and at x number of pounds of resistance by the prisoner according to his strength and punishment) occupied the prisoner until industrial labor, in most cases oakum picking, replaced it. Mat making had been abandoned because it threatened manufacture on the outside. And even oakum picking—separating strands of rotten rope—soon became entirely profitless when iron replaced wooden ships. As late as 1896 Du Cane was still arguing the "unavoidable uselessness of prison labor" with some cause, despite its demoralizing effects on the prisoner. The morally desirable industrial labor was impractical, for the great majority of prisoners would not serve long enough to learn a trade sufficiently to compete in outside markets. Consumers did not want the inferior products of prison labor; and even when the products were not inferior, there were legal prohibitions that prevented prisons from underselling outside manufacturers. As Du Cane saw it, the only possibility was that the government treat prisons as government workshops, use the prisoners as free labor, and consume the goods itself. Between the punitive enforcement of profitless hard labor and the market constraints on industrial labor that could conceivably contribute to "rehabilitation," the unwilling prisoner was rendered entirely unproductive. Wilde's *Epistola: in Carcere et Vinculis*, which occupied him obsessively for a quarter of a year, was an indirect response to the uselessness of prison labor.

One effect of total government control of prisons, with all appointments emerging from the same office, was the relatively small amount of bad press concerning the internal workings of prisons. But the public could not help but hear of the high rate of recidivism, especially through the efforts of the Du Cane Regime's most effective critic, William Morrison, chaplain of Wandsworth Prison.

Using statistics that Du Cane disputed, Morrison based his case for the failure of the bureaucratic system on the increase of recidivism, for him the true test of the growth of the criminal classes, and of the anarchism that resulted from recidivism. He measured the deterrence factor by the high rate of insanity among prisoners, arguing that insanity was generally found among recidivists and that it had doubled since the introduction of the centralized system. Moreover, Morrison considered the increase of crime in the context of the increase of police, the multiplication of laws to be broken, and the increasing concentration of population in the large cities. He wanted more public support for the locally funded Discharged Prisoners' Aid Societies, better educated prison governors, and a government inquiry into the current administration.[5]

Largely in response to Morrison's publicity, when Asquith became Home Secretary in 1892, he appointed Herbert Gladstone as chair of a Prison Committee. The Committee's report of 1894-95 stated that imprisonment failed to reform convicts and produced a debilitating effect on first offenders. The Committee recommended that the government support Prisoners' Aid Societies (which, Du Cane pointed out, opened up the question of general unemployment), that the ban on prisoners' talking be lifted, that education not be individual and in cells, and that there be a gradual introduction of labor in association. Asquith appointed Evelyn Ruggles-Brise to replace Du Cane as Chairman of Prison Commissioners, but unfortunately for Wilde, because of a change of government, the reforms recommended in 1895 (the first year of his sentence) were not effected until the Prisons Bill of 1898, the year after his release. Even then Morrison was driven to question how far the new Bill would decentralize the administration and allow for the individual case among prisoners, especially among mentally unstable prisoners for whom the effects of solitary confinement were often catastrophic and irreversible. Morrison also protested the secrecy of the proceedings and the vagueness of the general prison regulations under consideration. His article, "Prison Reform," composed while the 1898 Bill was before the House of Commons, begins with an account of Wilde's collapse under "the great silent machine." Here the specific details of Wilde's imprisonment are relevant.

After the trials, Alfred Douglas and More Adey wrote that Wilde's conviction was political, that Queensberry had certain information about very high persons in the Liberal government that would be made public unless Wilde were convicted.[6] (See Appendix B.) There is some support for such an argument, including the fact that by June 1895 Richard Burdon Haldane, who had served on Gladstone's Committee, was already arranging privileges for Wilde, probably at the encouragement of Asquith. Consequently, on an absolute scale, such as the number of regulations relaxed and privileges granted, Wilde's imprisonment was made easier than that of most prisoners of the time. But his special treatment through the intervention of friends did not prevent his feeling the brutality of centralization, or what he usually called "the system," during his confinement in five different institutions.

Before his first trial, he was imprisoned for three weeks at Holloway, which housed London's pre-trial prisoners, those under remand, women, and first-class misdemeanants. Since he was convicted on a Saturday at the Old Bailey, he was kept until Monday afternoon in the adjacent and notorious Newgate, marked by the history of the great rogues, executed murderers, and confined masses. At the modern Pentonville, where Mayhew had been impressed by separate cells even in chapel and where he had explored the dark cells generally housing Irish Cockneys ("nine-tenths of the habitual criminals" with "the natural quickness of the Hibernian race for good or evil"), Wilde was committed to a cell $13' \times 7' \times 9'$ with one window of opaque glass $6'9''$ above the floor.

At Pentonville Wilde encountered the general regime that, with the exception of type of labor, would change little during the next two years. His friend George Ives, in his *History of Penal Methods*, devotes an entire chapter to the "Monotony" that he perceived as the most destructive force in prison: 6 A.M., clean cell; 7, porridge and brown bread; exercise for an hour, oakum picking until noon; dinner of bacon, beans, bread, potatoes (cold meat once a week); 12:30-6 P.M., oakum picking; tea or gruel and eight ounces bread; 7 P.M., lights out. No personal possessions were allowed in the cell, which included only a plank bed, a blanket, a hard pillow, and a small table. Each morning, on pain of punishment, the prisoner would arrange these items symmetrically for inspection. (After his release, Wilde's friends noticed that he was incapable of allowing common objects to rest without comparable ordering.) One letter could be sent and received per quarter, but letters were allowed for the "purpose of enabling [prisoners] to keep up a connection with their respectable friends and not that they may be kept informed of public events."[7] No books were allowed the first month, during the second and third only a Bible, a prayer-book, and a hymnbook. Afterwards, one book a week from the prison library was permitted. But as early as June 1895, Haldane arranged for Wilde to have outside books that the governor deemed appropriate so that he "would be free to produce."

In July Haldane and Ruggles-Brise had Wilde transferred to Wandsworth, which was thought to benefit from the anti-bureaucratic watchfulness of Morrison. (Wilde had found the chaplain at Pentonville intolerable. On their first meeting, he had asked Wilde whether he had been accustomed to morning prayer at home. "I am sorry. I fear not," Wilde responded. "You see where you are now," said the chaplain.) Yet his health was failing, and in October he collapsed. As he improved in the infirmary, which because of staff limitations did not have continuous supervision, he was caught entertaining other convalescents. The Secretary of the Prison Board immediately reprimanded the governor and ordered that a guard be present at all times, day and night, in the infirmary room Wilde inhabited. The Secretary especially stressed that the guard himself not be susceptible to Wilde's conversation.

At Wandsworth Wilde made post bags in his cell, but when he told the physicians that he disliked Nature and found no pleasure in walking or physical exercise of any kind, the physicians recommended that he be removed to a country prison where he might have outdoor labor and gardening, always under the stricture of silence. Thus he went to Reading Gaol, his fifth and last prison.

From entertaining other prisoners to refusing to consider exercise a privilege, Wilde continued the strategy that he had developed during his first trials and indeed during most of his previous work: to refuse to meet authority on its own ground, to change the terms. At Reading, his major fear was of insanity, but both of his petitions to the Home Office for reduction of the sentence (in July and November 1896) were denied—rather ironically. Wilde pleaded a fear of mental breakdown and decline of literary capability, and the physicians observed that his prose style was too lucid, orderly, and polished to cause apprehension on those scores. On the outside, Wilde had been treated as an exemplary case of Lombroso and Nordau's theoretical connections between style and madness, but when he appealed to these theories in prison the official physicians maintained a less paradoxical science. Yet he was granted books and writing materials, that he "might be free to produce," and was encouraged by friends like Adela Schuster to perhaps write down the fairy tales that had formerly charmed his friends. He wrote instead *Epistola: in Carcere et Vinculis* to Alfred Douglas.

It was a three-month labor. Not until *The Ballad of Reading Gaol*—after his release, when he had been treated like one of the criminal classes—did he fully identify with the prisoners. In the letter his object is still to resist the effects of the prison bureaucracy by insisting on his individual "style" and to resist the prison regimentation with an incorrigible imagination. In fighting the threat that isolation and silence posed to sanity, Wilde had to reconstitute the world outside as precisely as possible (hence the meticulous naming of places and specific chronology in his account of his relationship with Douglas) and he had to make sense of his own confinement and its relationship to his life after prison in such a way that society would have to take him back. Hence the great joke on a Christian society of making Jesus Christ his hero. The structure of the letter functions precisely so: alternating passages of realism and romance so as to pose a total imaginative world against the frozen time and alien space of imprisonment.

Wilde fought silence and isolation by writing a biography of Alfred Douglas, whose remembered image recreated for him the world outside; yet even when this world was successfully recreated, the prison influenced the memory. He tries to concentrate on "the quality of the friendship while it lasted, rather than the appalling results" (427), but early in the letter he is so far from the relationship, so contaminated by the prison, that he refers to it as if it were a bygone broadsheet for the Newgate Calendar: "Our ill-fated and most lamentable friendship" (424). The focused intimacy of the first part of the letter seeks to bridge the distances: geographical, historical, and stylistic. As he begins to reconstruct the world before prison, however, he does so according to a time scheme as rigid as that in prison. To paraphrase a much longer account of an ordinary day with Douglas: "I arrived at St. James's Place to work every morning at 11:30. At 12 you drove up, chatted and smoked until 1:30, when I had to take you to lunch at the Café Royal or the Berkeley. Lunch and liqueurs lasted until 3:30. You went to White's club for an hour. We had tea together, then you stayed until time to dress for dinner. We dined at either the Savoy or Tite Street, and supped at Willis's, not separating until after midnight. This ruined my art" (426). In this first half of the letter, Wilde forces the presence of Douglas in the prose in order to make the pre-prison Wilde a reality. Sometimes he becomes hopelessly confused, as in the crazy syntactical subordination of subject and object, e.g., "But most of all I blame myself for the entire ethical degradation I allowed you to bring on me" (429).

Not yet able to vivify the world of art, Wilde says that Douglas also ruined his finances, willpower, and aesthetic perspective, yet when he explains why he stayed with the fatal Douglas, the explanation merely reinforces a positive image of Wilde's own personality: "Through deep if misplaced affection for you . . . through great pity . . . through my own proverbial good-nature and Celtic laziness . . . through an artistic aversion to coarse scenes . . . through [my] incapacity to bear resentment . . .

An Audience of Peers

through my dislike of seeing life made bitter . . . I gave up to you always" (429). Similarly, after Douglas's outrageous behavior at Brighton and Wilde's resolve to leave him forever, Wilde hears of the death of Douglas's brother and returns because of "my idea of what your own sorrow would be . . . my consciousness of the misery awaiting your mother . . . my consciousness of your own isolation . . . and the mere sense of the *lacrimae rerum*" (439). As Douglas becomes more and more hopelessly shallow and (necessarily) unresponsive—less, in fact, real—Wilde accumulates a positive personality in very detailed material surroundings.

But as yet the details remain tainted with prison habits. He meticulously describes their break-ups at three-month intervals—the largest unit of measure operative in the official prison regulations posted in his cell. Throughout the letter, the three-month unit functions heavily to order experience: "Three more months go over and my mother dies"; three more months go over, he is distraught to hear that Douglas tactlessly wants to dedicate to him a volume of poems (458-59). He recounts with determination the minutiae of their meetings. After one disassociation that was meant to be final, Douglas begged so persistently for a reconciliation that Wilde met him in Paris, "at dinner first at Voisin's, at supper at Paillard's afterwards" and finally back home for "luncheon with me at the Café Royal" (435). When he is not depicting times and places, he calculates expenses: from £12 to 20 per day at London, at £80 to 130 per week, and £1,340 (including rent) at Goring. These he contrasts with a 3 franc 50 c. *table-d'hôte* with Robbie.

The rest of the first part of the letter alternates between vividly dramatic scenes of his life with Douglas—for example, at the Grand Hotel at Brighton where Wilde imagines that Douglas might have knifed him (437-38)—and passages in which he broods on the deadening effect of imprisonment: the former are the antidote to the latter. Some examples of these phenomenologies of time and space in prison are worth quoting at length, since most accounts of the mental effects of solitary confinement are astonishingly similar. They are separated in the text by pages of minute appraisal of Douglas's former conduct, and they seek to explain why such appraisals are both necessary and inevitable for prisoners. They reflect on the process of composition and form of the letter:

Three years is a long time for you to go back. But we who live in prison, and in whose lives there is no event but sorrow, have to measure time by throbs of pain, and the record of bitter moments. We have nothing else to think of. Suffering—curious as it may sound to you—is the means by which we exist, because it is the only means by which we become conscious of existing; and the remembrance of suffering in the past is necessary to us as the warrant, the evidence, of our continued identity. . . . I spoke of your conduct to me on three successive days, three years ago, did I not? (435-36)

Here the colons mark the rapid shift of memories according to the regimentation of the prison day:

The memory of our friendship is the shadow that walks with me here: that seems never to leave me: that wakes me up at night to tell me the same story over and over till its wearisome iteration makes all sleep abandon me till dawn: at dawn it begins again: it follows me into the prison-yard and makes me talk to myself as I tramp round: each detail that accompanied each dreadful moment I am forced to recall: . . . every twitch and gesture of your nervous hands, every bitter word, every poisonous phrase comes back to me: I remember the street or river down which we passed . . . what figure on the dial stood the hands of the clock. (444)

And here the prison regimen imposes itself on the reconstruction of prior events, so that the outside is reified in the terms and cycles of imprisonment:

The paralysing immobility of a life, every circumstance of which is regulated after an unchangeable pattern, so that we eat and drink and walk and lie down and pray, or kneel at least for prayer, according to the inflexible laws of an iron formula: this immobile quality, that makes each dreadful day in the very minutest detail like its brother, seems to communicate itself to those external forces the very essence of whose existence is ceaseless change. . . . A week later, I am transferred here. Three more months go over and my mother dies. (457-58)

Each time Wilde so reflects on the monotony of prison he shifts to reconstructing scenes of remarkable variety with Douglas, until he is finally *with* Douglas, asking questions and answering for him. Each time he begins to lose Douglas's voice, he reflects on the barrenness of prison life, the emptiness that makes men mad. Then the upsurge of reconstruction, with all the detail of variety, begins again. I paraphrase another litany: "My bankruptcy, for which you were responsible, cost me my Whistlers, Monticelli, Simeon Solomons, Burne-Joneses, China; library from Hugo to Whitman, Swinburne to Mallarmé, Morris to Verlaine; mother's and father's works, college and school prizes," and so on (451).

Yet once Wilde has established through repetition the contours of his life before prison, he begins a transition to romance. If memories of the outside protect the prisoner from insanity, fantasy can punish the outside that sent the prisoner to prison and provide the prisoner with images of a future. Fantasy is also the particular province of the prisoner; on the outside, temporal change interferes with the life of the mind. When Wilde begins the great paean to individualism, sorrow, Christ, and art, he seems to forget Douglas altogether. (And in fact this was the popular romance that Ross published in 1905, with all references to Douglas deleted.) Yet in the romantic aestheticizing of Christ, Wilde is able to ally himself with the forces of universal sympathy against the shallowness of society, prison, and especially Douglas. He has in fact reconstructed the world in order to show that he is above it, and to some extent the old iconoclastic—aesthetic— Wilde returns for a while. Upon his release, he will go on, but "neither Religion, Morality, or Reason can help me" (468). He mocks the philistine interpretations of these with his own: in religion, he imagines himself as the priest of a brotherhood of the fatherless (a punning rebuke to Douglas, who was too much fathered); in morality, "I am one of those who are made for exceptions, not for laws"; and in reason, he knows that he was convicted under wrong and unjust laws and committed into a wrong and unjust system. He imagines, against the policy of deterrence, that whether or not he should have been imprisoned depends upon his will: "If one is ashamed of having been punished, one might just as well never have been punished at all" (464).

In his romance, Wilde first makes Jesus Christ banal, a celebrity of fascinating personality who walked abroad with a crowd of devoted young men and captured the imagination of the historical media (478), which identifies him with Wilde, though never as a martyr. Then Christ goes beyond the artist, as giving voice even to the silenced, which puts him in the service of all prisoners, including Wilde. And finally, Christ is all that prison is not, fully aestheticized and autonomous: "For him there were no laws: there were exceptions merely" (485). He surpassed the philistine reformers on the outside as completely as he surpassed the former prison governor Major Isaacson, whose greatest fault, as Wilde told André Gide, was his entire lack of imagination: "[Christ's] primary desire was not to reform people. . . . To turn an interesting thief into a tedious honest man was not his aim. He would have thought little of the Prisoners' Aid Society. . . . The conversion of a Publican into a Pharisee would not have seemed to him a great achievement by any means" (486).

During this otherwise sublime fantasy, Wilde is at his strongest, and his former empowering conversational style returns. He can insult Douglas lightheartedly, without pain or passion. He casually mentions that he reads from the Gospels in Greek each morning in his cell and says that it would be a capital habit for Douglas to cultivate "in your turbulent, ill-disciplined life," adding that "The Greek is quite simple" (483). In one of Shaw's favorite passages, in which Wilde describes the lesson of Love as analogous to his eating whatever crumbs of white bread may be granted him, he adds the breezy rebuke, "I do so not from hunger—I get now quite sufficient food" (482). It is at his most reverent that he turns to Douglas with the litotes that would be a literary embarrassment if it were not so absurdly, charmingly familiar, "There is something so unique about Christ" (487).

As long as this vision holds, until Wilde remembers the prison environment, he can, and does, claim that only sinners (that is, aestheticized prisoners) can alter the past (that is, pre-prison time), for the mind can repent in prison. On the unreflective and impenitent (that is, by now desublimated) outside, people cannot change. He uses a Paterian philosophy to justify making the world with his mind: "I said in *Dorian Gray* that the great sins of the world take place in the brain, but it is in the brain that everything takes place. We know now that we do not see with the eye or hear with the ear. They are merely channels for the transmission, adequate or inadequate, of sense-impressions. It is in the brain that the poppy is red, that the apple is odorous, that the skylark sings" (483). But when he must consider the facts of imprisonment, rather than the mind of the prisoner, he returns to Douglas and, through him, to the world outside.

This shift occurs in the discussion of one of Wilde's imagined future writing projects, the Artistic Life in Relation to Conduct. He describes his scene of humiliation at Clapham Junction to demonstrate to Douglas that people who laugh at souls in pain are unbeautiful. But Clapham Junction reminds him of why he is in prison, and after Christ, St. Francis, and Art, he suddenly writes, "This urging me, forcing me to appeal to Society for help, is one of the things that make me despise you so much" (492). He returns now to the excitement of his past, in the well-known "feasting with panthers" passage, only to contrast it with the images of Douglas and a society as stifling and sterile as the prison: "Clibborn and Atkins [witnesses against Wilde] were wonderful in their infamous war against life. . . . What is loathsome to me is the memory of interminable visits paid by me to the solicitor Humphreys in your company, when in the ghastly glare of a bleak room you and I would sit with serious faces telling serious lies to a bald man" (493).

Between the desublimated social world of artifacts with Douglas and the aestheticized, transcendent, mental world of Christ, Wilde finally emerges with a spiritual message solidly in the world outside: Christ's beloved sinner will pay for his salvation in the terms of his relationship to Douglas:

Even when I am stripped of all I have, and am ever to have, and am granted a discharge as a hopeless Insolvent, I have still got to pay my debts. The Savoy dinners—the clear turtle-soup, the luscious ortolans wrapped in their crinkled Sicilian vine-leaves, the heavy amber-coloured, indeed almost amber-scented champagne—Dagonet 1880, I think, was your favourite wine?—all have still to be paid for. The suppers at Willis's, the special *cuvée* of Perrier-Jouet reserved always for us, the wonderful *pâtés* procured directly from Strasburg, the marvellous *fine champagne* served always at the bottom of great bell-shaped glasses that its bouquet might be the better savoured by the true epicures of what was really exquisite in life—these cannot be left unpaid, as bad debts of a dishonest *client*. Even the dainty sleeve-links—four heart-shaped moonstones of silver mist, girdled by alternate ruby and diamond for their setting—that I designed, and had made at Henry Lewis's as a special little present to you, to celebrate the success of my second comedy—these even—though I believe you sold them for a song a few months afterwards—have to be paid for. . . . And what is true of a bankrupt is true of everyone else in life. For every single thing that is done someone has to pay. (507)

Here, with the remembrance of French, French food, and French style, and the repetition of how things "always" were "served" and "reserved" for him, the pre-prison world is triumphantly reconstituted in the kind of timelessness that fixed the world of imprisonment. And Wilde's debts, romantically transformed, become the link between his past and future. The human situation as Wilde describes it is to be in debt and to be able neither to repay nor to declare bankruptcy and nullify the debt—a situation not merely economic but also social, at the basis of human society, which he has imaginatively rejoined. It is also the condition of loving, which he has successfully remembered.

By counterposing realism and romance, Wilde kept a positive past and created a possible future, both in contrast to the frozen time of imprisonment. With its romance and realism, its romance and finance, the letter has also defeated the prison system, embodied the individual voice of the silenced, whose name was otherwise "merely the figure and letter of a little cell in a long gallery" (454). (When Wilde later spoke out on behalf of a mentally disabled prisoner, he found it rhetorically effective to write of the man as A.2.11., the number of his cell.)

Here we might also reverse the historical judgment on the style of the letter. In the course of composition Wilde has moved from a style as stilted as "our ill-fated and most lamentable friendship" to one as royal and fantastic as "I was a man who stood in symbolic relations to the art and culture of my age" (466), "The gods had given me almost everything" (466), and "I, once a lord of language, have no words in which to express my anguish and my shame" (458), to one as strikingly banal as "There is something so unique about Christ." The long, beautifully balanced sentences and the conversational realism resist the terse uniformity of prison life. The penal philosophy of deterrence had led to a regime where time was meaningless. If the prisoner's only function was to serve as an image to deter others from crime, then the prisoner's time, or the purposelessness of his labor, was irrelevant. Art could be quite useless, as Wilde had said in the Preface to *The Picture of Dorian Gray*, for it need only satisfy the contemplative spirit. But prison labor, whose only use under the philosophy of deterrence was punitive, surpassed the limits of uselessness: it made the prisoner feel used.

Although both the system and prisoners have changed during the past hundred years, Wilde's letter in fact illustrates most of the elements of prison literature under modern conditions.[8] These include a grandeur and authority of statement, frequently in the form of spectacular fantasies and largely in response to the monotony of prison life and the size of the bureaucracy; the necessary positing of a specific reader or listener whom the narrator engages in dialogues and whom the narrator frequently loves; a particular disruptive style of detail and romance in response to isolation and best described by prisoners familiar with solitary confinement; and, often after the prisoner's release, a collective voice—literally, as in books written by a group of prisoners, or in multiple, shifting points of view representing different prisoners, or in the collective ballad voice, as in Wilde's *Reading Gaol*. The grandeur and authority of statement, the pontificating attitude that in prison one can "see things as they really are," to use Wilde's own phrase, matches the conditions of mass convict labor under a strong centralized system, the existence of which makes life outside appear more uniformly explainable than it is. To counter the grandness of the system and to diminish the monotony, prisoners construct elaborate fantasies. If a prisoner is held in solitary confinement, such fantasies need to be disrupted and grounded to something real and particular lest they grow into insanity. Even if the prisoner is not in solitary, the fantasies, short of real madness, cannot endure, for the system can always show the prisoner the tenuousness of his illusions of grandeur. Wilde had been granted the privilege of writing his long letter to Douglas, but he still had to face the wall when first offenders walked by.

Even today prisoners' accounts of the mental effects of solitary confinement vary remarkably little, especially in disruptive outbursts against the system, sexual and other fantasies, the rehearsal of dialogues from previous times, and the specific reconstruction of local life outside. Solitary confinement, in fact, appears to be a great leveler among prisoners of diverse backgrounds and tempers. To cite just two accounts from very different prisoners will, I believe, indicate how pertinent they are to an understanding of Wilde's mental process in his letter to Douglas. *Prison Etiquette: The Convict's Compendium of Useful Information* contains several accounts of solitary confinement by extreme pacifist conscientious objectors in 1941. Referred to as "constructive meditation" by the prison authorities, solitary confinement began with overwhelming sexual desires, alternating with anger against the system and endless dialogues from former scenes from the life world.

> You think until your head aches and then you fall into a daze. After a while you start thinking again. You think about the prison setup, which Federal Prisons Director James V. Bennett calls "the most authoritarian in the world." You think about the screws who keep you locked in like an animal because they get orders from their superiors who get orders from higher officers who get orders from Washington. . . . Then you get tired of thinking and lapse into a daze again. But before long you find yourself thinking some more—you can't help it. You relive incidents and episodes; what you said, what the other person said, what you answered. Then you go over the entire scene again, but this time you think of what you should have said and what the other person would have answered. Then you mull over the names of places you have been, names of streets, names of night joints, names of girls.[9]

Jack Abbott writes about painful memories, what we have called the prisoner's realism in Wilde, and grand ideals, what we have called romance, in solitary confinement:

> I have my memories. I have the good ones, the bad ones, the ones that are neither of these. So I have *myself*. . . . I think. I remember. I think. I remember. Memory is arrested in the hole. I think about each remembered thing, study it in detail, over and over. I unite it with others, under headings for how I feel about it. Finally it changes and begins to tear itself free from facts and joins my imagination. . . . It travels the terrain of time in a pure way, unfettered by what is, reckless of what was, what will become of it. Memory is not enriched by any further experience. It is *deprived* memory, memory deprived of every movement but the isolated body traveling thousands of miles in the confines of my prison cell. . . . Every memory has an element of pain or disappointment. . . . In the hole after a while the painful elements begin to throw out shoots and sprout like brittle weeds in the garden of memory—until finally, after so long, they choke to death everything else in the garden. . . . It is the same with ideals. . . . As life in the hole, in the pure terrain of time, continues, your passions are aroused less and less with the hope of memories and more and more by your ideals. Love, Hate, Equality, Justice, Freedom, War, Peace, Beauty, Truth—they all eventually become Idols, pure and empty abstract gods that demand your fealty, your undying obedience.[10]

Like Wilde, Abbott also writes about the mental time expansion in the physical space of confinement:

> There are always voices in the hole. It's a strange thing. I have seen *wars* take place in the hole. I have seen sexual love take place in the hole. I have seen, as a matter of fact, the most impossible things *happen* under these conditions. Let us say a kind of movement that is not really movement exists there. To illustrate: to walk

ten miles in an enclosed space of ten feet is not really movement. There are not ten miles of space, only time. You do not go ten miles. . . . The real world is out of place in the hole, but the hole is nonetheless really there. It is time that no longer moves forward in human experience. You can walk, placing one foot before the other, across eternity in time. All the space you need is six or seven feet. The hole furnishes only that provision: you are living a demonstration of the theory of the infinite within the finite; the dream within the reality.

The collective voice often comes later, after release. This was Wilde's in *The Ballad of Reading Gaol*—with an emphasis on the collective form of the ballad. If in his letter to Douglas he feared the debilitation of his mind and extinction of his soul, in *Reading Gaol* he defended the dignity of the body. The prisoners are constituted as a class during exercise in the yard and united against the warden, doctor, and chaplain, the symbolic pillars of society, around the body of the hanged man. Their sexual nightmares and their crimes uniformly related to love have their counterparts in a great part of twentieth-century prison literature. Wilde wrote about the same time, "Of course I side with the prisoners: I was one, and I belong to their class now."[11]

Through writing as productive labor, Wilde had achieved a resilient form of rehabilitation, one which, as the drastically edited first edition and the subsequent versions trivialized by later critics indicate, could not be consumed by the public. But his wittiest act of resistance—perhaps ever— came in a letter to Leonard Smithers concerning where to publish *Reading Gaol*. It was his last line for the audience: "My idea is *Reynolds's*. . . . It circulates widely among the criminal classes—to which I now belong—so I shall be read by my peers—a new experience for me."[12]

Rooted in the public school, the press, the theater, and the prison, the Aestheticism of the 1890's produced a critical art world that was also but one commodity-spectacle among many on the shelves of the modern age. On his deathbed Wilde was received into the Roman Catholic Church, having flirted with Catholicism and having been a Freemason since his university days. His references to the Church in his letters most frequently concerned the beauty of the Pope's robes.

Appendixes

Appendix A
Art as Propaganda in Wartime: The Pemberton-Billing Trials on *Salome*

*T*RANSCRIPTS of the Pemberton-Billing case, first heard by Sir John Dickinson at Bow Street Police Court, then later by Mr. Justice Darling at the Old Bailey, were included in Noel Pemberton-Billing's private subscription paper the *Vigilante*, founded in 1916 as the *Imperialist* (see vols. 7-8; 6, 13, and 20 April and 15 June 1918). The transcripts from Bow Street are allegedly verbatim; those from the Old Bailey were edited, perhaps due to the entirely chaotic nature of the later trial. Prolific press reports supply what the *Vigilante* deleted, but it seems that this constituted relatively little, for Pemberton-Billing himself was not a close man.

During the trials Pemberton-Billing conducted his own defense and called his own witnesses. Although one of his staff, Capt. Harold Sherwood Spencer, actually wrote the libelous articles, Pemberton-Billing emphasized that he took full responsibility for everything printed in his paper, as indeed he was legally bound to do. The front page of every edition of the *Vigilante* bore the caption "THE ONLY NEWSPAPER THAT DOES NOT ACCEPT ADVERTISEMENTS AND THEREFORE IS FREE TO SPEAK THE TRUTH." Pemberton-Billing also emphatically reiterated in court that he had been libeling hundreds of persons, generally government officials, for some years in order to expose and end corruption in all its forms. Both he and Spencer testified that they had merely waited for Maud Allan to prosecute and were indeed surprised that she and J. T. Grein had taken so long to do so. Pemberton-Billing's paper, he and his witnesses stressed, functioned as the organ of the Vigilante Society, of which Pemberton-Billing was president and which had been "founded to fight for purity in public life."

First the trial concerned possible impurity among artistic circles. At Bow Street Allan testified that she took Spencer's article, entitled "The Cult of the Clitoris," to mean that her representation of Salome was an inducement to lesbianism and that she herself was a lesbian. ("A more horrible libel to publish of any woman," said her counsel Travers Humphreys—one of Wilde's counsel in 1895, "it is impossible to find.") Pemberton-Billing claimed that *Salome* directly ministered to "sexual perverts, Sodomites and

Appendix A

Lesbians," and argued at the Old Bailey that Allan's knowledge of the word "clitoris" proved her association with deviants:

"Clitoris" is an anatomical term; a Greek word; understood of the few. I had never heard it in my life before, and I doubt if any member of the Jury had ever heard it in his life before. The word was calculated to be understood only of those people who in their ordinary common parlance would refer to these things—and it was so understood. Grein told us that when he picked [the article] up he knew immediately what it meant. He takes it to Miss Allan. She knows immediately what it means.

(Out of hundreds of press clippings on the case, only one article actually quoted the libelous phrase.)

An editorial note concluding the transcripts from Bow Street included an article on the twelve-month prison sentence for "a certain offense" of Christopher Millard, Wilde's bibliographer; the testimonial for services to literature presented to Robert Ross, Wilde's literary executor, by Asquith and other prominent figures, about which Alfred Douglas had published his scathing *Rossiad* (1916), contrasting the homosexual Ross with boys dying at the front—at the height of Douglas's infighting with Ross and repudiation of Wilde, which he would in calmer times retract; and letters and articles concerned with the Ross and Douglas litigation. Pemberton-Billing matched this continuous journalistic attention to Wilde's friends by his claims during the trial that Wilde was "a great moral pervert"; that contrary to Grein's aesthetic defense of *Salome*, the play was about sex, specifically about sadism, defined in court as the love of dead bodies; and that the play consequently did not "assist us to concentrate on the great national problem which presents itself to every Britisher today." For further examples of the language of perversion, at the Old Bailey Pemberton-Billing had his then obliging witness Alfred Douglas read some of Wilde's letters. In Judge Darling's summing up, he conceded that "Oscar Wilde wrote filthy works, as you know: he was guilty of filthy practices: he was convicted in this Court and suffered imprisonment, and social extinction, and death in due course." After the jury's verdict of not guilty for Pemberton-Billing, the judge condemned *Salome* and suggested reform of the drama and of the dress code for actresses.

Yet Darling's sympathy with Pemberton-Billing's assessment of Wilde's work did not satify the M.P., who insisted to the end on inflating the issues of the trial well beyond a mere attack on the dancer and the Independent Theatre. In his article, Spencer had predicted that were the subscription members of Grein's theater to be apprehended, the "first of the 47,000" would be duly rooted out. The 47,000, to whom the *Vigilante* had devoted considerable space, were, according to Pemberton-Billing and his staff, 47,000 British citizens who, through indulgence in various sexual practices, had been found out by German spies and were consequently German sympathizers through fear of exposure. Their names were allegedly inscribed in a secret German Black Book, which Spencer, in various alleged military and diplomatic capacities, had seen and brought to the attention of Pemberton-Billing and one of his zealous witnesses, Mrs. Eileen Villiers-Stuart. Although the existence of such a book was never verified, and Spencer's testimony, as well as his claim to official posts, was discredited by various ministers, the Black Book received considerable attention during the trials and in the press.

Pemberton-Billing claimed that before the war Germany had devised a plot to infiltrate the British government and armed services with lesbians and homosexuals and in wartime used spies to blackmail civilians and debilitate the troops. Such German sympathizers were those for whom Allan danced and Grein produced his plays. At Bow Street, Pemberton-Billing concerned himself with the Dutch Grein's theatrical connections with neutral countries, his holding certain German Orders, and his having founded the German Theatre in London. In one astonishing scene of shouting and handwaving which came to be typical of the trial's conduct at the Old Bailey, Pemberton-Billing and Mrs. Villiers-Stuart charged Darling himself with considerable status in the Black Book and went on to include Asquith and Lord Haldane among its lists. Darling proceeded with his own hilarity in the form of jokes at Pemberton-Billing's expense, until Alfred Douglas, who had followed the entire proceedings squatting on a lower step in the courtroom, jumped up and loudly denounced the judge as a liar and damned liar.

All this, of course, was duly lapped up by the press: "GERMAN BOOK REVEALS . . ." "JUDGE IMPLICATED . . ." "ASQUITH HEADS LIST . . ." and so on ran the headlines. In general, the press represented the seriousness of the trial until Pemberton-Billing was acquitted, and then it ridiculed the jury for taking a contemptible Pemberton-Billing seriously. When it was all over, angry editorials flourished which denounced him for using such shenanigans to divert readers from more serious wartime news. The *Jewish World* of 12 June 1918 warned, however, that Pemberton-Billing's insubstantial evidence and the claims it supported were comparable to current calumny against Jews and that the consequences of such shenanigans could eventually become quite serious.

Appendix A

In his historical study of the case, *Salome's Last Veil: The Libel Case of the Century* (1977), Michael Kettle saw the event as a curious mixture of high politics and sex—reminiscent, actually, of political *affaires* more common in France than England. Pemberton-Billing, Allan, Grein, and company were merely pawns in a plot to overthrow the coalition government. The War Office and Admiralty feared that the peace talks (or prisoner-of-war exchanges) then being considered by the government would prolong the war, since Germany would use returned prisoners in the field. Lt. Col. Charles à Court Repington, the foremost military correspondent of his day—who had been embittered by the destruction of a brilliant career in the Army due to a woman—enlisted Pemberton-Billing to join the conspirators and help bring Lloyd George down. If Pemberton-Billing could smear various politicians at the Old Bailey and work up anti-German feeling in the House of Commons by persistent questions about aliens—German banks were still active in Britain—the peace talks could be prevented, Lloyd George brought down, and the war run properly.

Lloyd George learned of the generals' conspiracy to bring him down, take over the War Cabinet, and sabotage the peace talks, and decided to discredit Pemberton-Billing and the generals in the same way they intended to discredit his politicians: by allegations of sexual perversion (practically indistinguishable from German sympathy at this point). To this end Lloyd George sent Villiers-Stuart as *agent provocateur* to entrap Pemberton-Billing (as notorious a womanizer as Lloyd George himself), who would then be used to discredit the generals and admirals. Unfortunately for the coalition government, Villiers-Stuart apparently fell in love with Pemberton-Billing, became his mistress, and changed sides. Hence her appearance in court as witness for the defense.

The trial was then specially given to Darling, a former Tory M.P. who still retained close links with the Conservative Party. Pemberton-Billing had to be put away. Unfortunately again for the politicians, as Spencer cheerfully accused the judge and counsel of positions in the Black Book, cited the late Edward VII's mistress as a chief intermediary between Britain and Germany, and cast aspersions on the Germanic roots of the royal family name, the jury increasingly sided with Pemberton-Billing. It did not help that Pemberton-Billing, who had spent four years on stage as a professional actor, packed the gallery with wounded soldiers—and this before the war had turned in favor of the Allies.

Although the generals' conspiracy ultimately failed to defeat the politicians, Pemberton-Billing's spectacular seduction of the British Public was

Art as Propaganda in Wartime

not just political. It was an hysterical configuration of art, politics, military strategy, medicine, and sex. Presided by a judge who was, like Herod, a known wit and who amused the public with jokes from the bench, the trial became the scene of chaos and lunacy that made the moon-gazing in *Salome* look mild.

Consider how Spencer's cross-examination on art criticism is riddled with political suggestions and how he uses medical knowledge politically to discredit an ignorant counsel and judge.

Counsel: You think [Salome] desired [Iokanaan] to be killed in order that she might indulge this strange passion of hers for a dead body? Is that your reading?

Spencer: It is my reading that it aroused lust in a woman who was eventually satisfied with a dead head. . . .

Counsel: Bearing in mind the earlier parts of the play, do you give as your considered opinion that this act of this disappointed and revenged woman, because the man was dead, and had refused her lips in his lifetime, is Sadism?

Spencer: I think the Germans were very justified in their opinion of the play.

Judge: You are not asked that. You are not being asked whether the Germans were justified, or anything about what the Germans do. Get them out of your head for a moment.

Spencer: I wish more people would get them in. . . .

Counsel: You give it now as your considered opinion that the kisses on the lips which had been refused to her during his lifetime were Sadism?

Spencer: And produced an orgasm.

Counsel: What?

Judge: What is the word you used?

Spencer: I am quoting from the German writer Bloch.

Judge: Repeat the word you used.

Spencer: Orgasm.

Counsel: Some unnatural vice?

Spencer: No, it is a function of the body.

Dr. Serrell Cooke, in charge of the mentally disabled at Paddington Hospital and a student of Krafft-Ebing's *Psychopathia Sexualis*, gave as evidence a detailed medical synopsis of the play, finding it a museum of sexual pathology. Yet the height of critical lunacy was reached in Pemberton-Billing's contention that since the moon could influence female erotomaniacs— Salome gazes at the moon—Grein had probably scheduled the productions during the maddening phases.

Salome's casualty in 1918 emphasized that art could have no aesthetic function in wartime, being inevitably reduced to one of the two terms of propaganda. In this case, the Germans were barbarians and perverts while the British were noble patriots. Yet at the time of the trial the Germans were

Appendix A

winning. Unable to develop a consistent pro-war discourse or stratagem, Britain developed scapegoatism with a sort of sexual obsessiveness. A philistine, homophobic, xenophobic M.P. out-Heroded Herod and dragged Salome, with her delicate imagination, into the national wartime press. Then the fantasy and indeterminacy of art became the scapegoat of demagogues who closed off interpretation in the only way that could make sense of evil victors: by locating the evil in the good—that is, home—audience.

Appendix B
Alfred Douglas's Political Interpretation of Wilde's Conviction

*A*FTER 1895 Alfred Douglas turned his reckless courage and aristocratic arrogance from the superannuated dons he teased at Oxford to the government that convicted his friend. In August 1895, he composed an article entitled "Oscar Wilde" for the *Mercure de France* that claimed that Wilde's conviction was political.[1] After pointing out that Queensberry's assault on Wilde had merely duplicated that of an 1893 assault on Lord Rosebery (then Foreign Secretary, by 1894 Prime Minister), Douglas went on to expose his father's bribing and threatening of witnesses against Wilde, especially through the mediation of the lawyer Bernard Abrahams. Thus discrediting the witnesses, Douglas turned to certain peculiar circumstances of Wilde's trials: (1) that Wilde was refused bail after his arrest; (2) that a request to defer the trial in order to prepare the defense was refused—a refusal that Wilde's attorneys allegedly told Douglas was without precedent and constituted a denial of justice; and (3) that when a divided jury did not obtain a verdict of guilty, a new trial was immediately scheduled with the solicitor general to direct the prosecution.

Douglas attributes the extraordinary circumstances to political intrigue rather than personal animosity on the part of the government. He claims that Wilde's enemies and the Queensberry party told the government that unless Wilde were condemned, new revelations would be made that would incriminate important members of the Liberal party. "I know *for an absolute fact* that the London police has on its books the names of more than 4000 persons known as habitual pederasts, and yet none of them are prosecuted, and many of them occupy the highest and most respected positions in politics, art and society." The reason, for example, says Douglas, that a Maurice Schwabe mentioned in the trial was not permitted to appear was that he was the nephew of Lockwood, the solicitor general. The article went on to implicate higher figures in the government and to view Wilde as "a victim . . . sacrificed to save a party": "Give me 2000 pounds and the same lawyers [i.e., as his father's] and I will guarantee to work up material for a good suit against any man in England, high or low, starting with the Prime Minister." The article, which continued in this spirit for some twenty pages, concludes with an impassioned plea for a policy of laissez faire in adult sexual matters.

In "Une introduction à mes poèmes, avec quelques considerations sur l'affaire Oscar Wilde" (*La Revue Blanche*, 1 June 1896, pp. 484-90), Douglas intensified his defense of homosexuality and continued his attacks on the government:

> I want to ask Mr. Asquith, then Home Secretary and an old friend of Oscar Wilde, if on a certain occasion he was not informed by Lord Rosebery that unless a second trial was instituted and Mr. Wilde convicted, the Liberal Party would be out of power. . . . The fact is that the Liberal Party contained a large number of men whom I have already called the salt of the earth [i.e., homosexuals]. The mock moralists threatened a series of actions against members of the government which would have produced a scandal without precedent. If Oscar Wilde were found guilty and punished, there would be an end of the matter. Thus it became necessary to obtain a verdict of guilty at any price. . . . Oscar Wilde's conviction was one of the last acts of the discredited Liberal Party, which is now reduced to an exceptional minority in the House of Commons. [My translation]

Whatever the truth of Douglas's grander allegations about the government, there is little doubt today that Douglas was correct in some of his specifics. In 1892 his brother Francis, Viscount Drumlanrig, was appointed assistant private secretary to Rosebery, then Foreign Minister in Gladstone's government. In 1893, Rosebery persuaded Gladstone, who persuaded the Queen to grant Drumlanrig a seat in the House of Lords. Queensberry, who had lost his seat because of his refusal to take the customary oath of allegiance, sent abusive letters to the Queen, Gladstone, Rosebery, and Drumlanrig, threatened to horsewhip Rosebery for his "bad influence" on Drumlanrig, and was only persuaded to desist by the Prince of Wales. In 1894 Drumlanrig was found dead from a gunshot wound at a shooting party in Somerset. His nephew Francis, who became the 11th Marquess of Queensberry, told H. Montgomery Hyde that he was positive that Drumlanrig had taken his own life to avoid a scandal in which his and Rosebery's homosexual affair would become public.[2]

In June 1895 More Adey, a close friend of Robert Ross and a tireless worker for Wilde's material comforts and legal rights until Wilde's death, wrote but did not send a letter that supports Douglas's allegations. The identity of the intended receiver has not been established, but the letter at the Clark Library indicates that it was a French author who covered the trials in the French press. Adey desires the correspondent to emphasize that Wilde was convicted on insufficient and tainted evidence for political purposes. After describing the Crown's use of disreputable witnesses, Adey offers the following explanation of the conviction:

A. It has long been reported that a person—indeed several persons—but one in particular, in very high authority has been implicated in unisexual practises which are in England illegal.

B. I am certain that the Treasury were forced by a body of private persons some of whose names I know, headed by the infamous Lord Queensberry, to obtain a conviction by some means or other against Mr. Wilde. These individuals, I believe, *blackmailed* the Treasury, holding over the Treasury the threat that, if Wilde were not convicted, damning evidence would be produced against important and exalted persons.

Of course, in the 1914 *Oscar Wilde and Myself*, after Douglas's embattled litigations with Ross and Arthur Ransome concerning *De Profundis*, Douglas entirely repudiated his "vicious" opinions in the *Revue Blanche* article, going so far as to say that they had not been his at all but were inserted by the translator. (In the later *Autobiography*, he repudiated *Oscar Wilde and Myself*.) Yet even after he had changed his terminology from the "salt of the earth" to the "vicious," he continued to denounce, in both private correspondence and letters to editors in the press, British hypocrisy concerning sexual matters.

Appendix C
Commodity Fetishism as Poetry in *A Florentine Tragedy*

> The man is but a very honest knave
> Full of fine phrases for life's merchandise,
> Selling most dear what he must hold most
>   cheap,
> A windy brawler in a world of words.
> I never met so eloquent a fool.
> *A Florentine Tragedy*

*B*EFORE WILDE went to prison he had completed all but the opening scene of *A Florentine Tragedy*, which Sturge Moore composed at the request of Robert Ross in 1906 so that the play could be performed. Despite its title, the play is a kind of comic version of *Othello*, in which Othello is the merchant of Florence. The plot advances through the breaking of boundaries or culturally charged pairs familiar in Wilde's life and work: youth/age, beauty/decay, nation/world, domus/state, marriage/adultery, Nature/Art, value/price, subject/object. The triteness of these symbolic or semantic configurations would make the play a candidate for popularity if not for the disruptive poetry of the merchant Simone: disruptive, that is, of syntactic progress, or plot.

Guido, a Florentine prince, goes to seduce a merchant's wife, Bianca. At curtain rise she has refused his 40,000 crowns for her favor, for she believes that youth should not be exchanged for money but for youth, measure for measure. Her complaint against her aged husband consists in his blindness to beauty. "His soul," she testifies repeatedly, "stands ever in the marketplace. . . . His eyes meet mine and with a shudder I am sure he counts / the cost of what I wear." Yet although her marriage has but made her "perfect in the price of velvets," the lovers themselves cannot help but speak in economic metaphor. Sturge Moore emphasizes this with little subtlety in the scene he added to the work.

> *Guido:* It is thyself, Bianca, I would buy.
> *Bianca:* O, then, my lord, it must be with Simone
>   You strike your bargain.
> . . .

Commodity Fetishism as Poetry

Guido: Love is? Love is the meeting of two worlds
In never-ending change and counter-change.
Bianca: Thus will my husband praise the mercer's mart.

This Shakespearean love contaminated by trade is only heightened by the entrance of the merchant and husband Simone, who appears on stage wanting only to sell his wares. Estimating Guido a client, Simone displays his wares and commands his wife to spin for profit. As Guido and Bianca make a fool, nearly a cuckold, of him before his eyes, he appeals to the Prince concerning the plight of Florentine merchants losing their markets to English intruders selling wool at illegally low rates and the danger to Florence of the Pope's betrayal of Italy to France, summoned to put down internecine feuds. As love is blind—like autonomous art—to matters of state, Guido disclaims these concerns as his, and Simone laments the narrowness of the romance he begins to perceive:

> Is all this mighty world
> Narrowed into the confines of this room
> With but three souls for poor inhabitants?
> . . . Alas! my lord!
> How poor a bargain is this life of man,
> And in how mean a market are we sold!

The play ends with the merchant's phallic challenge to the Prince to duel ("I never touched so delicate a blade. / I have a sword too, somewhat rusted now"), the Prince's death ("He who filches from me something that is mine / Perils his soul and body in the theft"), and the repossession of Bianca. Now, for the first time, she sees her husband's strength: "Why did you not tell me you were so strong?" As the curtain falls, the previously negligent Simone kisses her on the mouth responding "Why did you not tell me you were beautiful?"

The choices that the play has posed and that romance has superficially resolved are shown to be false: English merchants still financially compromise a state courting military invasion from France, princes abandon rule, and Simone remains an old man with a young wife. That is, the romantic plot advanced through serial cultural dualisms like youth/age, beauty/decay, and Nature/Art is imposed upon, even masks, less pliant antitheses like nation/world, domus/state, value/price, and subject/object. The play reveals romance as the opiate of youth and the victim of power: it affirms not romance but finance. This probably explains why Wilde called the play a tragedy, despite its felicitous domestic closure.

Appendix C

Yet, like Marx and Engels's representation of the historical triumph of the bourgeoisie, the fictive tragedy is also ambivalent and dialectical. Simone's speech accompanying the parade of his merchandise is magic, the poetry of an erotic relationship to objects. Unsuspecting of his imminent and tactless cuckolding, he draws out the robes and caps and jewels, fondling them, getting lost in them. As he displays and fetishizes his commodities, always talking, he talks himself into a knowledge of his auditors' betrayal as well as of the Prince's romantic disregard for Florence and the state.

The play transforms beauty into a commodity and love into an object in the most exhilarating fashion. Simone's poetry is the poetry of objectification and glorious materialism: beyond the lovers' mere economic metaphors, Simone can only love what he *sees* and what he sees is made visible, not by its value, but by its price: the logical conclusion of the play is that the husband and wife see each other for the first time, value each other for the first time, because the strength of one has been activated, and the beauty of the other has been objectified, by a competitor. Simone's is the poetry of spectacle. The revolutionary desire of the play—the annihilation of the aristocrat, the repossession of beloved and made objects by the bourgeoisie, class and national solidarity in the face of evil empires—situates the merchant in a commercial world, a world with promise of production and, with considerable extension of the imagination, reproduction. It is a world inhabited, as Alfred Douglas would say, without apology, but tragically.

Reference Matter

Notes

Complete authors' names, titles, and publication data for sources cited in short form are given in the Selected Bibliography, pp. 235-43.

Introduction

1. Unless otherwise noted, quotations by Wilde are cited from the editions of his works listed in the Selected Bibliography, p. 243.
2. Richard Ellmann, "Oscar at Oxford," *New York Review of Books*, March 29, 1984, pp. 23-28.
3. I owe the compactness of this comparative formula to Stacey Vallas, who summarized it in my Decadents and Aesthetes Seminar, Stanford University, autumn 1984.
4. Although this study will treat British Aestheticism locally and specifically, there is no doubt that Wilde owed much of his affect and many of his themes to the French symbolists and decadents. Like Mérrimées he had a penchant for literary forgeries, and like Baudelaire he composed poems in prose; like Nerval—especially in his late life—he assumed vagabondage and was sometimes thought mad; like the Goncourts he produced histories of sensations; and like de l'Isle-Adam, he opposed a nobility and Church against middle-class materialism. With Verlaine he believed that geniuses were antagonistic to modern society; with Huysmans he shared a love of books and interest in modern psychology, and with Rimbaud a love of youth. Like many of the *décadents*, he believed that satire was the revenge of beauty upon ugliness and art the creation of heaven out of earth. These things were in the air. See A. Symons, *Symbolist Movement*, esp. pp. 45, 74, 117, 129, 138, 145, 210, 248, 271-72, 293, and 326.
5. For a history of Anglo-American criticism of the decadents, see Ch. 2, n. 34.
6. "No More Masterpieces" in Artaud, *Theater*, p. 79.
7. Debord, *Society of the Spectacle*, p. 195.
8. See Baudrillard, *Mirror of Production*.
9. See "The Author as Producer" in Benjamin, *Reflections*, pp. 220-38.
10. Debord, *Society of the Spectacle*, pp. 206-8. These ideas are quoted directly in Ch. 1; see p. 32.
11. Appleton, et al., *Essays*, pp. 22-23. See also Heyck's parallel analysis of aestheticism and the university reform movement in *Transformation*, p. 180. For

Notes to Pages 14-27

Cambridge, see Rothblatt, *Revolution of the Dons*; for Oxford, Engel, *Clergyman to Don*.

12. Chesterton, *Victorian Age*, p. 110; Borges in Ellmann, *Wilde: Critical Essays*, p. 172.

13. Hobsbawm, *Workers*, esp. ch. 11, "The Making of the Working Class 1870-1914," pp. 194-213.

14. Leverson, *Letters to the Sphinx*, pp. 19-20.

Chapter 1

1. "The Truth of Masks: A Note on Illusion" was first published in *Nineteenth Century*, May 1885, as "Shakespeare and Stage Costume"; "The Decay of Lying: An Observation" in *Nineteenth Century*, January 1889; "Pen, Pencil, and Poison: A Study in Green" in *Fortnightly Review*, January 1889; and "The Critic as Artist" as "The True Function and Value of Criticism" in *Nineteenth Century*, July and September 1890. Twentieth-century criticism of Wilde's literary theory can be divided between critics concerned with Wilde's themes and those concerned with his style. On Wilde and the form of Platonic dialogue, see Roditi, *Oscar Wilde*, ch. 5. On Wilde and Romantic and late-Victorian Hegelian dialectics, see Chamberlin, *Ripe Was the Drowsy Hour*, ch. 4. For Wilde's demonstration of Paterian flux in the forms of his essays, see Sussman, "Criticism as Art." For the themes, as opposed to the forms, of Wilde's critical writing, see Ericksen, *Oscar Wilde*, ch. 4; Shewan, *Wilde: Art and Egotism*, ch. 3; and San Juan, *Art of Wilde*, ch. 3.

2. "The Portrait of Mr. W. H." was first published in *Blackwood's Magazine*, July 1889. After a long history of delays the expanded version was published in 1921. "The Soul of Man Under Socialism" was published in *Fortnightly Review*, February 1891.

3. Sherard, *Life of Oscar Wilde*, pp. 129-32.

4. Cited in Gross, *Rise and Fall*, p. 1. I owe many of the following quotations to the attentiveness and energy of Deidre Lynch in my seminar on Victorian lives, Stanford University, autumn 1983.

5. Ruskin, *Genius*, p. 394. 6. Ibid., p. 443.
7. Leavis, *Fiction*, p. 163. 8. Ruskin, *Genius*, p. 444.
9. Charles Dickens, *Our Mutual Friend*, ed. Stephen Gill (Middlesex, 1971), p. 191.
10. Ruskin, *Genius*, p. 436.
11. See Heyck, *Transformation*, p. 204.
12. Gissing, *New Grub Street*, pp. 496-97.
13. Ibid., p. 114. 14. Ibid., p. 138.
15. Ibid. 16. Ibid., p. 213.
17. Ibid., pp. 397-98. 18. Leavis, *Fiction*, p. 157.
19. Ibid., p. 191. 20. See Gross, *Rise and Fall*, p. 26.

21. Sydney Colvin, "Fellowships and National Culture," *Macmillan's* (June 1876), p. 141; cited in Heyck, *Transformation*, p. 229.

22. Critics today are only beginning to appreciate this aspect of Arnold. See "Function of Matthew Arnold."

Notes to Pages 28-45

23. Empson, *Seven Types*, pp. 236-37.

24. For a discussion of Wilde's linking individualism and socialism, which were generally considered antithetical in the last decades of the nineteenth century, see Thomas, "The Soul of Man Under Socialism." Thomas also draws an explicit connection between the Fabians, especially Sydney Olivier, Shaw, Morris (see especially p. 93 n. 10) and Wilde; and he deals with sources cited by other Wilde critics but which he considers spurious, like Godwin, Kropotkin, and Chuang-tze. Masolino D'Amico, on the other hand, sees Kropotkin's anarchism as the major source of Wilde's formulation of individualism. D'Amico traces socialist references and sympathies in Wilde's major works and concludes that he was more anarchist than socialist. See D'Amico, "Between Socialism and Aestheticism."

25. See Rowbotham and Weeks, *Socialism*, pt. I, secs. 2-5; and Hobsbawm, *Labour's Turning Point*.

26. Although recent critics (e.g., Ellmann and Ericksen) frequently emphasize the effect of Ruskin's social thought on Wilde, the latter's contemporaries saw Wilde as much more radical than his alleged master. See Sherard, *Life of Oscar Wilde*, pp. 129-31.

27. The debate over the "sincerity" of Wilde's socialism in "The Soul of Man" is aged and prolific. For an example of the opposing sides see George Woodcock, "The Social Rebel," in Ellmann, *Wilde: Critical Essays*, pp. 150-68, and Ericksen, *Oscar Wilde*, pp. 90-95. In "Irony of a Socialist Aesthete" (*Crazy Fabric*, pp. 138-50), A. E. Dyson considers Wilde's socialism as well as his oblique style.

28. Pearson, *Wilde: Life and Wit*, p. 152.

29. Engels, *Condition of the Working Class*, pp. 312-13.

30. Ibid., pp. 370, 313-14, 82.

31. Bakhtin, *Dostoevsky's Poetics*, p. 234.

32. Debord, *Society of the Spectacle*, pp. 206-8.

33. For a discussion of the Newgate drama and its sources in popular fiction, see Stephens, *Censorship*.

34. "The Poetic License to Kill," *Time*, 1 Feb. 1982, p. 82.

35. Pearson, *Wilde: Life and Wit*, p. 58.

36. Wilde's 1880's commonplace book of notes, now at the Clark Library, indicates his familiarity with Kant and Hegel, with the then current debates between metaphysics and positivism, and his own conclusion that studies in metaphysics should be revised as studies in method, that metaphysics should be limited to metacriticism.

37. Reade, *Sexual Heretics*, pp. 47, 160n. For the "Terminal Essay," see Burton, *Thousand Nights*, vol. 10, pp. 63-302.

38. I have come to this analysis of homoeroticism in "The Portrait of Mr. W. H." with the help of Ira Livingston in my Decadents and Aesthetes Seminar, Stanford University, autumn 1984.

39. For a brief biography of the strange but enchanting John Moray Stuart-Young, see Appendix A in Smith, *Love in Earnest*, pp. 202-19.

40. Douglas's correspondence with Adrian Earle is at the Clark Library, as are Shaw's letters on the matter of William Hewes.

41. Wilde, *Letters*, p. 319.

42. Cited in Letwin, *Gentleman in Trollope*, p. 272 n. 32.
43. See "The Intellectuals" in Gramsci, *Prison Notebooks*, esp. p. 18.

Chapter 2

1. See Presbrey, *Advertising*; Turner, *Shocking History*; and Wood, *Story of Advertising*. (Chapter 3 will develop the theoretical and psychological appurtenances of advertising.) This chapter was written before the current academic interest in advertising practices, so I have not been able to make use of such studies of advertising in the U. S. as Stephen R. Fox, *The Mirror Makers: A History of American Advertising and Its Creators* (New York, 1984) and Michael Schudson, *Advertising: The Uneasy Persuasion: Its Dubious Impact on American Society* (New York, 1984). However, as these studies show, the effect of advertising upon consumers has changed dramatically in the last 20 years. Here I am concerned with the beginning of modern advertising practices, when they had a more pronounced impact on society.
2. Turner, *Shocking History*, p. 160.   3. Ibid., p. 94.
4. Ibid., p. 146.   5. Wood, *Story of Advertising*, p. 13.
6. Turner, *Shocking History*, p. 107.
7. For the little magazines, see Ian Fletcher, "Decadence and the Little Magazines," in Fletcher, *Decadence*, pp. 173-202; for the productions of the Bodley Head, see Nelson, *Early Nineties*.
8. Turner, *Shocking History*, p. 83.
9. See Wood, *Story of Advertising*, pp. 10-12.
10. A. J. A. Symons, "Oscar Wilde in America," manuscript of 193-? in the Clark collection. See also A. J. A. Symons, "Wilde at Oxford."
11. A. Symons, *Symbolist Movement*, p. 9.
12. *St. James's Gazette*, 24 June 1890. The most important reviews of *Dorian Gray* have been collected by Stuart Mason in *Wilde: Art and Morality*.
13. Ibid., pp. 43-44; and see Wilde's letter to the *Daily Chronicle*, pp. 72-73.
14. Ibid., pp. 137-39, 147, 199. Since recent critics tend to read Wilde's work in the light (or dark) of the events of 1895, they frequently psychologize *Dorian Gray*; the characters—which the *St. James's Gazette* called "puppies" (see ibid., pp. 27-34)—are seen as contradictory impulses in Wilde. The post-war history of *Dorian Gray* has until very recently illustrated this psychologizing with varying degrees of sophistication. For Edouard Roditi, the paradoxical Wotton is beyond good and evil, possessing the Taoist identity of contraries in which conscience and temptation are equal but transcended. Maintaining his philosophy of inaction, Wotton never acts and never falls (Roditi, *Oscar Wilde*, p. 214). G. Wilson Knight, who sees Wilde himself as a Christlike figure, suggests but does not elaborate that the novel is a critique of Platonic Eros (*The Christian Renaissance* [New York, 1962], pp. 287-300, cited in Ellmann, *Wilde: Critical Essays*, p. 143). Ellmann, in order to demonstrate Wilde's progressive attitudes toward his own homosexuality, reads *Dorian Gray* as Wilde's early recognition of sin as being useful for the artist: through Dorian's fatal "expiation and regeneration," a *felix*

culpa, Wilde could pass to the trivialization of sin in Jack's check to the bailiff and the baptism concluding *The Importance of Being Earnest* (see Ellmann, Johnson, and Bush, *Wilde and the Nineties*, pp. 10, 20; this essay, in an altered form, was used by Ellmann as the introduction for Wilde, *Artist as Critic*). For Ellmann, Wotton is a critique of Pater and Pater's Marius, "a spectator of life," who has disastrous effects upon young Dorian; and Basil is a triumph, of sorts, of Ruskin, in that with his death Dorian pays his moral debt to the artist and art critic ("Overtures to Salome," *Yearbook of Comparative and General Literature* 17 [1968]: 17-28; cited in Ellmann, *Wilde: Critical Essays*, pp. 88-89). Epifanio San Juan, Jr. emphasizes the backgrounds as symbolist stages for the personalities, and the agons between characters as forerunners of the psychological topography of Jamesian and twentieth-century novels (San Juan, *Art of Wilde*, pp. 58-62). Unlike Roditi, Donald Ericksen reads Wilde's tripartite statement regarding the novel—"Basil Hallward is what I think I am . . ."—as applying not to conflicts in Wilde himself but rather to his theories of art and criticism: Dorian, Basil, and Sybil all fall from art to living and self-gratification. Wotton, the only one true to Wilde's critical tenets, remains unscathed (Ericksen, *Oscar Wilde*, pp. 103-4). Philip Cohen, who reads all Wilde's works as struggles between sin and redemption—not for his homosexuality, but for his final reunion with his soul/sister Isola, whose early death was the source of Wilde's self-division—sees Basil as representing New Testament vengeance. In this reading Dorian's final destruction of the portrait is the triumph of conscience, a break with the sterile art-loving Pater and La Gioconda (Cohen, *Moral Vision*, pp. 126, 146). Christopher Nassaar, dating Wilde's post-1886 works "as a new beginning, for he definitely regarded homosexual contact as evil and now wrote in full awareness of a demonic impulse within himself," sees *Dorian Gray* as a first presentiment of the demon universe (Nassaar, *Into the Demon Universe*, p. xiii). And Jeffrey Meyers, who appreciates the "complexity," "repression," and "expression" of what he claims are the older examples of homosexual literature, finds that "the emancipation of the homosexual has led, paradoxically, to the decline of his arts." *Dorian Gray*, for Meyers, "is really about the jealousy and pain, the fear and guilt of being a homosexual" (Meyers, *Homosexuality*, pp. 3, 20).

15. Mason, *Wilde: Art and Morality*, pp. 199-200.
16. Ibid., pp. 29-30, 34-37.
17. Ibid., pp. 65-66.
18. For the full controversy in the *Scots Observer*, see ibid., pp. 75-135. For details of the anonymous notice cited, see Wilde, *Letters*, p. 265n.
19. Hyde, *Trials*, pp. 344-45.
20. Reade, *Sexual Heretics*, pp. 228-45; and see Hyde, *History of Pornography*, pp. 141-45.
21. Mason, *Wilde: Art and Morality*, p. 81.
22. Wilde, *Letters*, p. 268.
23. These deletions are included in Mason, *Wilde: Art and Morality*, pp. 223-57.
24. Ibid., pp. 43-44, 72-73.

25. See, for example, J. A. Symonds in Reade, *Sexual Heretics*, pp. 276-77.
26. See Cohen, *Moral Vision*, pp. 85-99; Ericksen, *Oscar Wilde*, ch. 3; and Shewan, *Wilde: Art and Egotism*, ch. 2.
27. Mason, *Wilde: Art and Morality*, pp. 200-201.
28. Ibid., p. 201.
29. *Athenaeum*, 1 Sept. 1888, p. 286; *Saturday Review*, 20 Oct. 1888, p. 472.
30. *Universal Review*, 15 June 1888, p. 305.
31. *Athenaeum*, 23 Jan. 1892, p. 113; *Nation* (New York), 11 Feb. 1892, p. 114.
32. *Athenaeum*, 6 Feb. 1892, p. 177; *Pall Mall Gazette*, 30 Nov. 1891, p. 3; *Nation*, 16 June 1892, p. 451.
33. *New Review* 6 (Jan. 1892): 121.
34. A brief history of criticism of the decadents follows. By the 1890's, critics like Arthur Symons, Richard Le Gallienne, Lionel Johnson, and Havelock Ellis distinguished "decadent" literature by its impressionism and its break with organic form. Chesterton called it "an attitude in the flat" (see *Victorian Age*, pp. 99-101). Arthur Symons contrasted it with both romantic and classic: "If what we call the classic is indeed the supreme art—those qualities of perfect simplicity, perfect sanity, perfect proportion, the supreme qualities—then this representative literature of to-day, interesting, beautiful, novel as it is, is really a new and beautiful and interesting disease" ("Decadent Movement"). Conceiving of "decadence" as the proliferation of limited perspectives representing no organic whole, 1890's critics were able to analyze it in terms later used by intellectual historians, phenomenologists, and Marxists.

In *The Eighteen-Nineties* (1913), Holbrook Jackson said that strictly "decadent" literature could be characterized by perversity, artificiality, egoism, and curiosity; and the new realism, by effeminacy and brutality; but that, ultimately, the period "of a thousand movements" produced no "final interpretation of reality." His idea of the period's unifying characteristic—"a widespread concern for the correct . . . mode of living"—was too vague but accurate.

The post-war and Freudian critics were attracted to what they termed agony, journeys through despair, and dark passages, yet their analyses were purely literary or vaguely cultural. For Mario Praz in *The Romantic Agony* (1933), "decadence" crystallized the Romantic movement into set fashion and lifeless decoration: romanticism's frenzied action gave way to the decadent's sterile contemplation and a sexual excitement largely mental. Taking seriously Barbey's statement of alternatives to Huysmans—the muzzle of a pistol or the foot of the cross—in *Art for Art's Sake* (1936) Albert Leon Guérard saw decadence as a path to conversion: "The Decadents were nearer orthodox belief than were the coolly rational, the self-satisfied Philistines. They had the deep conviction of human depravity" (p. 77). In *Romantic Image* (1957), a book designed, we should remember, to kill that image and its new criticism and to herald a return to Milton, Frank Kermode, too, saw the 1890's as a fall. (For more romantic-to-decadent images and myths, often viewed considerably more sympathetically, see Fletcher, *Romantic Mythologies* [1967], a collection of essays by various authors.)

In the early 1960's Wendell Harris began his serious, pioneering surveys of "decadent" fiction of the 1890's, which he divided into three categories: the new realism; the sentimental, melancholy stories of love and romance; and "aesthetic" prose or, using Wilde's definition, "the telling of beautiful untrue things." (See "Identifying the Decadent Fiction of the Eighteen-Nineties," *ELT* [*English Literature in Transition*] 5 [1962]: 1-13; "John Lane's Keynotes Series and the Fiction of the 1890's," *PMLA* [*Publication of the Modern Language Association*] 83 [Sept.-Dec. 1968]: 1407-13; and especially "Short Fiction." Also Richard Long and Iva Jones, "Towards a Definition of the 'Decadent Novel,'" *College English* 22 [1960-61]: 245-49; and Ellmann, *Edwardians*.)

In 1962, 35 people attended Helmut Gerber's sixth *EFT* (*English Fiction in Transition*, now *ELT*) Conference on Aestheticism and Decadence in Washington, D.C., at which Gerber reported that decadence and aestheticism were a reaction against, or a rejection of, what aesthetes and decadents associated with Victorianism ("The Editor's Fence," *EFT* 6 [1963]: iv-v). The artistic products of such reaction or rejection, Gerber also reported, "generally" entailed "a falling off in quality." Indeed, throughout the 1960's, relatively conservative academics generally emphasized what the 1890's lacked, and the attributes of contemporary student revolt began to be ascribed to the earlier era. See Swart, *Sense of Decadence* (1964); Gelpi, *Dark Passages* (1965); Lester, *Journey Through Despair* (1968); and Johnson, *Aestheticism* (1969). The adversarial view to the scholar's was of course Susan Sontag's "Notes on Camp" (1964). See also Daiches, *Attitudes*.

The 1970's brought more moralistic reaction against the British decadents, not for their immorality but for their lack of psychological depth. See, for example, Munro, *Decadent Poetry* (1970). Yet in addition to more of the same, the 1970's advanced the cultural criticism that tried to locate (not pity or judge) the 1890's in terms of an open market and theories of literary production. Such are Bradbury's *Social Context* (1971) and most of the contributions to Fletcher, *Decadence* (1979), in which several authors use the models of Terry Eagleton in *Criticism and Ideology: A Study in Marxist Literary Theory* (New York, 1978); Pierre Macherey in *A Theory of Literary Production*, trans. Geoffrey Wall (Boston, 1978); and Renato Poggioli in *The Theory of the Avant-Garde*, trans. Gerald Fitzgerald (Cambridge, Mass., 1968).

35. Wilde's typewritten copy of *Dorian Gray* with his manuscript revisions was the version printed in *Lippincott's* July 1890 and is now in the Clark Library. He deleted the original title of the "fascinating book" and changed all later reference to Catulle Sarrazin to "the book's author" and references to "Raoul" to "the young Parisian." In an unpublished letter to an American friend, Arthur Howard Pickering, Wilde said that "the fatal book that Lord Henry lent to Dorian is one of my many unwritten works. Some day I must go through the formality of putting it to paper" (June or July 1890, in the Clark Library).

36. *Woman's World*, Nov. 1888, pp. 53-56. At least two critics have noticed the duplicated passage: Stuart Mason in the *Woman's World* section of his *Bibliography of Oscar Wilde* and Richard Aldington in his Introduction to the *Portable Oscar Wilde*, but neither the bibliographer nor the editor makes anything of it.

37. *Woman's World*, Jan. 1888, p. 135. For an excellent article on the popular art-literature by women and men, see Powell, "Tom, Dick, and Dorian Gray."

Notes to Pages 66-76

38. See Wilde, *Letters*, for the year 1887.
39. Meyers, *Homosexuality*, p. 20.
40. Nassaar, *Into the Demon Universe*, p. 72.
41. Cited in Moers, *Dandy*, p. 227.
42. Lytton, *Pelham*, p. 314.
43. See Jesse, *Beau Brummell*, vol. 1, p. 12; Woolf, "Beau Brummell," pp. 148-56.
44. Jesse, *Beau Brummell*, vol. 2, p. 289.
45. Laver, *Dandies*, pp. 24, 34.
46. For an example of Jesse's manly, complacent irony at Brummell's expense see vol. 2, pp. 55-56: "Though buried in India during the preceding six years, I had heard, nay read, of Brummell—his superlative taste, and unquestionable authority in all 'that doth become a man': but the mysteries of *mufti* were to me a sealed book: when yet in my teens, my round jacket was supplanted by a full-dress regimental coat, and my ankle boots, by Wellingtons! Of the perfect contour of a shoestring I was, alas! in utter ignorance, and I had been saved all the trouble of overcoming the difficulties of a tie by our colonel, who, in his very laudable anxiety to preserve strict uniformity in the corps, fitted us all with glazed leather stocks, as stiff as blinkers, which were fastened with brass clasps behind. . . . What marvel, then, that with such disadvantages an awful dread came over me when I thought of the cauterizing that might be my fate, on being introduced to this satirical epitome of elegance."
47. Moers, *Dandy*, p. 185.
48. Jesse, *Beau Brummell*, vol. 2, p. 252.
49. Ibid., p. 274.
50. Ibid., p. 283.
51. Ibid., p. 286.
52. Hazlitt in the *Examiner*, 18 November 1827; included in Hazlitt, *Fugitive Writings*, pp. 343-47. Lockhart in *Quarterly Review*, 36 (1827): 269. For a discussion of the paradoxical social implications of the Regency novel, from its roots in Fanny Burney and Maria Edgeworth to its culmination in Disraeli and Bulwer Lytton, see Francis Russell Hart, "The Regency Novel of Fashion," in Mintz, *Smollett to James*, pp. 84-133.
53. For a current Marxist account of the anti-organic interpretation of decadence, see John Goode's "The Decadent Writer as Producer" in Fletcher, *Decadence*, pp. 105-29.
54. See Turner, *Shocking History*, pp. 53-57, and Wood, *Story of Advertising*, pp. 119-23.
55. Lytton, *Pelham*, pp. xxxiii-xxxiv.
56. Jesse, *Beau Brummell*, vol. 1, p. 3, vol. 2, pp. 277-78.
57. Lytton, *England*, vol. 1, p. 154.   58. Ibid., vol. 2, p. 109.
59. Davidoff, *Best Circles*, p. 21.   60. See Moers, *Dandy*, pp. 84-86.
61. Cited in ibid., p. 104. Jerome McGann has informed me that this quotation is a pastiche made out of Byron's letters and journals, which had recently been published (1832). Disraeli is imagining himself as the great Lord redivivus in

thus ventriloquizing. It is a most trenchant illustration, McGann points out, of a life being lived in what Baudrillard calls the "hyperreal."

62. This and the description of Idle that follows are cited in Moers, *Dandy*, p. 240.

63. Kempf, *Sur le dandysme*, p. 58. I have translated the quotations from Balzac's "Traité."

64. Ibid., pp. 51-54, 89.
65. Ibid., p. 84.
66. Ibid., pp. 51-54, 89.
67. Barbey, *Dandyism*, pp. 18-21.
68. Ibid., p. 23.
69. Morris, *News from Nowhere*, p. 77.
70. Barbey, *Dandyism*, p. 102.
71. Ibid.
72. Shaw, *Theatres*, vol. 1, pp. 153-54, vol. 2, p. 113. See also John Stokes, "The Legend of Duse," in Fletcher, *Decadence*, pp. 150-71.
73. Barbey, *Dandyism*, pp. 135-38.
74. When Wilde's collected *Works* was published in the Sunflower Edition of 1909, *What Never Dies: A Romance, By Barbey D'Aurevilly: Translated into English by Sebastian Melmoth* was erroneously included in the canon. *Ce qui ne meurt pas*, an intense tale of latent lesbianism, adultery, metaphorical sex changes, and unrequited loves, was not Wilde's chosen text to repair a vulnerable reputation. However, he had read and appreciated Barbey's work, and Barbey was probably the first to analyze the relationship of dandiacal wit to conflict with "puritans" that later critics have found in Wilde's works. "Dandyism," writes Barbey, "while still respecting the conventionalities, plays with them. While admitting their power, it suffers from and revenges itself upon them, and pleads them as an excuse against themselves; dominates and is dominated by them in turn" (*Dandyism*, p. 23).
75. Baudelaire, *Painter*, pp. 28-29.
76. See "The Work of Art in the Age of Mechanical Reproduction" in Benjamin, *Illuminations*, pp. 219-59.
77. Baudelaire, *Oeuvres Complètes*, vol. 1, pp. 676-708; and *My Heart Laid Bare and Other Prose Writings*, ed. Peter Quennell, trans. Norman Cameron (London, 1950), pp. 175-210, 213. On Baudelaire, women, and dandyism in the English tradition see also Jerry Palmer, "Fierce Midnights: Algolagniac Fantasy and the Literature of the Decadence," in Fletcher, *Decadence*, pp. 86-106.
78. Wilde, *Letters*, p. 191; see also pp. 253-54.
79. See "The Work of Art in the Age of Mechanical Reproduction" in Benjamin, *Illuminations*, and Gramsci, *Prison Notebooks*, p. 308.
80. "A Defense of Cosmetics" in *Yellow Book*, vol. 1, pp. 65-82.
81. Maturin, *Melmoth the Wanderer* (1968), p. 540.
82. See Introduction and Bibliographies to Maturin, *Melmoth the Wanderer* (1892).
83. Balzac, *Studies*, p. 38.
84. Ibid., p. 105.
85. Ibid., pp. 125-26.
86. Baudelaire, *Painter*, pp. 152-53.
87. Ibid.
88. Ibid.
89. Cited in Chamberlin, *Ripe Was the Drowsy Hour*, p. 161.

Notes to Pages 89-105

90. A. Symons, *Study*, p. 85.
91. Preface to the 1820 edition, in *Melmoth the Wanderer* (1968), p. 6.
92. Moers, *Dandy*, p. 155.
93. For the gentleman, see Best, *Mid-Victorian Britain*; Girouard, *Return to Camelot*; Letwin, *Gentleman in Trollope*; and Wiener, *English Culture*. For the public schools, see Bamford, *Public Schools*; Honey, *Tom Brown's Universe*; and, of course, the most popular of all school boy memoirs, Hughes's *Tom Brown's School Days*.
94. O. F. Christie, *A History of Clifton College, 1860-1934* (1935), pp. 122-23, cited in Girouard, *Return to Camelot*, p. 172.
95. Arthur Ponsonby, *The Decline of the Aristocracy* (1912), pp. 207-8, cited in Bamford, *Public Schools*, pp. 82-83.
96. Honey, *Tom Brown's Universe*, p. 138.
97. Ibid., p. 141.
98. Russell, *The Autobiography of Bertrand Russell, 1872-1914* (Boston, 1967), p. 220; cited in Buckley, *Turning Key*, p. 53.
99. Cyril Connolly, *A Georgian Childhood* (London, 1949), p. 253; cited in Buckley, *Turning Key*, p. 50.
100. The nine were Charterhouse, Eton, Harrow, Merchant Taylors', Rugby, St. Paul's, Shrewsbury, Westminster, and Winchester.
101. Cited in Curtin, "Etiquette and Society," p. 125.
102. Chesterton, *Victorian Age*, p. 101.
103. Cited in Curtin, "Etiquette and Society," p. 199.
104. Ibid., p. 146.
105. F. Harris, *Wilde: Life*, vol. 1, p. 153; and Shaw, "My Memories of Oscar Wilde," in ibid., vol. 2, p. 19.
106. Cited in Davidoff, *Best Circles*, p. 92.
107. Wilde, *Letters*, p. 352.
108. Artaud, *Theater*, p. 152.

Chapter 3

1. James, *Tragic Muse*, p. 48. Although, as Leon Edel says, the character Nash's judgments concerning theater audiences are entirely consistent with James's own, in Nash's capacity of aesthete he is also the popular image of Wilde, Whistler, and Robert de Montesquiou. (See Edel's Introduction to James, *Guy Domville* and vols. 3 and 4 of Edel, *Henry James*.) In the final episodes, Gabriel Nash and his disappearing portrait are particularly reminiscent of Wilde and Dorian Gray.
2. See Stephens, *Censorship*, pp. 140-53.
3. Ibid., pp. 142-43.
4. For a fuller history of Wilde's scenario and the critical reception of Harris's play, see H. Montgomery Hyde's Introduction to F. Harris, *Mr. and Mrs. Daventry*.
5. Wilde, *Letters*, pp. 360-62.
6. See, for example, Stephens's comparative assessment of Wilde's *A Woman of*

No Importance and Pinero's *The Second Mrs. Tanqueray* in *Censorship*, p. 144. Edel, in those volumes of *Henry James* that deal with James's involvement in the theater, offers constant comparisons between Wilde's and James's drama that amount to lessons in literary taste. Wilde's plays are "tinsel and pasteboard," James's are supersubtle characterizations and scenic frameworks. Wilde was utterly indifferent to his public but knew how to please it; James was forsaking his private religion either to make money or to elevate the great "Form" of drama.

7. See H. G. Wells's review of the first production of *Guy Domville* at the St. James's in the *Pall Mall Gazette*, 7 Jan. 1895. The young Shaw also reviewed the premiere in the *Saturday Review*, 12 Jan. 1895. On the one hand, Shaw chastized the vulgarity of the audience for not appreciating the predominantly "intellectual" life and "artistic taste" of Guy Domville; on the other, he admitted that these did not interest him either. The play, he wrote, represents "a certain calm spot where cultivated ladies and gentlemen live on independent incomes or by pleasant artistic occupations. . . . If it is real to Mr. James, it must be real to others." These reviews are appended to James, *Guy Domville*.

8. Debord, *Society of the Spectacle*, p. 24.

9. For the paradoxical themes of the comedies, see Eric Bentley, "The Importance of Being Earnest," in Ellmann, *Wilde: Critical Essays*, pp. 111-15; Bird, *Plays of Wilde*, pp. 112-33 and p. 182; Cohen, *Moral Vision*, p. 224; Ericksen, *Oscar Wilde*, pp. 136-48; Ellmann, Johnson, and Bush, *Wilde and the Nineties*, p. 19; Guralnick and Levitt, "Allusion and Meaning"; Mary McCarthy, "The Unimportance of Being Oscar," in Ellmann, *Wilde: Critical Essays*, pp. 107-10; San Juan, *Art of Wilde*, pp. 136-37; and Shewan, *Wilde: Art and Egotism*, pp. 169-83, 192. These works discuss the paradoxes in the comedies, but not their paradoxical appeal.

10. For the issues involved in late-Victorian upper- and middle-class analysis, see *Cambridge Economic History*; Cipolla, *Fontana Economic History*; Hobsbawm, *Labour's Turning Point*; and Morazé, *Triumph*.

11. See chapters 3 and 4 on respectability and Society drama in Rowell, *Victorian Theatre*.

12. Macqueen-Pope, *Haymarket*, p. 336.

13. Macqueen-Pope, *St. James's*, p. 16.

14. Ibid., p. 121.

15. See Webb, *My Apprenticeship*, pp. 46-54.

16. See Beerbohm's letter of 21 April 1893 in *Max Beerbohm's Letters to Reggie Turner*, ed. Rupert Hart-Davis (London, 1964), cited in Beckson, *Wilde: Critical Heritage*, p. 18.

17. Cited in Bird, *Plays of Wilde*, pp. 109-11.

18. Ibid., p. 112.

19. Green, *Children of the Sun*, p. 415.

20. Debord, *Society of the Spectacle*, p. 42.

21. Artaud, *Theater*, p. 48.

22. Ibid., p. 126.

23. Artaud, *Collected Works*, vol. 2, p. 34.

24. Ibid., p. 15.

Notes to Pages 110-23

25. Artaud, *Theater*, p. 96.
26. In the Introduction to Artaud, *Collected Works*, vol. 2, p. 9.
27. Introduction to Jarry, *The Ubu Plays*, p. 16.
28. Wilde's virgin Salome also speaks in metaphor.
29. Shaw cited in Pearson, *Wilde: Life and Wit*, p. 228. Also see the *Times*, 15 Feb. 1895; *Athenaeum*, 23 Feb. 1895; *Punch*, 23 Feb. 1895; *World*, 20 Feb. 1895.
30. Webb, *My Apprenticeship*, p. 42.
31. Artaud, *Collected Works*, vol. 2, p. 33.
32. Wilde, *Letters*, p. 382.
33. The eminent dramatic critic William Archer wrote of the "sudden glory" of the audience's laughter when John Worthing entered in deep mourning (*World*, 20 Feb. 1895). And years later Allan Aynesworth, who had played Algernon, told Hesketh Pearson, "In my fifty-three years of acting, I never remember a greater triumph than the first night of *The Importance of Being Earnest*. The audience rose in their seats and cheered and cheered again." (Pearson, *Wilde: Life and Wit*, p. 228.) That the play is satirical is the verdict of most critics today. *Earnest* has remained Wilde's most popular play and has frequently been revived on stage and film. Although Mary McCarthy attacked the play as depraved and by a depraved author ("The Unimportance of Being Oscar," in Ellmann, *Wilde: Critical Essays*, pp. 107-10), and Clive Barnes wrote that the wit in *Earnest* was "horribly dated" (*New York Times*, 6 July 1968), in general recent American critics have joined their contemporary British counterparts in recognizing that if the play is depraved it is because it is a superb satire on a depraved society. Helen Dawson wrote in *Plays and Players* that Wilde's play was "the best way of puncturing the bombast of social nonsense at the end of the last century" (15, no. 7 [Apr. 1968]: 26-29). Geremy Kingston wrote later in the same journal that someone should even revive the original four-act version. Wilde, he wrote, "is sharp without being bitchy, pithy without being trite" (22, no. 8 [May 1975]: 26-27).
34. Artaud, *Collected Works*, vol. 2, pp. 59-60.
35. Bird, *Plays of Wilde*, p. 110.
36. Davidoff, *Best Circles*, pp. 51-52.
37. At the conclusion of the performance and the calls for "Author," Wilde stunned the audience and offended a good many critics by strolling onto the stage with a burning cigarette. A member of the St. James's Theatre staff took his speech down in shorthand, indicating the actual words he stressed: "Ladies and Gentlemen: I have injoyed [sic] this evening *immensely*. The actors have given us a charming rendering of a *delightful* play, and your appreciation has been *most* intelligent. I congratulate you on the *great* success of your performance, which persuades me that you think *almost* as highly of the play as I do myself." Mikhail, *Wilde: Interviews*, vol. 2, p. 398n.
38. Frank Marcus, "The Smell of Rancid Champagne," *Plays and Players*, 14, no. 3 (Dec. 1966): 23.
39. This was the virtually unanimous response of writers on the play. For the most concise formulations see the *Times*, 20 April 1893; *Athenaeum*, 22 April 1893; William Archer in *World*, 26 April 1893. In America, see *World*, 12 Dec. 1893; *New York Herald*, 12 Dec. 1893. For Archer's identification of Mrs. Ar-

Notes to Pages 123-34

buthnot with some of Ibsen's strong women characters, see Bird, *Plays of Wilde*, pp. 122, 132.

40. Wilde himself archly responded to his rigorous critics: "I wrote the first act of *A Woman of No Importance* in answer to the critics who said that *Lady Windermere's Fan* lacked action. In the act in question there is absolutely no action at all. It was a perfect act." (Pearson, *Wilde: Life and Wit*, p. 210.)

41. Ibid., p. 220.

42. Guralnick and Levitt, "Allusion and Meaning."

43. Paul Dehn's revision of the play in New York and London, 1953, "removed some of the dated melodrama and replaced it with epigrams generally indiscernible from those of Mr. Wilde." See Henry Hewes in the *Saturday Review* (New York), 1 Aug. 1953, p. 24. Modern audiences have apparently opted for Illingworth's urbanity over Arbuthnot's histrionic morality. See also Hugh Leonard in *Plays and Players*, 15, no. 5 (Feb. 1968): 18-19.

44. Webb, *My Apprenticeship*, p. 50.   45. Lytton, *Pelham*, p. 134.
46. James, *Tragic Muse*, p. 194.   47. Davidoff, *Best Circles*, p. 88.
48. See, for example, McCormack, "Masks Without Faces."
49. Hyde, *Wilde: Biography*, pp. 156-57.
50. Webb, *My Apprenticeship*, p. 52.

51. *Pall Mall Gazette*, 4 Jan. 1895. Wells, a young journalist in the 1890's, watched Wilde's career with some interest. In 1895 he wrote *The Island of Doctor Moreau*, inspired, he said, by Wilde's trials: "There was a scandalous trial about that time, the graceless and pitiful downfall of a man of genius, and this story was the response of an imaginative mind to the reminder that humanity is but animal rough-hewn to a reasonable shape and in perpetual internal conflict between instinct and injunction. This story embodies this ideal, but apart from this embodiment it has no allegorical quality. It is written just to give the utmost possible vividness to that conception of men as hewn and confused and tormented beasts." Wells, Preface to *Island of Dr. Moreau*, p. ix.

52. Cited in Bird, *Plays of Wilde*, p. 148.

53. See Green, *Children of the Sun*, pp. 366-73. Green frequently discusses twentieth-century works concerned with British treachery and the collusion of the Establishment in protecting the traitors from punishment.

54. James, *Tragic Muse*, p. 177.

55. See, for example, the review of a 1967 production, which states that the character of Goring, one "of shrewdness and principle," is to be contrasted with that of Chiltern, "whose high moral tone conceals a certain shallowness" (*Plays and Players* 14, no. 5 [Feb. 1967]: 24).

56. The *New York Times*'s reviewer wrote that the play's dandy, Lord Goring, "in his daily life is an idiot. He devoted hours to the discussion of buttonhole bouquets" (13 March 1895, p. 5).

57. Bird, *Plays of Wilde*, pp. 165-66.

58. See *Sunday Special*, 9 and 16 December 1900, and *Sunday Times*, 8 December 1901; cited in Beckson, *Wilde: Critical Heritage*, pp. 233-36, 238-40.

59. Wilde, *Letters*, pp. 568-74, 722-25.

60. Artaud, *Theater*, p. 83.

Notes to Pages 135-46

61. For the theories of advertising that helped me formulate the dynamic of Wilde's comedies and their audience, see Boorstin, *The Americans*, pt. II, "Consumption Communities," and pt. VII, "From Packing to Packaging: The New Strategy of Desire"; and Steinberg, *Creation of Consent*, chs. 3-5.

Chapter 4

1. Grosskurth, *Symonds*, p. 271.
2. See John D'Emilio, "Capitalism and Gay Identity," in Snitow, Stansell, and Thompson, *Powers of Desire*, pp. 100-113; and Foucault, *History of Sexuality*, especially p. 4.
3. For the complicated events leading to Beardsley's dissociation from the *Yellow Book*, see Mix, *Study in Yellow*, ch. 15, pp. 140-47; and for the business aspects of the event, see the chapter "Poisonous Honey and English Blossoms" in Nelson, *Early Nineties*, especially p. 211.
4. Beardsley, *Letters*, p. 158.
5. Yeats, *Autobiography*, p. 121.
6. *L'Affaire Oscar Wilde* in Raffalovich, *Uranisme*, pp. 241-78.
7. Yeats, *Autobiography*, p. 195.
8. See Reade, *Sexual Heretics*, pp. 14-15, 18, 30-31; S. Marcus, *Other Victorians*, p. 263; and Jerry Palmer in Fletcher, *Decadence*, pp. 88-106.
9. For the "Terminal Essay" see Burton, *Thousand Nights*, vol. 10, pp. 63-302. Swinburne's "Memorial Verses" and Richard and Isabel Burton's correspondence with Smithers are in the Huntington Library.
10. In Reade, *Sexual Heretics*, p. 225.
11. Dowson, *Letters*, pp. 127-28, 378n.
12. Beardsley, *Letters*, pp. 58, 92, 394, 440.
13. Yeats, "Memoirs," p. 1956.
14. For the distinction between Wilde's trivial and profound paradoxes see Chamberlin, *Ripe Was the Drowsy Hour*, chs. 4-5. For discussions concerning the form and function of Wilde's epigrams and paradoxes, see (in Mikhail, *Wilde: Interviews*): Percival W. H. Almy, *The Theatre*, vol. 1, pp. 233-34; Coulson Kernahan, *In Good Company*, vol. 2, p. 312; Frank Harris, *Contemporary Portraits*, vol. 2, p. 389; Richard Le Gallienne, *The Romantic '90s*, vol. 2, p. 389; and Stuart Merrill, *Le Plume*, vol. 2, p. 466. Also Hough, *Last Romantics*, p. 203; George Woodcock, "The Social Rebel," in Ellmann, *Wilde: Critical Essays*, p. 152; San Juan, *Art of Wilde*, p. 201 and passim; Shewan, *Wilde: Art and Egotism*, p. 4; Dyson, *Crazy Fabric*, pp. 138-50; Ericksen, *Oscar Wilde*, pp. 78-81; and Jan Gordon, "'Decadent Spaces': Notes for a Phenomenology of the *Fin de Siècle*," in Fletcher, *Decadence*, pp. 51-52.
15. Hyde, *Trials*, pp. 11-12, 64-75; and Holland, *Son of Oscar Wilde*, p. 268.
16. In "The Priest and the Acolyte," a priest and his altar boy commit suicide before their "perfect love" is degraded by the congregation that has found them out. The story, by John Francis Bloxam, is included in Reade, *Sexual Heretics*, pp. 342-60.
17. Hyde, *Trials*, p. 133.

18. Ibid., pp. 165-66.

19. See Reade, *Sexual Heretics*, pp. 40-48. Reade includes many publications from *The Artist* and *The Studio* in his anthology. For more on the "little" (art) magazines and homosexuality, see Fletcher's "Decadence and the Little Magazines," in Fletcher, *Decadence*.

20. Letter in the Clark Library.

21. Wilde, *Letters*, pp. 401-5.

22. Lombroso, *Genius*, pp. 359-61.

23. Lombroso, *Crime*, pt. II, ch. 2, pp. 255-61.

24. For further speculation on the historical alliance of Anglo-Catholicism and homosexuality, see Hilliard, "Un-English."

25. See Lombroso, *Crime*, pt. II, pp. 255-61. This type of sanctioned vice to remedy vice, heavily weighted against women, was the target of the middle-class feminists' campaign of the early 1870's against the English Contagious Disease Acts. To protect troops from venereal disease, women in certain garrison towns could be stopped by the police on suspicion of prostitution and had to submit to examination for sexually transmitted diseases or appear before a magistrate. Josephine Butler and her supporters objected to the Acts as an example of the double standard of sexual morality, which punished women and not men and which disregarded middle-class notions of social purity. See Rowbotham and Weeks, *Socialism*, p. 13.

26. Lombroso, *Crime*, pt. II, p. 418. Within Lombroso's biological tradition, both Richard von Krafft-Ebing in *Psychopathia Sexualis* (trans. Charles G. Chaddock, London, 1892) and Havelock Ellis in *Sexual Inversion* (Philadelphia, 1915) made the same distinction. Thus Ellis distinguished between occasional and circumstantial "homosexuality" (or "perversion") and "inversion," defined as a congenital condition.

27. Shaw's attack on Nordau uses the scientist / literary critic's weapons against him. Nordau claims that rhyme, poetic inconsistency, and repetition indicate general softening of the brain and body, and Shaw cites examples of Nordau's own echolalia (*Sanity of Art*, p. 80). Nordau denounces socialism and other forms of discontent and social critique in the arts as stigmata of degeneracy, and Shaw cites Nordau's own lengthy passages expressing dissatisfaction with the social order (*Sanity of Art*, pp. 94-97).

28. After personal contact with Theodor Herzl in 1895, Nordau reaffirmed his Jewish background and worked in the new Zionist movement. See George L. Mosse's Introduction to the 1968 edition of *Degeneration*.

29. Nordau, *Degeneration* (1920), p. 557.

30. Cited in Mosse's Introduction to *Degeneration* (1968), p. xxxii.

31. Shaw, *Sanity of Art*, p. 5.

32. These interviews and reviews are among the news clippings at the Clark Library.

33. Chris Healy, "Oscar Wilde and Zola," *Today*, 26 Nov. 1902, p. 145. In *Today* of 8 Oct. 1902, Healy had claimed that Wilde "was one of the direct instruments in freeing Alfred Dreyfus."

34. Galton, *Hereditary Genius*, p. ix.

35. The articles quoted here appeared in Pemberton-Billing's private subscription paper, the *Vigilante*, on 13 Apr. and 15 June 1918.
36. See Nelson, *Early Nineties*, pp. 211-16, 260-61.
37. For more appreciative reviews of the "decadents," see Le Gallienne, *Retrospective Reviews*.
38. Hichens, *Green Carnation*, pp. 109, 125-26.
39. In Reade, *Sexual Heretics*, pp. 248-85.
40. Letter of 4 September 1913 in the Clark Library.
41. S. Marcus, *Other Victorians*, pp. 271-72.
42. See Rowbotham and Weeks, *Socialism*, and Weeks, *Coming Out*.
43. *Pall Mall Gazette*, 25 Jan. 1889, p. 3; included in Wilde, *Artist as Critic*, pp. 121-25.
44. *Five Unknown Letters of Oscar Wilde to George Ives*, introduced by Louis Marlow (1950), in the Clark Library manuscript collection.
45. Letters of 22 October 1897 in the Clark Library.
46. S. Marcus, *Other Victorians*, ch. 1. Marcus does not discuss homosexual pornography, but see pp. 22 and 274. Marcus states that "inside of every pornographer there is an infant screaming for the breast from which he has been torn" (p. 274), and his general view of sex is that it is all a matter of grimness, sadness, and defeat, a matter of repetitious attempts to repossess a wholeness once lost. Such Freudian premises in conjunction with terms of condescension toward his material such as "disgusting" and "it is all rather like 'The Solitary Reaper' written in a sewer" (p. 102) may put off many present-day readers.
47. Foucault, *History of Sexuality*, p. 104.
48. In Reade, *Sexual Heretics*, pp. 313-19.
49. Grosskurth, *Symonds*, p. 95.
50. In Reade, *Sexual Heretics*, pp. 324-47.
51. In ibid., p. 226.
52. This and the poems that follow are cited in Smith, *Love in Earnest*, pp. 176-78.
53. Wilde, *Letters*, p. 621 and throughout.
54. This and the letters that follow are included in Alfred Douglas's wide correspondence at the Clark Library. Wilson's letters were addressed to More Adey.
55. *Spirit Lamp* 4, no. 1 (May 1893): 45.
56. Robertson, *Time Was*, pp. 130-38; also in Mikhail, *Wilde: Interviews*, vol. 1, p. 212.
57. Hyde, *Trials*, app. E, p. 370.
58. In an article published in 1968, Richard Ellmann defended Wilde's *Salome* from a long critical line of accusations of derivativeness ("Overtures to *Salome*," *Yearbook of Comparative and General Literature* No. 17 [1968]: 17-28; also in Ellmann, *Wilde: Critical Essays*, pp. 73-91). This line culminated in Mario Praz's contention (*Romantic Agony*, pp. 298-303) that the play was so derivative as to be virtually a parody of decadence. Despite Wilde's repeated statements that *Salome* meant more to him than any of his other works and that *Salome* alone permitted him to assert himself as an artist (*Letters*, p. 656), and despite his hurt response when a contemporary laughed at what he thought Wilde intended as "a

burlesque of Maeterlinck" (W. Graham Robertson in Mikhail, *Wilde: Interviews*, vol. 1, p. 212), literary critics have generally followed the review in the *Pall Mall Gazette*, that is, that *Salome* was "the daughter of too many fathers . . . the victim of heredity." To save the play from literary historians who see Wilde's Salome as descended from Heine's, Flaubert's, Mallarmé's, Huysmans's, and Laforgue's, and his style as derived from Maeterlinck or Ollendorf (as one caustic contemporary critic sneered of Wilde's French [the *Times* (London), 23 Feb. 1893]), Ellmann proposed to inquire into "what the play probably meant to Wilde and how he came to write it." Ellmann's argument "includes, at any rate, those fugitive associations, often subliminal, which swarm beneath the fixed surface of the work, and which are as pertinent as is that surface to any study of the author's mind." Thus the critic moves from literary descendence to psychological ascendence, a movement that in fact has characterized Wilde criticism through the years.

Ellmann's argument is briefly that *Salome* is a sort of Wildean *drame à thèse*, a dialectic in which Wilde's tutelary masters, Ruskin and Pater, appear in diseased forms as Iokanaan and Salome, respectively. Wilde, contends Ellmann, sees himself as Herod, who triumphs over Iokanaan's asceticism and Salome's extreme sensuality. Other critics have for the most part psychoanalyzed Wilde and read the play entirely from what they discerned as the male characters' point of view. See, for example, Christopher Nassaar, who insists on seeing Salome as evil. Nassaar's highly suspect and teleological line of descent runs from Keats to Rossetti to Pater to Wilde: "Wilde offered the Victorians the chillingly evil Salome as an erotic-divine object of worship. . . . He elevated the demonic to the status of a religion and tried to terminate the nineteenth century with a religion of evil, an unholy worship of evil beauty" (*Into the Demon Universe*, "Introduction," p. xii). Frank Kermode (*Romantic Image*, pp. 73-74) sees Salome as innocent but totally destructive: hers is a beauty inhumanly immature and carelessly cruel. Kermode's is a reading entirely depoliticized.

Recently socio-historical readings of *Salome* have begun to replace the literary-historical and psychoanalytic. See, for example, Elliott L. Gilbert, "Tumult of Images." But even Kate Millett in *Sexual Politics* can only see Salome as a "product of Wilde's homosexual guilt and desire" (pp. 152-56). My own reading of the play has certain affinities with Jane Marcus's in "*Salome*: The Jewish Princess Was a New Woman," but I differ from Marcus in that for me the New Woman was not nearly so radical as Salome: she certainly was not revolutionary in the sense Marcus claims for Salome and Iokanaan. More importantly, the New Woman was not *sexual*. Marcus's reading of a spiritualized, saintly Salome coupled with an ascetic Iokanaan as brother and sister of the revolution continues to avoid the strong sexuality of Wilde's Salome, just as Marcus's remarks on Maud Allan (based largely, it is true, on O. G. Brockett, "J. T. Grein and the Ghost of Oscar Wilde," *Quarterly Journal of Speech* 52, no. 2 [1966]: 131-38) avoid the politics of the lesbian's horrible persecution at the hands of the crazed M. P.

59. See Robertson, *Time Was*, p. 126, cited in Bird, *Plays of Wilde*, p. 60; and (in Mikhail, *Wilde: Interviews*) Henry Mazel, *Everyman*, 18 Oct. 1912, vol. 2, p. 446 and Gomez Carrillo, "Comment Oscar Wilde rêva *Salome*," vol. 1, pp. 192-95. Sarah Bernhardt never performed the play, for, composed in 1891, it was

banned from public performance by the British Censor until 1931. The ostensible basis for prohibition was an archaic law forbidding representation of biblical figures on stage.

60. This and the following quotes are from "The First Manifesto," included in Artaud, *Theater*, pp. 89-100.

61. See Beardsley's decoration on the title page (Wilde, *Salome*), in which a dubious angel prays at the altar of a Satanic hermaphrodite. Beardsley, Wilde said, was the only artist besides himself who knew what the dance of the seven veils was and could see that invisible dance (*Letters*, p. 348n). Beardsley captured the sexual ambiguity of *Salome* in his androgynous characters and in his representations of Wilde as "The Woman in the Moon," that is, as the source of the sexual lunacy of the play.

62. A paraphrasing of Luke 3:16-17.

63. And see Wilde, *Letters*, p. 589.

64. For a most obvious illustration, see Beckson, *Wilde: Critical Heritage*, in which Beckson deletes the portions of criticism of *Salome* that deal with the performances and production and in effect includes only textual criticism.

65. Cited in Stephens, *Censorship*, p. 112.

66. When *Reading Gaol* was published in 1898, it was a popular and critical success. In their biographies of Wilde, Robert Sherard and Frank Harris maintain that its favorable reception indicated the British public's repentance for the severity of Wilde's sentence. Although this is doubtless an exaggeration, it is clear that most British reviewers found the poem remarkable for its biographical significance rather than its poetry. As poetry most reviewers found it derivative. Arthur Symons, among others, compared it to Hood's "Dream of Eugene Aram" and Henley's "In Hospital"; "S. G.," in the *Pall Mall Gazette*, to Kipling's "Danny Deever"; and Frank Harris to "The Ancient Mariner" and A. E. Housman's "A Shropshire Lad." See Symons, *Saturday Review*, 12 Mar. 1898, pp. 365-66, and *Study*, ch. 3; *Pall Mall Gazette*, 19 Mar. 1898, p. 4; Harris, *Wilde: Life*, pp. 387-93; and Sherard, *Life of Oscar Wilde*, pp. 411-14. Yet with the exception of W. E. Henley (who had so violently attacked *Dorian Gray* and who maintained that Wilde's description of an English Tommy with "blood and wine"—rather than the more probable blood and beer—on his hands simply indicated an elitist aesthete in a slumming posture), critics felt that the poem was the most sincere of Wilde's works and praised it accordingly; see Henley, *The Outlook*, 5 Mar. 1898, p. 146, cited in O'Sullivan, *Aspects*, p. 95. Symons saw it as a turning point for the author, a long-needed "humanizing" of the man of superior, but abstract, intellect. The writer in *The Academy* (26 Feb. 1898) also saw the poem's strength in its descriptions of the author's feelings and sensations. "In the present work," the reviewer says approvingly of Wilde, "he is not a thinker."

When Chesterton came to summarize and pass judgment on what he called "the age of Oscar Wilde," the "interregnum of art" between the civic and religious ideals he saw crumbling by 1870 and turn-of-the-century socialism, he found Wilde the only transitional figure among the "decadents"; see *Victorian Age*, ch. 4. And this transition occurred, Chesterton believed, with *Reading Gaol*: "To return to the chief of the decadents [i.e., Wilde], I will not speak of the end of the

Notes to Pages 172-79

individual story: there was horror and there was expiation. And as my conscience goes, at least, no man should say one word that could weaken the horror—or the pardon. But there is one literary consequence of the thing which must be mentioned, because it bears us on to that much breezier movement which first began to break in upon all this ghastly idleness—I mean the Socialist Movement. . . . I mean the one real thing he ever wrote: *The Ballad of Reading Gaol*, in which we hear a cry for common justice and brotherhood very much deeper, more democratic, and more true to the real trend of the populace to-day, than anything the Socialists ever uttered even in the boldest pages of Bernard Shaw" (p. 227).

If we take Henley's view that Wilde in *Reading Gaol* is merely posing and Chesterton's that for possibly the first time he is sincere, we typify the two poles—and there is little between them—of later criticism of the poem. After Henley, all subsequent critics of Wilde have seen *Reading Gaol* as radically disjoined from his earlier work. Those who find the earlier work insincere find in *Reading Gaol* Wilde's redeeming sincerity. For George Woodcock, "this poem alone would have justified [Wilde] as a writer. . . . Beneath all his superficial callousness, he was a great humanist, and made the freedom of individual men the first article of his social creed. Wherever else he may have seemed insincere, in these matters he always spoke with a conviction that cannot be held in doubt" (in Ellmann, *Wilde: Critical Essays*, p. 108). For Rodney Shewan, in *Reading Gaol* Wilde turned from individualism and "style" to anonymity (*Wilde: Art*, p. 199). For him, the poem is as formless as the proletarian cry and as "collective" in voice: its author is C.3.3.—the number of Wilde's prison cell. Yet for W. H. Auden and psychoanalytic critics, *Reading Gaol* is either inauthentic or dispensable; see Auden, "An Improbable Life," in Ellmann, *Wilde: Critical Essays*, p. 134.

I have already shown the socialist tendencies in even Wilde's earliest works, particularly in his criticism, so here I do not intend to belabor an argument against Chesterton's and others' surprise at finding them in *Reading Gaol*. Wilde was consistent, but until he went to prison, his contemporaries could not reconcile, and in fact could barely recognize, socialist attitudes with a dandy's dress. Alternatively, once Wilde was punished, many of his contemporaries saw him as redeemed, with changed attitudes and a sincerity newly found in suffering. But writing *Reading Gaol* in Naples, living once again with Douglas, Wilde was neither changed nor redeemed.

67. In Mason, *Bibliography*, pp. 426-27.
68. Wilde, *Letters*, p. 730n.
69. Sartre, *Saint Genet*, p. 350.
70. For variations on this theme see Sir Henry Hall Caine's *The Deemster* (1887); excerpts in Reade, *Sexual Heretics*, pp. 204-22.
71. Letter of 18? April 1895 in the Clark Library.

Chapter 5

1. "A shining light of literary purity reflected from a dark background of insincerity and depravity. . . . odious pretensions. . . . Oscar Wilde was a poser to the last . . . until the world was rid of his empty pratings" (*The Theatre Magazine*

Notes to Pages 179-84

5 [May 1905]: iii); "There was something about Wilde's personality that renders it difficult for the reader to believe in his sincerity when he is writing a purely personal apologia" (*Pall Mall Gazette*, 25 Mar. 1908, pp. 1-2); "This is not sorrow, but its dextrously constructed counterfeit. . . . [Wilde] grew to be incapable of deliberately telling the truth about himself or anything else. . . . By nature a witty and irresponsible Irishman. . . ." (*Times Literary Supplement*, 24 Feb. 1905); "[In *De Profundis* Wilde was] almost unable to call up the language of sincerity" (*Saturday Review*, 20 Oct. 1962, p. 26); "The veil of artifice is seldom lifted" (*New York Herald Tribune Book Review*, 28 Oct. 1962, p. 5); "Wilde was totally devoid of an interior life" (*Time and Tide*, 28 June 1962, pp. 18-20); "He may never really have existed, except as a performance" (*Hudson Review* 15 [Winter 1962-63]: 620-22); "Oscar Wilde creates the myth and legend of himself . . . a mingling of artificial high comedy and grotesque and lurid melodrama" (*Yale Review* 52 [Dec. 1962]: 287-89). See also W. H. Auden, "An Improbable Life" in *New Yorker*, 9 Mar. 1963, included in Ellmann, *Wilde: Critical Essays*; Bernard Shaw cited in Weintraub, *Reggie*, p. 99; Barzun, "Introduction," pp. v-xix. There is no question but that criticism of Wilde's autobiographical letter has remained rather primitive. For recent and more sophisticated theories of Victorian and other autobiography, see Landow, *Approaches*; Roy Pascal, *Design and Truth in Autobiography* (Cambridge, Mass., 1960); Paul de Man, "Autobiography as Defacement," *MLN* 94 (Dec. 1979): 919-30; Louis A. Renza, "The Veto of the Imagination: A Theory of Autobiography," *New Literary History* 9, no. 1 (Autumn 1977): 1-26; Arnold Weinstein, *Fictions of the Self: 1550-1800* (Princeton, N.J., 1981); Buckley, *Turning Key*; Paul Jay, *Being in the Text: Self-Representation from Wordsworth to Roland Barthes* (Ithaca, N.Y., 1984); James Olney, ed., *Autobiography: Essays Theoretical and Critical* (Princeton, N.J., 1980); and William Spengemann, *The Forms of Autobiography: Episodes in the History of a Literary Genre* (New Haven, Conn., 1980).

2. The phrase "material matrix" is Nicos Poulantzas's in *State, Power, Socialism*, especially in Part I, "The Institutional Materiality of the State," but I do not wish to claim any relevance of Poulantzas's State theory to the concerns of this chapter.

3. Wilde, *Letters*, p. 425. All quotations from *De Profundis* are indicated in the text by page numbers of this edition.

4. On late nineteenth-century penal practice, see Du Cane, *Punishment*, "Decrease of Crime," "Prison Committee Report," and "Prison Labour"; Morrison, *Crime*, "Increase of Crime," "Prisons a Failure?" and "Prison Reform"; Mayhew and Binny, *Criminal Prisons*; Ives, *Penal Methods*; and Webb and Webb, *English Prisons*. For Wilde's experiences in, and after, prison, see Hyde, *Wilde: Aftermath* and Wilde's *Letters*.

5. In *Crime and Its Causes*, Morrison listed the qualifications of a good governor: a general education; an understanding of the economic and social causes of crime as well as of its individual causes, of the principles of sociology and political economy, of psychology, of the historical, philosophic, and legal aspects of criminal jurisprudence, of prison science, of the historical development of punishment by imprisonment, of the various modern prison systems, of the aim and object of

Notes to Pages 184-206

imprisonment, and of the legal and administrative arrangements; a ripened judgment and a heart for the miserable. "He must have a quick eye for all that is being done; he must see everything; he must hear everything; nothing should escape him; and still he ought to leave independence and initiative to every officer in his own department" (pp. 219-21).

6. See *La Revue Blanche*, 1 June 1896, pp. 484-90; a typescript of an unpublished article by Douglas for the *Mercure de France* in August 1895 at the Clark Library; a letter not sent from More Adey to a correspondent in the French press in June 1895, also at the Clark Library. And in support of Douglas's allegations about Prime Minister Rosebery, see Hyde, *Love*, pp. 146-47 and Appendix B of this book.

7. See Hyde, *Aftermath*, app. A, p. 201.

8. In reading prison literature, I have found two bibliographies especially useful: Engelbarts, *Books in Stir*, and that in Franklin, *Victim as Criminal and Artist*.

9. Inmates, *Prison Etiquette*, pp. 51-52.

10. Abbott, *Belly of the Beast*, pp. 43-53 for this and the following excerpt.

11. Wilde, *Letters*, p. 581.

12. Ibid., p. 663.

Appendix B

1. When Wilde heard in prison that the article included some of his letters to Douglas, he forbade its publication, and Douglas complied with his wishes. A typescript of the article in the Clark Library and other of Douglas's papers have convinced me that Douglas sincerely believed, when he encouraged Wilde to prosecute his father, that Wilde would win the case. For the history of this typescript see Wilde, *Letters*, p. 393n.

2. See Hyde, *Love*, pp. 146-47.

Selected Bibliography

Many reviews, reminiscences, and criticisms (both old and new) cited fully in the notes are not included in this bibliography. Some, though not all, of their dates and locations may also be found in the casebooks included below, in Mikhail's *Annotated Bibliography*, or in Dowling's *Aestheticism and Decadence*. The original texts have been consulted for all citations in the notes from newspapers, magazines, and journals, many of which are collected in the William Andrews Clark Memorial Library of the University of California, Los Angeles. The letters of Richard Burton cited in Chapter 4 are in the Huntington Library, San Marino, California.

Abbott, Jack Henry. *In the Belly of the Beast: Letters from Prison*. New York, 1981.
Adorno, Theodor W. *Aesthetic Theory*. Trans. C. Lenhardt. Ed. Gretel Adorno and Rolf Tiedemann. London, 1984.
Althusser, Louis. *Lenin and Philosophy and Other Essays*. Trans. Ben Brewster. London, 1971.
Anderson, Perry. *Considerations on Western Marxism*. London, 1976.
Appleton, Charles Edward, T. K. Cheyne, J. S. Cotton, W. T. Dyer, H. Nettleship, M. Pattison, A. H. Sayce, and A. C. Sorby. *Essays on the Endowment of Research*. London, 1876.
Arnold, Matthew. *Complete Prose Works*. Ed. R. H. Super. Ann Arbor, 1960-77.
Artaud, Antonin. *Collected Works*. 3 vols. Trans. Victor Corti and Alastair Hamilton. London, 1968-72.
———. *The Theater and Its Double*. Trans. Mary Caroline Richards. New York, 1958.
Bakhtin, Mikhail. *Problems of Dostoevsky's Poetics*. Trans. R. W. Rotsel. Ardis edition, n.p., 1973.
Balzac, Honoré de. *Philosophic and Analytic Studies*. Vol. 42 of *The Human Comedy*. Trans. George Burnham Ives. Philadelphia, 1899.
Bamford, T. W. *The Rise of the Public Schools: A Study of Boys' Public Boarding Schools in England and Wales from 1837 to the Present Day*. London, 1967.
Barbey D'Aurevilly, J. A. *Of Dandyism and of George Brummell*. Trans. Douglas Ainslie. London, 1897.
———. *What Never Dies*. [Translation mistakenly attributed to "Sebastian Melmoth (Oscar Wilde)."] In *The Works of Oscar Wilde*, Sunflower edition, vol. 13. New York, 1909.

Selected Bibliography

Barzun, Jacques. Introduction to *De Profundis*. New York, 1964.
Baudelaire, Charles. *Oeuvres Complètes*. Paris, 1975.
———. *The Painter of Modern Life and Other Essays*. Trans. and ed. Jonathan Mayne. London, 1964.
Baudrillard, Jean. *The Mirror of Production*. Trans. Mark Poster. St. Louis, 1975.
Beardsley, Aubrey. *The Letters of Aubrey Beardsley*. Ed. Henry Maas, J. L. Duncan, and W. G. Good. Rutherford, N.J., 1970.
Beckson, Karl, ed. *Oscar Wilde: The Critical Heritage*. London, 1970.
Beerbohm, Max. *And Even Now*. London, 1920.
———. *Zuleika Dobson*. New York, 1926.
Benjamin, Walter. *Illuminations*. New York, 1969.
———. *Reflections*. Trans. Edmond Jephcott. Ed. Peter Demetz. New York, 1978.
Berger, John. *Ways of Seeing*. London, 1972.
Best, Geoffrey. *Mid-Victorian Britain 1851-1875*. London, 1971.
Bird, Alan. *The Plays of Oscar Wilde*. London, 1977.
Boorstin, Daniel J. *The Americans: The Democratic Experience*. New York, 1974.
Bradbury, Malcolm. *The Social Context of Modern English Literature*. Oxford, 1971.
Braybrooke, Patrick. *Lord Alfred Douglas: His Life and Work*. London, 1931.
Buckley, Jerome H., ed. *The Pre-Raphaelites*. New York, 1968.
———. *The Turning Key: Autobiography and the Subjective Impulse Since 1800*. Cambridge, Mass., 1984.
Bürger, Peter. *Theory of the Avant-Garde*. Trans. Michael Shaw. Minneapolis, 1984.
Burton, Richard F. *The Book of the Thousand Nights and a Night*. 10 vols. Benares, 1885.
———. *Supplementary Nights*. 6 vols. Benares, 1885.
The Cambridge Economic History of Europe. Vols. 6 and 7. Cambridge, 1965 and 1978.
Carlyle, Thomas. *Sartor Resartus and On Heroes, Hero-Worship and the Heroic in History*. London, 1921.
———. "Shooting Niagara." *Macmillan's Magazine*, August 1867.
Chamberlin, J. E. *Ripe Was the Drowsy Hour: The Age of Oscar Wilde*. New York, 1977.
Chesterton, G. K. *The Victorian Age in Literature*. London, 1966.
Cipolla, Carlo M., ed. *The Fontana Economic History of Europe*. Vols. 3 and 4. London, 1973.
Cohen, Philip K. *The Moral Vision of Oscar Wilde*. London, 1978.
Critchley, Macdonald. *The Black Hole and Other Essays*. London, 1964.
Croft-Cooke, Rupert. *The Unrecorded Life of Oscar Wilde*. New York, 1972.
Curtin, Michael. "Etiquette and Society in Victorian England." Ph.D. diss. University of California, Berkeley, 1981.
Daiches, David. *Some Late Victorian Attitudes: The Ewing Lectures*. New York, 1969.

Selected Bibliography

D'Amico, Masolino. "Oscar Wilde Between Socialism and Aestheticism." *English Miscellany* 8 (1967): 111-39.
Davidoff, Leonore. *The Best Circles: Society Etiquette and the Season.* London, 1973.
Debord, Guy. *Society of the Spectacle.* Detroit, 1977.
Doughty, Oswald. *A Victorian Romantic: Dante Gabriel Rossetti.* London, 1960.
Douglas, Alfred. *The Autobiography of Lord Alfred Douglas.* London, 1929.
———. *My Friendship with Oscar Wilde.* New York, 1932.
———. *Oscar Wilde: A Summing-Up.* London, 1940.
———. *Oscar Wilde and Myself.* London, 1914.
———. *The True History of Shakespeare's Sonnets.* London, 1933.
———. *Without Apology.* London, 1938.
Dowling, Linda C. *Aestheticism and Decadence: A Selective Annotated Bibliography.* New York, 1977.
Dowson, Ernest. *The Letters of Ernest Dowson.* Ed. Desmond Flower and Henry Maas. London, 1967.
Du Cane, Edmund. "The Decrease of Crime." *Nineteenth Century*, Mar. 1893, pp. 480-92.
———. "The Prison Committee Report." *Nineteenth Century*, Aug. 1895, pp. 278-94.
———. *The Punishment and Prevention of Crime.* London, 1885.
———. "The Unavoidable Uselessness of Prison Labour." *Nineteenth Century*, Oct. 1896, pp. 632-42.
Dyos, H. J., and Michael Wolff, eds. *The Victorian City.* 2 vols. London, 1973.
Dyson, A. E. *The Crazy Fabric: Essays in Irony.* London, 1965.
Edel, Leon. *Henry James.* Vols. 3 and 4. Philadelphia, 1962 and 1969.
Ellmann, Richard. *Eminent Domain: Yeats Among Wilde, Joyce, Pound, Eliot and Auden.* New York, 1967.
———, ed. *Edwardians and Late Victorians: English Institute Essays 1959.* New York, 1960.
———, ed. *Oscar Wilde: A Collection of Critical Essays.* Englewood Cliffs, N.J., 1969.
Ellmann, Richard, E. D. H. Johnson, and Alfred L. Bush. *Wilde and the Nineties: An Essay and an Exhibition.* Ed. Charles Ryskamp. Princeton, 1966.
Empson, William. *Seven Types of Ambiguity.* London, 1947.
Engel, A. J. *From Clergyman to Don: The Rise of the Academic Profession in Nineteenth-Century Oxford.* Oxford, 1983.
Engelbarts, Rudolf. *Books in Stir: A Bibliographic Essay About Prison Libraries and About Books Written by Prisoners and Prison Employees.* Metuchen, N.J., 1972.
Engels, Friedrich. *The Condition of the Working Class in England.* Trans. W. O. Henderson and W. H. Chaloner. Stanford, Calif., 1968.
Ericksen, Donald H. *Oscar Wilde.* Boston, 1977.
Fletcher, Ian, ed. *Decadence and the 1890s.* London, 1979.
———, ed. *Romantic Mythologies.* London, 1967.
Foucault, Michel. *The History of Sexuality. Vol. 1: An Introduction.* Trans. Robert Hurley. New York, 1980.

Selected Bibliography

Franklin, H. Bruce. *The Victim as Criminal as Artist: Literature from the American Prison.* New York, 1978.
Fredeman, William E. *Pre-Raphaelitism: A Bibliocritical Study.* Cambridge, Mass., 1964.
Freeman, William. *The Life of Lord Alfred Douglas: Spoilt Child of Genius.* London, 1948.
"The Function of Matthew Arnold at the Present Time." *Critical Inquiry.* Mar. 1983 (entire issue on this topic).
Fussell, Paul. *The Great War and Modern Memory.* New York, 1975.
Galton, Francis. *Hereditary Genius.* London, 1978.
Gaunt, William. *The Aesthetic Adventure.* London, 1945.
———. *The Pre-Raphaelite Tragedy.* London, 1942.
Gelpi, Barbara Charlesworth. *Dark Passages: The Decadent Consciousness in Victorian Literature.* Madison, Wis., 1965.
Gettmann, Royal A. *A Victorian Publisher.* Cambridge, Eng., 1960.
Gide, André. *Oscar Wilde: A Study*, with Introduction, Notes, and Bibliography by Stuart Mason. Oxford, 1905.
Gilbert, Elliott L. "Tumult of Images: Wilde, Beardsley, and *Salome.*" *Victorian Studies* 26, no. 2 (Winter 1983): 133-59.
Gilbert, W. S. *Patience; or Bunthorne's Bride.* In *The Savoy Operas: Being the Complete Text of the Gilbert and Sullivan Operas as Originally Produced in the Years 1875-1896.* London, 1963.
Girouard, Mark. *The Return to Camelot: Chivalry and the English Gentleman.* New Haven, Conn., 1981.
Gissing, George. *New Grub Street.* Ed. Bernard Bergonzi. Middlesex, 1983.
Gramsci, Antonio. *Selections from the Prison Notebooks.* Ed. and trans. Quintin Hoare and Geoffrey Nowell Smith. New York, 1971.
Green, Martin. *Children of the Sun: A Narrative of "Decadence" in England After 1918.* New York, 1976.
Gross, John. *The Rise and Fall of the Man of Letters: A Study of the Idiosyncratic and the Humane in Modern Literature.* London, 1969.
Grosskurth, Phyllis. *John Addington Symonds.* London, 1964.
Guérard, Albert Leon. *Art for Art's Sake.* Boston, 1936.
Guralnick, Elissa S., and Paul M. Levitt. "Allusion and Meaning in Wilde's *A Woman of No Importance.*" *Eire-Ireland* 13, no. 4 (Winter 1978): 45-51.
Harris, Frank. *Mr. and Mrs. Daventry: A Play in Four Acts by Frank Harris: Based on the Scenario by Oscar Wilde.* London, 1956.
———. *Oscar Wilde: His Life and Confessions.* 2 vols. Published by the author, 1918.
Harris, Frank, and Lord Alfred Douglas. *New Preface to "The Life and Confessions of Oscar Wilde."* London, 1927.
Harris, Wendell. "English Short Fiction in the Nineteenth Century." *Studies in Short Fiction* 6 (1968-69): 1-93.
Harrison, Fraser. "Oscar Wilde." *Journal of the Eighteen Nineties Society* 11 (1980): 1-9.
Hazlitt, William. *Fugitive Writings.* Vol. 11 of the *Collected Works of William Hazlitt.* Ed. A. R. Waller and Arnold Glower. London, 1904.

Selected Bibliography

Heyck, T. W. *The Transformation of Intellectual Life in Victorian England.* New York, 1982.
Hichens, Robert. *The Green Carnation.* New York, 1894.
Hilliard, David. "Un-English and Unmanly: Anglo-Catholicism and Homosexuality." *Victorian Studies* 25, no. 2 (Winter 1982): 181-210.
Hobsbawm, Eric J. *Primitive Rebels: Studies in Archaic Forms of Social Movement in the Nineteenth and Twentieth Centuries.* New York, 1959.
———. *Workers.* New York, 1984.
———, ed. *Labour's Turning Point 1880-1900: Extracts from Contemporary Sources.* 2d. ed. Rutherford, N.J., 1974.
Holland, Vyvyan. *Son of Oscar Wilde.* London, 1954.
Honey, J. R. de S. *Tom Brown's Universe: The Development of the English Public School in the Nineteenth Century.* New York, 1977.
Horkheimer, Max, and Theodor W. Adorno. *Dialectic of Enlightenment.* Trans. John Cumming. New York, 1972.
Hough, Graham. *The Last Romantics.* London, 1949.
Houghton, Walter E. *The Victorian Frame of Mind 1830-1870.* New Haven, Conn., 1957.
Hughes, Thomas. *Tom Brown's School Days.* New York, 1891.
Hunt, W. Holman. *Pre-Raphaelitism and the Pre-Raphaelite Brotherhood.* 2 vols. New York, 1905.
Hyde, H. Montgomery. *A History of Pornography.* London, 1964.
———. *The Love That Dared Not Speak Its Name: A Candid History of Homosexuality in Britain.* Boston, 1970.
———. *Oscar Wilde: The Aftermath.* New York, 1963.
———. *Oscar Wilde: A Biography.* London, 1976.
———, ed. *The Three Trials of Oscar Wilde.* New York, 1956.
The Inmates. *Prison Etiquette: The Convict's Compendium of Useful Information.* Ed. Holley Cantine and Dachine Rainer. Preface by Christopher Isherwood. Bearsville, N.Y., 1950.
Ives, George. *A History of Penal Methods.* London, 1914.
Jackson, Holbrook. *The Eighteen-Nineties.* N.p., 1913.
James, Henry. *Guy Domville.* Philadelphia, 1960.
———. *The Tragic Muse.* New York, 1978.
Jarry, Alfred. *The Ubu Plays.* Trans. Simon Watson Taylor. London, 1968.
Jesse, Captain [William]. *The Life of Beau Brummell.* 2 vols. London, privately printed, n.d.
Johnson, Robert Vincent. *Aestheticism.* London, 1969.
Kempf, Roger, ed. *Sur le dandysme: Balzac, Barbey d'Aurevilly, Baudelaire.* Paris, 1971.
Kermode, Frank. *Romantic Image.* London, 1957.
Kettle, Michael. *Salome's Last Veil: The Libel Case of the Century.* London, 1977.
Landow, George P., ed. *Approaches to Victorian Autobiography.* Athens, Ohio, 1979.
Langtry, Lillie. *The Days I Knew.* 2d ed. London, n.d.
Laver, James. *Dandies.* London, 1968.
Leavis, Q. D. *Fiction and the Reading Public.* London, 1932.

Selected Bibliography

Le Gallienne, Richard. *English Poems.* London, 1892.
———. *Retrospective Reviews: A Literary Log.* 2 vols. London, 1896.
Lentricchia, Frank. *Criticism and Social Change.* Chicago, 1983.
Lester, John A., Jr. *Journey Through Despair.* Princeton, 1968.
Letwin, Shirley Robin. *The Gentleman in Trollope: Individuality and Moral Conduct.* London, 1982.
Leverson, Ada. *Letters to the Sphinx from Oscar Wilde: With Reminiscences of the Author.* London, 1930.
Lombroso, Cesare. *Crime: Its Causes and Remedies.* Trans. Henry P. Horton. Boston, 1911.
———. *The Man of Genius.* 3d ed. London, n.d.
Lowther, Aimee, ed. "Unpublished Stories by Oscar Wilde." *The Mask: A Quarterly Journal of the Art of the Theatre* 4 (Jan. 1912): 190; 4 (Apr. 1912): 283-85; 5 (July 1912): 17-19; 5 (Oct. 1912): 162.
Lytton, Edward George Bulwer. *England and the English.* London, 1833.
———. *The Last Days of Pompeii.* 2 vols. London, 1859.
———. *Pelham: or the Adventures of a Gentleman.* Ed. Jerome J. McGann. Lincoln, Neb., 1972.
Macqueen-Pope, W. *Haymarket: Theatre of Perfection.* London, 1948.
———. *St. James's: Theatre of Distinction.* London, 1958.
Marcus, Jane. "*Salome*: The Jewish Princess Was a New Woman." *Bulletin of the New York Public Library* 78 (1974-75): 95-112.
Marcus, Steven. *The Other Victorians: A Study of Sexuality and Pornography in Mid-Nineteenth-Century England.* New York, 1964.
Mason, Stuart [Christopher Sclater Millard]. *Bibliography of Oscar Wilde.* London, 1914. New ed., London, 1967.
———. *Oscar Wilde and the Aesthetic Movement.* Dublin, 1920.
———. *Oscar Wilde: Art and Morality: A Record of the Discussion Which Followed the Publication of "Dorian Gray."* London, 1907. Rev. ed., 1912.
Maturin, Charles Robert. *Melmoth the Wanderer.* 3 vols. London, 1892.
———. *Melmoth the Wanderer: A Tale.* Ed. Douglas Grant. London, 1968.
Mayhew, Henry, and John Binny. *The Criminal Prisons of London.* London, 1862.
McCormack, Jerusha. "Masks Without Faces: The Personalities of Oscar Wilde." *English Literature in Transition* 22, no. 4 (1979): 253-69.
Meyers, Jeffrey. *Homosexuality and Literature.* London, 1977.
Mikhail, E. H. *Oscar Wilde: An Annotated Bibliography of Criticism.* London, 1978.
———, ed. *Oscar Wilde: Interviews and Recollections.* 2 vols. London, 1979.
Millett, Kate. *Sexual Politics.* New York, 1970.
Mintz, Samuel I., ed. *From Smollett to James: Studies in the Novel and Other Essays.* Charlottesville, Va., 1981.
Mix, Katherine Lyon. *A Study in Yellow: The Yellow Book and Its Contributors.* Lawrence, Kans., 1960.
Moers, Ellen. *The Dandy: Brummell to Beerbohm.* Lincoln, Nebr., 1960.
Morazé, Charles. *The Triumph of the Middle Class.* Trans. George Weidenfeld and Nicolson Ltd. London, 1966.

Selected Bibliography

Morris, William. *News from Nowhere: or An Epoch of Rest; Being Some Chapters from a Utopian Romance.* 2d ed. London, 1891.
Morrison, William. "Are Our Prisons a Failure?" *Fortnightly Review*, Apr. 1894, pp. 459-69.
———. *Crime and Its Causes.* London, 1891.
———. "The Increase of Crime." *Nineteenth Century*, June 1892, pp. 950-57.
———. "Prison Reform." *Fortnightly Review*, May 1898, pp. 781-89.
Munro, John M. *The Decadent Poetry of the Eighteen-Nineties.* Beirut, 1970.
Nassaar, Christopher. *Into the Demon Universe: A Literary Exploration of Oscar Wilde.* New Haven, Conn., 1974.
Nelson, James G. *The Early Nineties: A View from the Bodley Head.* Cambridge, Mass., 1971.
Nordau, Max. *Degeneration*, translated from the 1893 edition of the German. London, 1920.
———. *Degeneration.* Introduction by George L. Mosse. New York, 1968.
O'Sullivan, Vincent. *Aspects of Wilde.* London, 1936.
Pearson, Hesketh. *Oscar Wilde: His Life and Wit.* New York, 1946.
Poulantzas, Nicos. *State, Power, Socialism.* Trans. Patrick Camiller. London, 1980.
Powell, Kerry. "Tom, Dick, and Dorian Gray: Magic-Picture Mania in Late Victorian Fiction." *Philological Quarterly*, Spring 1983, pp. 147-70.
Praz, Mario. *The Romantic Agony.* Oxford, 1933. Rev. ed., 1951.
Presbrey, Frank. *The History and Development of Advertising.* Garden City, N.J., 1929.
Raffalovich, Marc-André. *Uranisme et unisexualité.* Paris, 1896.
Reade, Brian, ed. *Sexual Heretics: Male Homosexuality in English Literature from 1850 to 1900: An Anthology.* New York, 1970.
Renan, Ernest. *The Life of Jesus.* Trans. Charles Edwin Wilbour. New York, 1864.
Robertson, W. Graham. *Time Was.* London, 1931.
Roditi, Edouard. *Oscar Wilde.* Norfolk, 1947.
Rothblatt, Sheldon. *The Revolution of the Dons: Cambridge and Society in Victorian England.* London, 1968.
Rowbotham, Sheila, and Jeffrey Weeks. *Socialism and the New Life: The Personal and Sexual Politics of Edward Carpenter and Havelock Ellis.* London, 1977.
Rowell, George. *The Victorian Theatre 1792-1914.* 2d ed. Cambridge, Eng., 1978.
Ruskin, John. *The Genius of John Ruskin.* Ed. John D. Rosenberg. Boston, 1980.
Sambrook, James, ed. *Pre-Raphaelitism: A Collection of Critical Essays.* Chicago, 1974.
San Juan, Epifanio, Jr. *The Art of Oscar Wilde.* Princeton, 1967.
Sartre, Jean-Paul. *Saint Genet: Actor and Martyr.* Trans. Bernard Frechtman. New York, 1963.
Shaw, Bernard. "My Memories of Oscar Wilde." In Frank Harris, *Oscar Wilde: His Life and Confessions*, vol. 2. Published by Harris, 1918.
———. *Our Theatres in the Nineties.* 3 vols. London, 1932.

Selected Bibliography

———. *The Sanity of Art: An Exposure of the Current Nonsense About Artists Being Degenerate*. London, 1908.
Sherard, Robert. *The Life of Oscar Wilde*. London, 1906.
———. *Oscar Wilde: The Story of an Unhappy Friendship*. London, privately printed, 1902.
———. *The Real Oscar Wilde*. London, n.d.
Shewan, Rodney. *Oscar Wilde: Art and Egotism*. London, 1977.
Smith, Timothy d'Arch. *Love in Earnest: Some Notes on the Lives and Writings of English "Uranian Poets" from 1889 to 1930*. London, 1970.
Snitow, Ann, Christine Stansell, and Sharon Thompson, eds. *The Powers of Desire: The Politics of Sexuality*. New York, 1983.
Sontag, Susan. "Notes on Camp." *Partisan Review* 31 (1964): 515-30.
The Spirit Lamp. Oxford, 1892-93.
Stein, Richard L. *The Ritual of Interpretation: The Fine Arts as Literature in Ruskin, Rossetti, and Pater*. Cambridge, Mass., 1975.
Steinberg, Charles S. *The Creation of Consent: Public Relations in Practice*. New York, 1975.
Stephens, John Russell. *The Censorship of English Drama 1824-1901*. Cambridge, Eng., 1980.
Stokes, John. *Oscar Wilde*. Essex, 1978.
———. *Resistible Theatres: Enterprise and Experiment in the Late Nineteenth Century*. London, 1972.
Stuart-Young, John Moray. *Osrac, the Self-Sufficient*. Sunderland, Eng., 1905.
———. *Osrac, the Self-Sufficient, and Other Poems: With a Memorial of the Late Oscar Wilde*. London, 1905.
Sussman, Herbert. "Criticism as Art: Form in Oscar Wilde's Critical Writings." *Studies in Philosophy* 70 (Jan. 1973): 108-22.
Swart, Koenraad. *The Sense of Decadence in Nineteenth-Century France*. The Hague, 1964.
Symons, Alphonse James Albert. "Wilde at Oxford." *Horizon* 3, no. 16 (April 1941).
Symons, Arthur. "The Decadent Movement in Literature." *Harper's New Monthly Magazine*, November 1893.
———. *A Study of Oscar Wilde*. London, 1930.
———. *The Symbolist Movement in Literature*. London, 1898. Rev. ed., New York, 1919.
Teleny. Ed. Winston Leyland. San Francisco, 1984.
Temple, Ruth Z. *The Critic's Alchemy: A Study of the Introduction of French Symbolism in England*. New Haven, Conn., 1953.
Thomas, J. D. "'The Soul of Man Under Socialism': An Essay in Context." *Rice University Studies* 51, no. 1 (Winter 1965): 83-95.
Thompson, E. P. *William Morris: Romantic to Revolutionary*. London, 1955.
Trilling, Lionel. *Sincerity and Authenticity*. Cambridge, Mass., 1971.
Trollope, Anthony. *The Way We Live Now*. London, 1962.
Turner, E. S. *The Shocking History of Advertising*. London, 1952.
The Vigilante. Vols. 6-8, nos. 79-81 (6 April-15 June 1918).

Selected Bibliography

Webb, Beatrice. *My Apprenticeship*. Cambridge, Eng., 1979.
Webb, Beatrice, and Sidney Webb. *English Prisons Under Local Government*, with a preface by Bernard Shaw. London, 1922.
Weeks, Jeffrey. *Coming Out: Homosexual Politics in Britain from the Nineteenth Century to the Present*. London, 1977.
Weintraub, Stanley. *Reggie: A Portrait of Reginald Turner*. New York, 1965.
Wells, H. G. Preface to *The Island of Doctor Moreau*. Vol. 2 in *The Works of H. G. Wells*. Atlantic Edition. New York, 1924.
Wiener, Martin J. *English Culture and the Decline of the Industrial Spirit, 1850-1980*. Cambridge, Eng., 1981.
Wilde, Oscar Fingal O'Flahertie Wills. *The Artist as Critic: Critical Writings of Oscar Wilde*. Ed. Richard Ellmann. New York, 1968. [This edition is the source for citations for Wilde's criticism, unless otherwise noted.]
———. *The Letters of Oscar Wilde*. Ed. Rupert Hart-Davis, New York, 1962. [For all letters, including *De Profundis*.]
———. *The Original Four-Act Version of the Importance of Being Earnest*. Ed. Vyvyan Holland. London, 1957.
———. *Plays*. Harmondsworth, Eng., 1954. Reprint 1979. [For the comedies.]
———. *The Plays of Oscar Wilde*. Vol. 4. Boston, 1920. [For what is left of *A Florentine Tragedy* and the text of *Salomé* in French.]
———. *The Portable Oscar Wilde*. Ed. Richard Aldington. Harmondsworth, Eng., 1977. [For *The Picture of Dorian Gray*.]
———. *Salome: A Tragedy in One Act: Translated from the French of Oscar Wilde by Lord Alfred Douglas: Pictured by Aubrey Beardsley*. London, 1894. Reproduction, New York, 1967.
———. *The Works of Oscar Wilde*. London, 1970. [For *The Happy Prince and Other Tales*, *A House of Pomegranates*, and *Lord Arthur Savile's Crime and Other Stories*.]
———. *The Works of Oscar Wilde*. 15 vols. Sunflower Edition. New York, 1909. [For works not listed above.]
Winwar, Frances. *Oscar Wilde and the Yellow Nineties*. New York, 1940.
The Woman's World. London, 1887-89.
Wood, James Playsted. *The Story of Advertising*. New York, 1958.
Woolf, Virginia. "Beau Brummell." In "Four Figures" in *The Common Reader*, 2d series. London, 1959.
Yeats, William Butler. *The Autobiography*. New York, 1965.
———. "Memoirs." In *The Norton Anthology of English Literature*. Ed. M. H. Abrams et al. 3d ed. Vol. 2. New York, 1974.
The Yellow Book, vols. 1 and 3. London, April and October 1894.
Young, Dal. *Apologia pro Oscar Wilde*. London, 1895.

Index

Abbott, Jack, 194-95
Academy, the, *see* Universities
Academy, The (journal), 171, 230
Addison, Joseph, 53
Adey, More, 163, 184, 206-7
Adorno, Theodor, 6
Advertising, 5, 9, 14f, 21, 27-28, 51-57 *passim*, 61, 65, 72-73, 135, 216, 226
Aestheticism, 3-15, 72, 82-83, 139; Wilde's, 11-12, 14, 21, 56, 67, 139; gender confusion and, 141-44; press attacks on, 146; symbols of movement, 163-64; and Christ, 190-92; British, French, 213. *See also* Decadence and Decadents
Ainsworth, Harrison, 34
"Alchemical Theater, The" (Artaud), 109-10
Aldrich, Richard, 170
Alexander, Florence, 108
Alexander, George, 104, 133
Alfred Jarry Theater of Cruelty, *see* Artaud; Theater of Cruelty
Allan, Maud, 153f, 199-204, 229
Anarchism, 215
Aphorisms, *see* Epigrams
Appleton, Charles Edward, 13
Archer, William, 104, 130, 224
A Rebours (Huysmans), 5, 65, 146
Arnold, Matthew, 27-29, 30, 31
Art: Wilde on, 3, 7-14 *passim*, 29-35 *passim*, 47, 66, 105-7, 193; for art's sake, 5-7, 39, 65, 159-62; consumers and consumption of, 15, 105-35; criminality and, 34-39, 147-52; truth and, 41f; acting, forgery, and, 42; -as-seduction, 44-47; morality and, 51, 59; homosexuality and, 61-62; life and, 105-7; politics as, 131; sex, love, and, 139-76; as propaganda in wartime, 199-204
Artaud, Antonin, 8, 109-11, 115, 117, 134-35, 166
Artist and Journal of Home Culture, The, 147
Art world, the, 6, 12, 19, 34-39, 139
Ashbery, John, 45
Asquith, Herbert Henry, 184, 200f
Athanaeum, 58, 62, 72, 90, 116, 131, 143
Auden, W. H., 179-80, 231
Audiences: Wilde's, 3-15, 19-47; nature of modern, 103-4; Wilde's manipulation of, 105-6, 117f, 120-24, 163-64, 170-71; first-night, 107-8; as consumers, 108-9, 114, 115-16, 133-35; Artaud and, 110-11; *Earnest* and, 111-12, 224; of peers, 177-95. *See also* Spectacle and spectators
Avant-garde, 6, 8
Aynesworth, Allan, 224

Bakhtin, Mikhail, 31-32
Ballad of Reading Gaol, The (Wilde), 4, 70, 134, 140, 152, 165, 180, 193, 195; male community and,

Index

173-76; reviews and criticism of, 230-31; socialism and, 231
Balzac, Honoré de, 78-79, 86-87
Bamford, T. W., 92f
Barbey d'Aurevilly, Jules, 80-81, 114, 121f, 132, 218, 221
Barford, John Leslie ("Philebus"), 161
Barnes, Clive, 224
Barratt, Thomas J., 53
Baudelaire, Charles, 81-89 *passim*, 133, 160, 213, 221
Baudrillard, Jean, 9-10, 221
Beardsley, Aubrey, 15, 141f, 144, 169, 230
Beerbohm, Max, 83, 85, 108, 141, 169-70
Benjamin, Walter, 10, 22, 84
Bernhardt, Sarah, 165, 169, 229
Best, Geoffrey, 91
Bettany, F. G., 62
Bird, Alan, 108, 117-18
"Birthday of the Infanta, The" (Wilde), 64
Blavatsky, Madame H. P., 141
Bloxam, John Francis, 147, 226
Bodies: souls and, 167; sexual politics using, 169; death of, 171-75; dignity of, 176. *See also* Sexuality
Bodley Head (firm), 55, 141, 154
Book of the Thousand Nights and a Night, The (Burton), 143
Borges, Jorge Luis, 14
Browning, Robert, 104
Brummell, George Bryan, 68-72, 74-81 *passim*, 133, 220
Bürger, Peter, 6, 7
Burton, Isabel, 143
Burton, Richard, 41, 141, 143
Butler, Josephine, 227
Butler, Samuel, 43
Byron, George Gordon, 68f, 220

"Canterville Ghost, The" (Wilde), 63
Carlyle, Thomas, 22, 76

Carpenter, Edward, 157f, 160-61
Carson, Edward, 146
Cassell, Ernest, 130
Catholicism: Wilde's, 195
Cecil; or the Adventures of a Coxcomb (Gore), 68
Cenci, The (Shelley), 103f
Censorship: official government, 103-5; of *Salome*, 165, 170, 230
Chamberlin, J. E., 214
Chameleon, 147, 149
Chesterton, G. K., 14, 95-96, 141, 218, 230-31
Children of the Sun (Green), 131
Chorley, Henry, 90
Christ, 175-80 *passim*, 187-91 *passim*
Christianity, 12
Christian Socialists, 91-92
Churchill, Winston, 54
Cohen, Philip, 217
Colburn, Henry, 72f, 75, 86
Cole, Alan, 66
Collins, Wilkie, 77
Colvin, Sidney, 26-27
Comedy, Wilde's wit and, 7-8, 19, 105-35, 167
Commodity: dandy as, 7; theorists of, 8-11; sex as, 141, 157-62; woman-as-, 159-61; fetishism, as poetry, 208-10. *See also* Spectacle and spectators
Conder, Charles, 141
Condition of the Working Class in England, The (Engels), 31
Connolly, Cyril, 93, 111
Conrad, Joseph, 141
Consumers and consumption: art from perspective of, 5, 15; of the sign, 9-10; advertising and, 51-57; audiences as, 105-35; male homosexual, 140-41; materialism, sexuality, and, 157-62
Contagious Disease Acts, 227
Cooke, Serrell, 153-54, 203
Corelli, Marie, 55
Corti, Victor, 111

246

Index

Costume, *see* Dress
Counterdecadents, the, 141, 154-55
Crime: criminology and, 5, 147-54; the arts and, 34-39, 147-52; homosexual love as, 173-76. *See also* Prison experience; Trials
Crime and Its Causes (Morrison), 232-33
Crime: Its Causes and Remedies (Lombroso), 148-49
Criminal Law Amendment Act, 143
"Critic as Artist, The" (Wilde), 20-21, 29, 42, 46f
Criticism: by Wilde, 3, 13-14, 19-22, 32-33, 47, 66, 214; of Wilde's works, *see* Reviews *and under titles of his works*
Croft-Cooke, Rupert, 42, 176
C.T.W. (Woolridge), 172f
Culture: cultural criticism, 12-13, 22-29, 47; popular, 22-29; advertising, art, and, 27-28, 52, 55, 85; "high," 34-39. *See also* Art
Culture and Anarchy (Arnold), 22, 23, 27-29
Curtin, Michael, 95-96
Cynicism, Wilde's, 19, 123-24, 130

Daily Chronicle, 58-59, 134, 145, 152, 181
Daily Telegraph, 145-46
D'Amico, Masolino, 215
Dandies and dandyism, 4-5, 7, 51-99, 220; Wilde's, 7, 85, 132-33; advertising and, 73; philosophies of, 76, 131-34, 221; French, 5, 76, 78, 80, 82, 221; women and, 80-83; 1890's form of, 84; banter of, 120-21; and gender confusion, 141; symbols of, 163. *See also* Gentleman
Dandy: Brummell to Beerbohm, The (Moers), 67
Darwinism and Politics (Ritchie), 98
Davidoff, Leonore, 75, 97, 120, 128
Davitt, Michael, 181
Dawson, Helen, 224

Days I Knew, The (Langtry), 118
Death (topic of), 171-76
Debord, Guy, 9-11, 21, 32, 41, 105, 109, 124
Decadence and decadents: French, 5, 213; of 1890's literature, 51-52, 72, 76-77, 154-55; Wilde's, 65-67, 156, 213; publishers of, 141; *Salome* as, 153-54; counterdecadents and, 154-55; symbols of, 163; history of criticism and critics of, 218-19
"Decay of Lying, The" (Wilde), 21, 41f, 46, 109
Degeneration (Nordau), 149-52 *passim*
Dehn, Paul, 225
De Profundis (Wilde), 4f, 69, 89-90, 145, 169, 173, 176, 179-95, 207; reviews and criticism of, 231-32
Dialogical language, 31-33. *See also* Diversion
Dickens, Charles, 22f, 25, 67, 76f
Disraeli, Benjamin, 53, 67, 75-76, 90, 130f, 220-21
Diversion, style of, 10-11, 32-33, 114
Dorian Gray, see Picture of Dorian Gray, The
D'Orsay, Count, 69, 90
Dostoevsky, Feodor M., 31-32
Double lives, homosexuals', 140, 158-59, 163-64. *See also* Posing
Double standard of sexual behavior, 130, 227. *See also* Prostitution
Douglas, Alfred: and Wilde together, 4, 85, 133, 144, 176, 179f, 186-93, 195, 233 (*see also De Profundis*); on *True History of Shakespeare's Sonnets*, 43; writing and editing by, 146-52 *passim*, 158, 162-63, 173, 200, 207, 210; and Wilde's trials, 146, 153, 201; in *The Green Carnation*, 155; political interpretation of Wilde's conviction by, 184, 205-7

247

Index

Dowson, Ernest, 141, 144
Dress, Wilde's, 56, 67, 150-51. *See also* Dandies and dandyism; Gentleman
Drumlanrig, Francis, 206
DuCane, Edmund, 182-84
Duchess of Padua, The (Wilde), 129
Dunne, Mary Chavelita, 155
Duse, Eleanora, 81
Dyson, A. E., 215

Earle, Adrian, 43-44
Earnest, see *Importance of Being Earnest, The*
Earthly Paradise, The (Morris), 142
Echo, 146
Edel, Leon, 125, 222f
Ellis, Havelock, 141, 148, 156, 218, 227
Ellmann, Richard, 3, 215, 216-17, 228-29
Empson, William, 28
Engels, Friedrich, 31
England and the English (Lytton), 75
Epigrams, Wilde's, 7-8, 113-14, 116, 121, 130, 167, 176, 226. *See also* Style; Wit
Epistola: in Carcere et Vinculis (Wilde), see *De Profundis*
Eriksen, Donald, 215-18 *passim*
Essays on the Endowment of Research (Oxbridge scholars, 1876), 12-13
Etiquette, 5; books, 95-98. *See also* Gentleman
Evans, Edith, 133
Evening News, 146

Faber, Frederick William, 149
Fabians, 215
Familialism, 94-99
Family Herald, The, 123
Ferri, Enrico, 152
Fetishes, Wilde's uses of, 112-13, 114, 125, 129, 133-34
"Fiction, Fair and Foul" (Ruskin), 22, 23

"Fisherman and His Soul, The" (Wilde), 63f, 175
Florentine Tragedy, A (Wilde), 141, 208-10
Fors Clavigera (Ruskin), 22
Fortnightly Review, 61
Foucault, Michel, 70, 82, 140f, 160
Fowler, N. C., Jr., 56
Frankfurt School, 6
Fraser's Magazine, 57, 70, 72, 78, 91
Freemason, 106-7
Frith, W. P., 55
Froude, Richard Hurrell, 149

Galton, Francis, 152-53
Gautier, Théophile, 6-7
Gay Sunshine Press, 60
Gender: "femininity" and, 65-67; "effeminacy" and, 69; construction of, 94-99; aestheticism and, 139-44; confusion, 141-44
Genius: Wilde's, 11; frequency of madness and, 150, 152f; Galton's study of, 152-53
Gentleman: dandies and, 4, 7 (*see also* Dandies and dandyism); criminality and, 38f; history and concept of British, 91-98, 143
Georgian Childhood, A (Connolly), 93
Gerber, Helmut, 219
Ghosts (Ibsen), 103-4
Gill, Charles Frederick, 147
Gissing, George, 21f, 23-25, 26
Gladstone, William Ewart, 53f, 206
Gonne, Maud, 144
Gore, Catherine, 68, 71, 76
Gramsci, Antonio, 13, 47, 84
Gray, John, 61, 142
Great Expectations (Dickens), 77
Green, Martin, 108, 131, 225
Green Carnation, The (Hichens), 155-56, 164
Green carnations (as symbol), 67, 163-64
Grein, J. T., 103f, 133, 153-54, 199-204

248

Index

Gross, John, 26
Grosskurth, Phyllis, 93
Guérard, Albert Leon, 218
Guralnick, Elissa S., 123f
Guy Domville (James), 105, 125, 223

Haldane, Richard Burdon, 184, 201
Happy Prince and Other Tales, The (Wilde), 62f, 175
"Harlot's House, The" (Wilde), 174
Harris, Frank, 20, 85, 96, 104-5, 159f, 230
Harris, Wendell, 218-19
Hawthorne, Nathaniel, 123
Haymarket: Theatre of Perfection (Macqueen-Pope), 107
Hazlitt, William, 72
Hearth and Home, 115
Hedda Gabler (Ibsen), 112
Henley, W. E., 57, 59, 171, 230f
Hereditary Genius (Galton), 152-53
Hermeneutics, 41
Heterosexuality, and homosexuality debate, 157-62. *See also* Gender; Prostitution; Sexuality; Women
Hewes, William, 43
Heyck, T. W., 213
Hichens, Robert, 155-56, 164
Hirsch, Charles, 60
Hirsh, Baron, 130
Hobsbawm, Eric, 14
Holland, Vyvyan, 133
Homogenic Love (Carpenter), 160
Homosexuality, 4-5; Wilde's, 20f, 57, 59-60, 139-47, 157-58; homoeroticism in Wilde's works, 41-47, 59-62, 66-67, 115, 157-58, 229, *and under titles of his works*; in British public schools, 93-94; homosexual communities, 139-41, 147-65, 173-76; and double lives, 140, 158-59, 163-64 (*see also* Posing); and homosexual identity, 140-41; press hostility toward, 145-46; literature supporting, 147; in twentieth-century literary tradition, 148-49, 162, 217; symbols of, 155-56, 163-64, 170; and heterosexuality debate, 157-62; rights and prison reform, 162-63, 227; female, 199-200; in wartime, 201; politics and, 205-7. *See also* Gender; Love; Sexuality
Honey, J. R. de S., 94
Household Words (Dickens), 77
Houseman, Laurence, 158
House of Pomegranates, A (Wilde), 62-63, 64
Humanité, 151
Huysmans, Joris Karl, 5, 65, 74, 213

Ibsen, Henrik, 103, 112, 150, 225
Ideal Husband, An (Wilde), 3, 117, 125-32, 225
Idealism: Wilde's, 19; satirizing of upper-class, 116-17; of sanctioned homosexual love, 158
Idylls of the King, The (Tennyson), 142
Imagination, 15
Importance of Being Earnest, The (Wilde), 8-9, 35, 105, 110, 111-17, 128, 133, 158, 217, 224
Independent Theatre Society, 103, 133, 153
Individualism, Wilde's, 28, 215
Insanity: Wilde's style compared with descriptions of, 148, 186; solitary confinement and, 178-89 *passim*. *See also* Crime
Intellectuals, 12-14
Intentions (Wilde), 19, 32, 61
Ironic reference, 7-8, 19
Ives, George, 147, 158, 162-63, 185

Jackson, Holbrook, 218
Jackson, Richard C., 143
James, Henry, 103, 105, 125, 131, 155, 222-23
Jarry, Alfred, *see* Theater of Cruelty

Index

Jesse, William, 68-72, 80, 133, 220
Johnson, Lionel, 141, 143-44, 218
Johnson, Samuel, 53, 54-55
Jones, Henry Arthur, 103
Journalism, 5; Wilde on, 10, 20-21; literature's decline, Wilde's critical theory and, 19-39, 45-47; truth and, 41. *See also* Advertising; Magazines; Press; Reviews

Kains-Jackson, Charles, 147, 157-63 *passim*
Kermode, Frank, 218, 229
Kettle, Michael, 200
Kingston, Geremy, 224
Kipling, Rudyard, 171
Knight, G. Wilson, 216
Knight Errant, The (Millais), 92
Krafft-Ebing, Richard von, 227

Lady Windermere's Fan (Wilde), 107f, 117-22, 133, 163, 224
Lane, John, 55, 141
Langtry, Lillie, 85, 118
Last Days of Pompeii, The (Lytton), 73-75
Laver, James, 69
Leaves of Grass (Whitman), 158
Leavis, Q. D., 22-23, 25-26
Le Galliene, Richard, 154-55, 218
Legislation: for homosexual rights, 156, 162-63; for prison reform, 181-84. *See also* Censorship: Prostitution
Lesbianism, 199-200
Letwin, Shirley, 91f
Leverson, Ada, 14-15, 45
Levitt, Paul M., 123f
Lewis, Henry, 133
Life of Beau Brummell, The (Jesse), 69-72
Lippincott's Monthly Magazine, 58f
Literary world, late-Victorian, 11-12, 14, 22-27 *passim*, 72-73. *See also under* Homosexuality; Prison experience

Little (art) magazines, 12
Livingston, Ira, 45, 215
Lloyd George, David, 202
Lockhart, J. G., 72
Lockwood, Frank, 147
Lombroso, Cesare, 148-53 *passim*, 159, 186
Lord Arthur Savile's Crime and Other Stories (Wilde), 62f
Love: secrets of, 115; art for sake of, 139-76; between males, 155-65 *passim*; physical, 172-76
Lugné-Poe, Aurélien-Marie, 111
Lynch, Deidre, 23, 214
Lyttleton, Alfred, 92
Lytton, Edward George Bulwer, 22-23, 34, 53, 67f, 72-75, 86, 131

Macaulay, Thomas Babington, 53-54
McCarthy, Mary, 224
McGann, Jerome, 220-21
Machen, Arthur, 25
Macqueen-Pope, W., 107
Madness, *see* Insanity
Magazines, advertising and, 55-56, 72-73
Manners, *see* Etiquette; Gentleman
Man of Genius, The (Lombroso), 149
Man of letters, 26. *See also* Literary world
Marcus, Frank, 122
Marcus, Jane, 229
Marcus, Steven, 157, 159, 228
Marginality, 10; social mobility and, 14-15; in *Ideal Husband*, 131-32; Wilde's, 176
Marlow, Louis, 158
Marriage, *see* Gender; Women
Mass literature and popular culture, 19-29. *See also* Advertising
Materialism: Victorian debate on sexuality, consumerism, and, 157-62
Maturin, Charles Robert, 85-86, 87
"Melmoth, Sebastian," 85, 176
Melmoth the Wanderer (Maturin), 83, 85-89

Index

Meredith, George, 104
Metaphysics, Wilde on, 215
Meyers, Jeffrey, 217
Middle class: life, values of, 51, 57f, 65, 67f, 76f, 134; reviewers, 105-7, 113, 116; Wilde as, 115; criticisms of, 117, 121; art world's divorce from, 139-40, 141-42, 147-48; press as, 146; feminists, 227
Millais, John, 55, 92, 142
Millard, Christopher, 200
Millett, Kate, 229
Mobility, social, 14-15; through posturing, 76; public schools and, 94
Moers, Ellen, 67f, 76ff, 84
Moore, Sturge, 208
Morality: middle-class, 51, 57f, 65, 67f, 76f, 134 (*see also* Middle class); art and, 51, 59. See also under *Picture of Dorian Gray, The*
Morning Post, 154
Morris, William, 30-31, 80, 142, 215
Morrison, William Douglas, 152, 182, 183-84, 186, 232-33
Morrow, Lance, 34
Morse, Colonel, 56
Mr. and Mrs. Daventry (Harris), 104-5
"Mr. W. H.," *see* "Portrait of Mr. W. H., The"
Mudie's circulating library, 12, 23
My Secret Life (anon.), 159

Nassaar, Christopher, 217, 229
Nation, 62
Nature and the "natural," 139-40, 155-57, 163, 176
"New Chivalry, The" (Kains-Jackson), 160, 162
New Culture, the, 162
Newgate Calendar, 34
New Grub Street (Gissing), 22, 23-25, 26
New Journalism, 26

Newman, John Henry, 149
News from Nowhere (Morris), 30-31, 80
New York Daily Tribune, 131
New York Times, 170
Nicolson, Harold, 131
Nietzsche, Friedrich, 150f
"Nightingale and the Rose, The" (Wilde), 63, 175
"No More Masterpieces" (Artaud), 134
Nordau, Max, 55-56, 149-52, 153, 159, 186, 227
November Boughs (Whitman), 157

Of Dandyism and of George Brummell (Barbey), 114, 221
"On the Essence of Laughter" (Baudelaire), 88
Order of Chaeronea, 158
Oscar Wilde and Myself (Douglas), 207
Osrac, the Self-Sufficient (Stuart-Young), 43
Ottinger, Ulrike, 51
Our Mutual Friend (Dickens), 23

"Painter of Modern Life, The" (Baudelaire), 81-82
Pall Mall Gazette, 106, 165, 171, 229, 232
Palmer, A. Smythe, 47
Paradoxes, Wilde's, 145, 176. See *also* Epigrams; Style; Wit
Parker, Charles, 146
Pater, Walter H., 5, 11, 35-39, 44, 72, 142ff, 191, 229
Pattison, Mark, 12-13
Pelham (Lytton), 68, 73
Pemberton-Billing, Noel, 153-54, 199-204
"Pen, Pencil, and Poison" (Wilde), 12, 33-39, 84, 158
Picture of Dorian Gray, The (Wilde), 3f, 51-67, 85, 90, 98-99, 180, 193; morality of, 7, 56-61, 65,

139, 157, 191; used in trial as evidence, 146; recent criticism of, 216-17
Picture of Dorian Gray in the Yellow Newspaper, The (Ottinger), 51
Pigott, Edward, 170-71
Pinero, Arthur, 103
Plagiarism: uses of, 10-11, 41f; Wilde's, 84, 104. *See also* Diversion
Platitudes, Wilde's uses of, 7-8, 10, 113-14
Ponsonby, Arthur, 92, 170
Pornography, Victorian, 157, 159-60, 228
"Portrait of Mr. W. H., The" (Wilde), 19-20, 21, 33, 39-46, 139, 158
Posing: Wilde's, 14, 57, 109, 125-29 *passim*, 155, 161-62, 163-64, 231-32; in Lytton's novels, 73; Disraeli's, 75-76; Wilde's post-prison repudiation of, 176. *See also* Double lives
Poulantzas, Nicos, 232
Pound, Ezra, 105
Praz, Mario, 218, 228
Press, the: dandies, gentlemen, and, 4-5, 11, 14, 51-67, 85, 90, 98-99, 180; and increased numbers of publications, 19-39, 45-47, 55-56, 72-73; hostility to psychological realism by, 103-7, 135; hostility toward Wilde (during trials) by, 145-47. *See also* Advertising; Journalism; Reviews
"Priest and the Acolyte, The" (Bloxam), 149, 226
Prison experience: Wilde's, 4f, 134, 145, 171-76, 179-95; literature of, 181, 193-95. *See also Ballad of Reading Gaol*; *De Profundis*
Prison reform: homosexual rights and, 162-63; Wilde's letters on, 134, 181; solitary confinement, insanity, and need for, 179-89 *passim*, 232-33; legislation for, 181-84
"Problem in Modern Ethics, A" (Symonds), 156, 158
Problem plays, 103-5
Problems of Dostoevsky's Poetics (Bakhtin), 31-32
Professional specialization, academic, 11-14, 21, 26
Professor of Aesthetics (Wilde), 11-12, 14, 21, 56, 67
Prostitution (female), 149, 227
Psychological realism, 103-6, 109, 113, 133ff
Public relations, 56; Wilde and, 135. *See also* Advertising
Public schools, English, 5, 52, 90-98, 141, 222
Punch, 116, 121, 123
Punishment, Wilde on, 137, 165, 190, 193. *See also* Prison experience

Raffalovich, Marc-André, 61, 142, 161
Ransome, Arthur, 207
Reade, Brian, 41, 60, 148-49
Reading: by mass publics, 22-29; women's, 66
Reading Gaol, see *Ballad of Reading Gaol, The*
Reading Mercury, 172
Realism: psychological, 103-5, 109, 113, 133ff; romance and, 179-80, 187-95 *passim*
Reform Bill, 75
"Renascence of the English Drama," 103-5
Research, university, 12-14, 21, 26
Reviews by Wilde, see *under* Criticism
Reviews of Wilde's works: *Dorian Gray*, 52, 56, 57-60, 62, 216-17; short fiction, 62-63; middle-class-

Index

ness of, 105-7, 113, 116; comedies, 106-7; *Earnest*, 115-17, 224; *Lady Windermere's Fan*, 117, 121-22; *Woman of No Importance*, 122-25; *Ideal Husband*, 129-31; *Salome*, 165, 169-71, 228-29; *Reading Gaol*, 171-73, 230-31; Wilde's critical theory, 214; *De Profundis*, 231-32
Revue Blanche, La, 152, 206
Reynolds's Newspaper, 145, 163, 195
Rhymers Club, 12, 141-45 *passim*
Rise and Fall of the Man of Letters, The (Gross), 26
Ritchie, David, 98
Rivière, Pierre, 70
Robertson, W. Graham, 163, 229
Roditi, Edouard, 216
Romance: Romantics and, 6, 12; realism and, 179-80, 187-95 *passim*
Rosebery, Lord, 205f
Ross, Robert, 42, 157, 163, 172, 179, 200, 206ff
Rossetti, Dante Gabriel, 142
Rossiad (Douglas), 200
Ruskin, John, 22-23, 142, 215, 229
Russell, Bertrand, 93

Saillet, Maurice, 99
St. James Gazette, 58
St. James: Theatre of Distinction (Macqueen-Pope), 107-8
Saintsbury, George, 63
Salome (Wilde), 4f, 139-41, 153-54, 165-71, 172-76 *passim*, 199-204, 224, 230; private productions of, 103, 111, 133; symbols in, 114, 163; censorship of, 165, 170, 230; sexuality of, 166-69, 230; and women, 166-71; history of criticism and antecedents of, 228-29, 230
Sand, George, 82, 160
Sanity of Art, The (Shaw), 150, 227
San Juan, Epifanio, Jr., 217

Satire, Wilde's, 106f, 116-17, 123, 130, 135, 167
Saturday Review, 62, 116, 170
Savoy, 55, 141
Scarlet Letter, The (Hawthorne), 123-24
Schuster, Adela, 186
Schwob, Marcel, 45
Science (natural), 12; *Contemporary Science Series*, 148
Scott, Clement, 104, 118, 121
Scott, Sir Walter, 22
Secrets of Love (Vitrac), 115
Seduction, art-as-, 19, 44-46, 47
Self-advertising, Wilde's, 56f, 61, 65, 216
Sentimentality, Wilde's uses of, 106, 122, 129-30, 135
Seven Types of Ambiguity (Empson), 28
Sexual Heretics (Reade), 60
Sexuality: art and, 139-41; Victorian debate on materialism, consumerism, and, 157-62; confronting audiences with own, 165; *Salome*'s, 166-69; in Pemberton-Billing trials, 199-204; British hypocrisy concerning, 207. *See also* Gender; Heterosexuality; Homosexuality
Shakespeare, William, 40-43
Shaw, George Bernard, 30, 81, 89, 96, 103, 105, 116, 135, 141, 149-50, 215, 223, 227
Shelley, Percy Bysshe, 103
Sherard, Robert, 20, 152, 230
Sheridan, Richard Brinsley, 104
Shewan, Rodney, 218, 231
Short fiction, Wilde's, 7, 58, 62-65, 175
Signification, 9-10, 17
Sincerity, Wilde's, 14, 114, 171-76, 215, 230-31, 232. *See also* Posing
Smith, Timothy d'Arch, 96
Smithers, Leonard, 60, 141, 195
Socialism: Wilde's, 29-34, 52-54,

253

56, 215, 231 (*see also* "Soul of Man Under Socialism, The"); Christian, 91-92
Society (high): in Wilde's plays, 105-9, 111-12; double standard in, 130
Society for the Checking of Abuses in Public Advertising (S.C.A.P.A.), 55
Society of the Spectacle (Debord), 9. *See also* Spectacle and spectators
Solitary confinement: Wilde's, 179-83, 185-86, 188-89; effects of, 184, 188-89, 193-95
Sonnets (Shakespeare), 39-44
Sorrows of Satan, The (Corelli), 55
"Soul of Man Under Socialism, The," 19-22 *passim*, 28f, 33, 54, 75, 109, 139
Specialization: spectacle and, 9; professional, academic, and research, 11-14, 21, 26; popularized, 25
Spectacle and spectators, 7-11, 14, 202-4; spectacular society, 56-57, 103-35; in Wilde's works, 57, 105, 109, 113, 117f, 126-27, 133-35; Artaud's, 134; *Salome* and, 165-71. *See also* Audiences
Spencer, Harold Sherwood, 199-201
Sphinx (Ada Leverson), 14-15
"Sphinx, The" (Wilde), 21, 44-45, 169
"Sphinx Without a Secret, The" (Wilde), 63
Spirit Lamp, 147, 149, 162
"Star-Child" (Wilde), 64
Strachey, Amy, 41
Strauss, Richard, 169f
Stuart-Young, John Moray, 43
Studio, The, 147f
Style: wit and, 4-5, 7; avant garde and, 6; Wilde's two styles, 19, 45-47; Shaw and Nordau on, 227. *See also* Epigrams; Wit
Swinburne, Algernon, 142-43

Symbolist Movement in Literature, The (Symons), 150
Symbols: Wilde's uses of, 67, 114; of homosexuality, 155-58, 163-64, 170. *See also* Posing
Symonds, J. A., 93, 139, 156-57, 158, 160, 162
Symons, A. J. A., 56
Symons, Arthur, 57, 62, 89, 141, 150, 171, 218, 230

Talent, Wilde's, 11
Tatler (Addison), 53
Taylor, Alfred, 145ff, 165
Taylor, M., 97
Teleny: A Physiological Romance of Today (anon.), 60
Tennyson, Alfred, 142
"Terminal Essay" (Burton), 41, 143
Thackeray, William Makepeace, 76, 90
Theater, 5, 103-35
Theater of Cruelty, 8, 109ff, 115, 134-35, 166. *See also* Audiences; Spectacle and spectators
Theory of the Avant-Garde (Bürger), 6
Thomas, J. D., 215
Three Imposters, The (Machen), 25
Times (London), 116, 121, 131, 232
Tolstoy, Leo, 150
Tono-Bungay: A Romance of Commerce (Wells), 23
Tractarians, 148-49
Tragic generation, the, 141-43, 144-45
Tragic Muse, The (James), 131, 163, 222
"Traité de la vie élégante" (Balzac), 78-79
Treasure Island (Stevenson), 26
Tree, Herbert Beerbohm, 107
Trembling of the Veil, The (Yeats), 19, 141
Trials: Wilde's, 11, 139-41, 145-47; Pemberton-Billing libel, 153-54,

254

Index

199-204; political circumstances around, 184, 205-7
Trollope, Anthony, 87-88
"Truth of Masks, The" (Wilde), 32-33, 41
Turner, E. S., 55
Tyrwhitt, Thomas, 41

Ubu Roi (Jarry), 8-9, 45, 111, 134
Ulrich, K. H., 156
Universal Review, 62
Universities: academic and professional specialization in, 12-14, 19, 21, 26; Morris on, 80; reform, 213
Upper class, *see* Society (high)

Vallas, Stacey, 213
Vaughan, C. J., 93
Vera; or the Nihilists (Wilde), 129
Victor, or the Children Are in Power (Artaud and Vitrac), 110, 117
Vigilante, 199
Vitrac, Roger, 110, 115, 117
Vivian Gray (Disraeli), 75-76

Wagner, Richard, 150
Wainewright, Thomas Griffiths, 34-39
Walkley, A. B., 121-22, 130-31
Watson, William, 154
Way We Live Now, The (Trollope), 87-88
Webb, Beatrice, 107-8, 113, 126, 128, 130
Webb, Sidney, 52-53
Weekly Sun, 151
Weeks, Jeffrey, 157-58

Wells, H. G., 106, 116, 129-30, 135, 225
Westminster, 151-52
Whistler, James Abbott McNeill, 14, 56, 83-84
White, Joseph Gleeson, 147
Whitehead, Evelyn, 93
Whitman, Walt, 150, 157-58
Wiener, Martin J., 91
Wilson, James H., 163
Wit, Wilde's, 7-10, 19; press and, 4-5. *See also* Comedy; Epigrams; Satire; Style
Woman of No Importance, A (Wilde), 117, 122-25, 133, 225
Woman's World: Wilde's editorship of, 66f, 98; advertising in, 85; *Dorian Gray* and, 219
Women: advertising images of, 51; literature for, 66; dandies and, 80-83; British public schools and, 94; middle- and upper-class, 97-99; in politics, 98; of the "tragic generation," 142-43; prostitution recommended for, 149, 227; Nordau on, 152; authors, 155; sexuality of, 157-62; *Salome* and, 166-71
Woodcock, George, 231
Woolridge, Charles Thomas (C. T. W.), 172f
Writers, kinds of, 25-26

Yeats, William Butler, 19, 56, 141-42, 144
Yellow Book, 55, 85, 141, 144, 154f
Young Things (Barford), 161

Zuleika Dobson (Beerbohm), 83

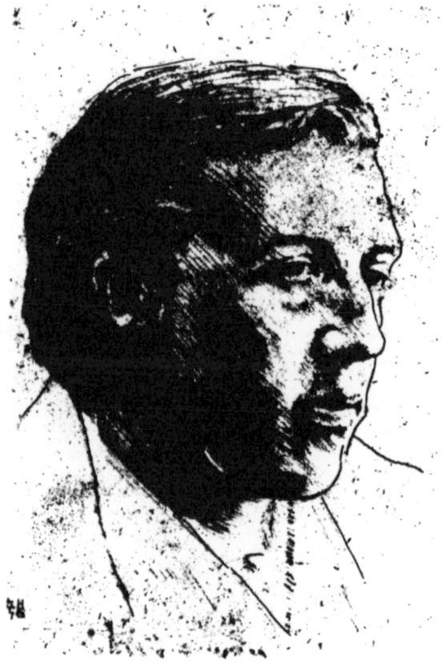

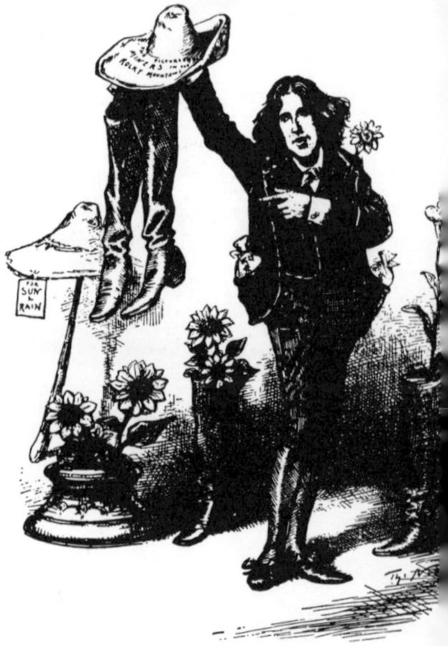
FOR
SUN
&
RAIN

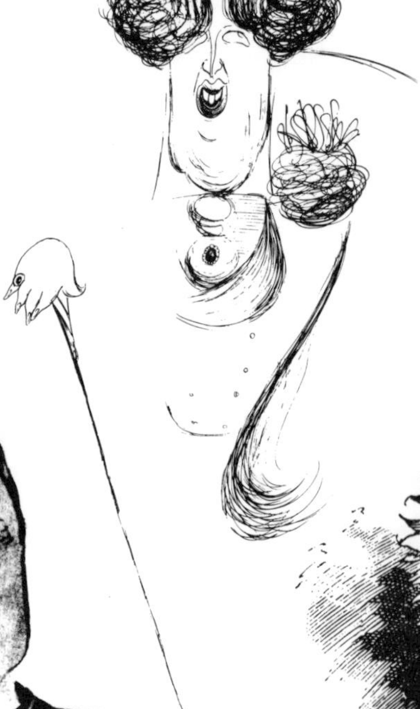

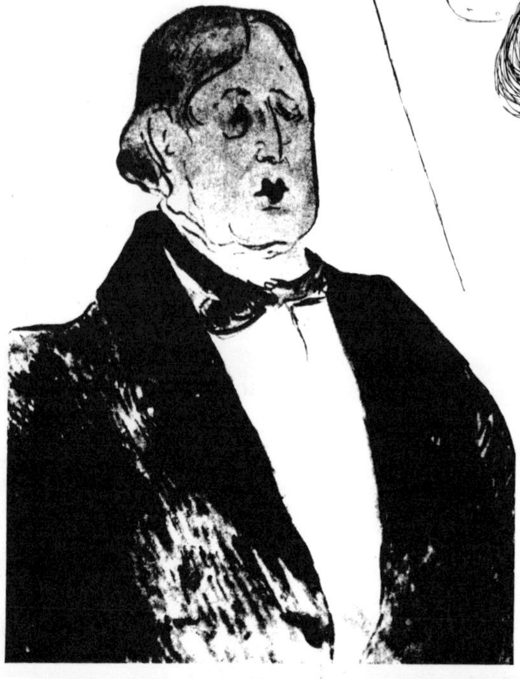

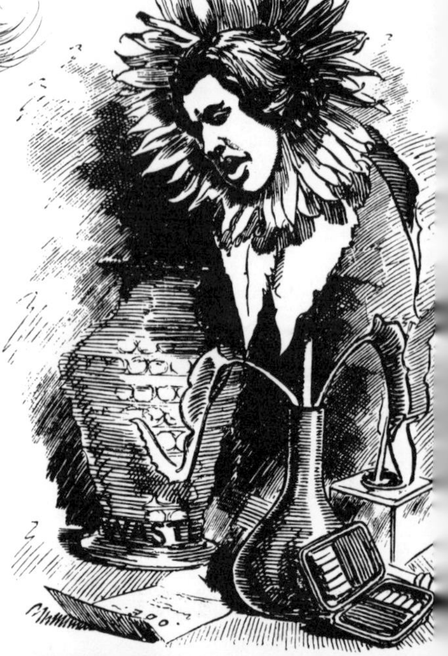